DISASTER PLANNING

A How-To-Do-It Manual for Librarians with Planning Templates on CD-ROM

Deborah D. Halsted
Richard P. Jasper
Felicia M. Little

*HOW-TO-DO-IT MANUALS
FOR LIBRARIANS*

NUMBER 129

NEAL-SCHUMAN PUBLISHERS, INC.
New York, London

Published by Neal-Schuman Publishers, Inc.
100 William St., Suite 2004
New York, NY 10038

Printed and bound in the United States of America.

The paper used in this publication meets the minimum requirements of American National Standard for Information Sciences—Permanence of Paper for Printed Library Materials, ANSI Z39.48-1992. ∞

Library of Congress Cataloging-in-Publication Data

Halsted, Deborah D.
    Disaster planning : a how-to-do-it manual for librarians with planning templates on CD-ROM / Deborah D. Halsted, Richard P. Jasper, and Felicia M. Little.
        p.   cm.—(How-to-do-it manuals for librarians ; no. 129)
    ISBN 1-55570-486-7 (alk. paper)
    1. Libraries—Safety measures—Handbooks, manuals, etc.   2. Library materials—Conservation and restoration—Handbooks, manuals, etc.   3. Emergency management—Handbooks, manuals, etc.   4. Library planning—Handbooks, manuals, etc.   I. Jasper, Richard P.   II. Little, Felicia M.   III. Title.   IV. How-to-do-it manuals for libraries ; no. 129.
Z679.7.H35   2005
025.8'2—dc22

                                                                                        2003065152

Thanks to the staff of the Houston Academy of Medicine-Texas Medical Center Library, for all their hard work following the June 2001 flood. Their dedication shows that teamwork can truly make what seems impossible happen!
Deborah D. Halsted

For Jeremy Corry, 1970–2001.
Richard P. Jasper

To Kenneth Little, my guiding light.
Felicia M. Little

The authors would also like to dedicate this book to the three librarians
Helen Belilovsky
Maureen Olson
Margaret Orloske
who lost their lives in the World Trade Center on September 11, 2001.

CONTENTS

LIST OF FIGURES

LIST OF SAMPLES

PREFACE

The terrorist attacks that caused the tragic events of September 11, 2001, in New York City and Washington, D.C., were a heartbreaking wake-up call that unimaginable disasters can happen to any one, any place, any time. Libraries are never immune from the danger; the ones in or near the World Trade Center and Pentagon were destroyed or damaged and at least three of the people who lost their lives were librarians.

Of course, the more imaginable kind of disaster caused by natural circumstances have always been a fact of life. We, the authors of *Disaster Planning: A How-To-Do-It Manual for Librarians with Planning Templates on CD-ROM*, as staff at the Houston Academy of Medicine—Texas Medical Center Library found out only too well how quickly Mother Nature can strike. During the early hours of June 9, 2001, Tropical Storm Allison hit Houston for a third time in four days as she made a circular route around the metropolitan area, dumping more than 14 inches of rain. As Allison raged, the library collected between three and four feet of water in the lower level. The good news? Many library managers kept a copy of the library's emergency plan on their desks. The bad news? The plan had not been updated in nearly ten years. At the moment of crisis, some library managers realized they did not even have a current list of staff phone numbers.

After recovering from our experience, we agreed that it is human nature to not relish planning for catastrophe but realize it is essential. We designed *Disaster Planning* as a straightforward yet comprehensive tool to help your library weather any storm. Indeed, it's key to remember that disasters arrive in all forms and levels of severity. They can strike as random acts of nature—hurricanes, tornadoes, tsunamis, or wildfires—or random acts of man—broken pipes, fires, or even terrorist attacks. They can be small and contained to one area or they can destroy the entire building and its contents. To minimize the effects, preparation is imperative. *Disaster Planning* is a practical guide for librarians and other information professionals concerned with the safety and protection of their facilities, materials, and staff.

Disasters may differ in their nature and scope, but several core elements tackle the proper level of preparedness. This guide stresses 11 key steps toward effectively planning for the seemingly impossible, including how to:

- create a response team;
- write a plan;

- plan for standard events such as floods, fire, tornadoes, etc.;
- prepare for new realities such as terrorism, bioterrorism, and computer viruses and/or worms;
- identify relief/recovery agencies such as the American Red Cross and FEMA; and
- construct a Web site with important information and instruction.

The main part of this guide is divided into three parts supplemented by a Disaster Recovery Quick Guide and a CD-ROM. The contents of this manual are designed to work as a collective whole, pulling together in a single source a broad array of basic, realistic information, tools, and resources for library managers to use in planning.

Part I, "Create an 11–Step Disaster Preparation Strategy," outlines a proven process to ready libraries for disastrous events. This section teaches how to look at a library with a critical eye—Risk Assessment; Understand the Vulnerabilities. It challenges staff to think through worst-case scenarios—Formulate a List and Stock Disaster Supplies; Establish Evacuation Plans; and Establish Disaster Communications. It stresses the importance of readiness and advanced planning—Create a Disaster Team; Gain Access to Finances; Secure the Building; Conduct Disaster Drills. All together, these components will help with the most important part of the process—Write the Disaster Plan; and Revise and Update the Plan. Some of these steps

Figure P-1. HAM-TMC Library Flood after Tropical Storm Allison

may seem basic, others may seem overly cautious, but ultimately they will prove integral to creating a staff and organization ready to respond to disastrous events that may arise.

Part II, "Prepare by Understanding the Most Common Disasters," helps familiarize staff with the unique needs and circumstances of several of the most universal and damaging disasters to affect libraries. This part includes valuable information on floods, fires, hurricanes, tornadoes, earthquakes, civil disorders, terrorism, computer terrorism (viruses and worms), mold, and infestation. Planning is not one-size-fits-all, and libraries should become aware of the unique attributes and necessary responses to the events they are most prone to.

Part III, "Resources on the Web," helps librarians locate additional tools readily available on the Web to help plan for and respond to disasters. This section includes an annotated bibliography as well as an annotated list of resources.

"The Disaster Recovery Quick Guides" includes the complete real-life sample of a library response plan, a roster of companies that specialize in disaster services and the same information laid out as an "at-a-glance" grid. There is a comprehensive disaster prevention and protection checklist. The last source, "How to Use the CD-ROM," features complete step-by-step instructions and materials to create a customized plan as well as a disaster mitigation Web site kit.

We wish libraries never need to come face to face with circumstances that require the information and guidance of *Disaster Planning*. In a world where anything can happen, the instruction provided here and valuable tools on the CD-ROM make sure that an institution can prepare for and respond to events appropriately and in a way that minimizes the damage incurred.

ACKNOWLEDGMENTS

The authors gratefully acknowledge the people and organizations listed below for their permission to reprint photographs, plans, and other library policies.

Amigos Library Services, Inc.
Dallas, Texas

Angelo and Jennette Volpe Library and Media Center
Cookeville, Tennessee

Technological University
Cookeville, Tennessee

Brown University Library
Providence, Rhode Island

Burlingame Public Library
Burlingame, California

California State University
San Marcos, California

Brooks Library, Central Washington University
Ellensburg, Washington

The City and Borough of Juneau
Juneau, Alaska

D. Hiden Ramsey Library, University of North Carolina
Asheville, North Carolina

E. Lingle Craig Preservation Laboratory, Indiana University Libraries
Bloomington, Indiana

Fairfax County Public Library
Fairfax, Virginia

Firewise.org

Fort Worth Public Library
Fort Worth, Texas

George A. Smathers Libraries, University of Florida
Gainesville, Florida

Houston Academy of Medicine—Texas Medical Center Library
Houston, Texas

James Gee Library, Texas A&M University—Commerce
Commerce, Texas

James Madison University
Harrisonburg, Virginia

Leyburn Library, Washington and Lee University
Lexington, Virginia

Lincoln County, Montana
Lincoln, Montana

Livingston Lord Library, Moorhead State University
Moorhead, Minnesota

Northeast Documents Conservation Center
Andover, Massachusetts

Oregon Department of Land Conservation and Development
Salem, Oregon

Oviatt Library, California State University Northridge
Northridge, California

Robert M. Bird Health Sciences Library, University of Oklahoma Health
Sciences Center
Oklahoma City, Oklahoma

San Diego County Library
San Diego, California

SOLINET, Inc.
Atlanta, Georgia

University of California, San Diego, Undergraduate Library
San Diego, California

University of California, Santa Cruz
Santa Cruz, California

University of Texas School of Public Health at Houston Library
Houston, Texas

U.S. Federal Emergency Management Agency
Washington, D.C.

U.S. Geological Survey
Washington, D.C.

Waupauca Area Public Library
Waupauca, Wisconsin

West Coast and Alaska Tsunami Warning Center
Palmer, Alaska

WHAT'S ON THE CD-ROM?

Note: For a complete description and step-by-step instructions, please turn to the Disaster Recovery Quick Guides, Guide 5.

The companion CD-ROM contains:

- the Disaster Plan Template,
- a Directory of Consultants, and
- the Disaster Mitigation Web Site Kit.

The **Disaster Plan Template** lays out the rudimentary elements of a strategic response to emergency events that present a potential threat to a particular facility. It is customizable by simply clicking on the prompt and entering the required information. It contains:

- the scope and purpose of the plan,
- disaster definitions,
- how often the plan will be updated,
- identification of the main author, and
- the location of the print and electronic copy of the disaster plan.

It will also help organize valuable info on:

- disaster teams,
- emergency contacts,
- library closure procedures,
- communications equipment,
- disaster supplies for immediate response,
- emergency systems, and
- plans for specific emergencies.

The **List of Consultants** contains a directory of experts that specialize in the recovery of general facilities and library collections, including company name, address, phone number and, if available, the hyperlinked Web address.

The **Disaster Mitigation Web Site Kit** provides a framework on which to build an online version of the disaster plan. Its purpose is to keep employees informed whether they are at their desktops or at remote locations. The site, if updated regularly, can:

- propagate details of and changes to the plan quickly,
- connect employees with information about conditions that can affect a facility locally,
- grant easy access to downloadable print copies of the plan, and
- serve as an effective communication tool during a disaster.

It also contains information to help you plan for recovering from a computer network attack or catastrophic damage to your facility, including how to:

- prepare for blackouts,
- establish back up power supplies, and
- keep key portions of the site accessible by a *Personal Digital Assistant* (PDA).

CREATE AN 11-STEP DISASTER PREPARATION STRATEGY

INTRODUCTION

The U.S. government defines both *disaster* and *emergency* in the U.S. Code of Federal Regulations, in the section discussing "Management of Vital Records." *Disaster* is defined as an unexpected occurrence inflicting widespread destruction and distress and having long-term adverse effects on operations. *Emergency* means a situation or an occurrence of a serious nature, developing suddenly and unexpectedly, and demanding immediate action. An emergency is generally of short duration, involving an interruption of normal operations. Examples of emergencies include electrical failures and minor flooding caused by broken pipes (U.S. CFR, 1998).

The government has taken the possibility of either natural or human-made disasters very seriously as evidenced by a number of federal Web sites dealing with disasters. The U.S. Federal Emergency Management Agency has long provided information on dealing with disasters on their Web site (www.fema.gov). Post-9/11 America has also prompted the creation of the U.S. Department of Homeland Security, which makes the Ready.gov site available (www.ready.gov). Recently, even the U.S. National Library of Medicine added a "Coping with Disasters" page to MedlinePlus (www.nlm.nih.gov/medlineplus/copingwithdisasters.html). Nongovernmental sites such as the American Red Cross (www.redcross.org) also offer advice on emergency planning and response.

Disasters occur on various levels and must be measured by the extent of their influence. Some disasters are community-wide, such as earthquakes, tornadoes, floods, power blackouts or acts of terrorism. Some disasters are local to one building, such as a water leak, arson, or a disgruntled employee destroying computer records. Disaster planning must account for all levels of emergencies. Additionally, human life should always be the first consideration in any emergency or disaster. No building or collection is worth the risk of injury or death (Rike, 2001). Just as some geographic areas are prone to specific natural disasters, the U.S. government has identified specific targets for terroristic threats based on seized terrorist documents. These targets include national symbols (World Trade Center, White House), monuments, landmarks, airports, harbors, transportation vehicles, nuclear facilities, power plants, fuel storage areas, bridges, buildings, mass gatherings, sports events, shopping malls, subways, and government facilities (Durham, 2002).

While disasters and emergencies can happen at any place or any time, a 2002 Gartner survey found that only 35% of small and mid-sized businesses have a comprehensive disaster recovery plan in place. Another Gartner report, *The Business Continuity Readiness Survey*, revealed that only 36% of the companies and governmental agencies surveyed have a plan for the complete loss of their physical assets and workspace (Rike, 2002). Many factors contribute to a lack of disaster planning. Figure 1.1 (D'Antoni, 2002) lists the major deterrents to disaster planning as defined by a survey sent to 100 companies without disaster plans.

Libraries are not unlike businesses and most likely suffer the same deterrents. So what is a library administrator to do? This chapter will discuss eleven steps in planning for disasters.

Fortunately, disasters, whether caused by nature such as Tropical Storm Allison in the Houston area or created by humans, are rare. On the other

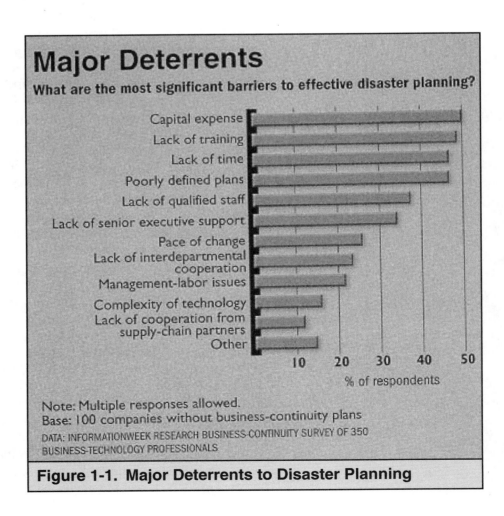

Figure 1-1. Major Deterrents to Disaster Planning

hand, since they are rare, library administrators often neglect disaster planning. Planning for disasters can seem to be an arduous task, with little obvious reward, unless the unthinkable happens. Too often, library administrators think they cannot justify the staff time to create an active disaster plan. What these administrators do not take into account is that when disaster strikes, it usually happens very quickly, without much time to respond or react. The library that has a disaster plan, complete with the chain of command, communication guidelines, emergency supplies on hand, and a dedicated disaster team who have a hand at creating the plan, is better equipped to minimize damage to staff and collections and is more likely to recover quickly from the disaster.

While disasters in libraries may seem unique, there are many similarities to other types of institutions. Often after a disaster, communication or the lack of communication is seen as the most important issue. After the terrorist attacks of September 2001, Frank Raymond, MD, director of emergency medicine at Peninsula Hospital Center in Far Rockaway, NY stated "From my direct experience, the most important thing is communication. . . . You have to frequent the dialog with the police, the fire department and other agencies" (Zablocki, 2002). By having a disaster team and a current disaster plan in place, staff of a library, or any other institution for that matter, can have on hand the most recent contact names and numbers. Additionally, libraries are not the only institutions that store paper materials. Tropical Storm Allison destroyed medical records at hospitals, scores and sheet music at the Houston Symphony, and scripts from the Alley Theater. Librarians and archivists can help other types of institutions in recovery of documents, but can learn from them as well.

So where does one begin in creating an effective disaster plan? The effort includes many steps including:

1.1	Step 1: Create a Disaster Team
1.2	Step 2: Risk Assessment
1.3	Step 3: Establish Disaster Communications
1.4	Step 4: Gain Access to Finances
1.5	Step 5: Secure the Building
1.6	Step 6: Formulate a List and Stock Disaster Supplies
1.7	Step 7: Understand the Vulnerabilities
1.8	Step 8: Establish Evacuation Plans
1.9	Step 9: Write a Disaster Plan
1.10	Step 10: Conduct Disaster Drills
1.11	Step 11: Revise and Update the Plan

1.1 STEP 1: CREATE A DISASTER TEAM

The very first step in creating an effective disaster plan is to appoint a disaster team. By creating a team, all members will know, in advance, individual duties if disaster strikes. Disaster team members should represent all areas of the library and should be responsible for various functions including: assessing risks, creating a communication plan, identifying agencies to aid in the event of a disaster, purchasing appropriate disaster supplies, writing and updating the disaster plan, and most important, to be the front line when disaster strikes. Therefore, the disaster planning team also serves as the official disaster recovery team.

Different types of libraries have different types of disaster teams. Large libraries have teams made up entirely of library staff, but might also be part of campus, city, or company-wide teams. In the case of a corporation or a hospital library with only one staff member, the librarian might be part of the corporate or hospital disaster team. No matter what the size of the library, it is imperative to have the planning in place to salvage collections and other library possessions in the case of a disaster. The most important benefit of a disaster plan is to minimize the possibility of personal injury to staff or clients in the case of a true disaster.

Each member of the disaster team should have a specific function in relation to his or her position in the library and will have assignments listed in the plan. A disaster team leader should also be named. The leader will be in charge during and immediately after a real disaster, ensures the team meets regularly, updates the disaster plan at least annually, and schedules drills.

The members of a disaster team will vary from library to library depending on size, but in a larger library should include some or all of the following staff members:

- Director or Deputy Director
- Collections Manager
- Accountant
- Security/Safety Officer
- Human Resources Representative
- Systems/Automation Head
- Public Relations Representative
- Facilities Manager

The library director may or may not be a member of the team. While the director is ultimately responsible for all areas of the library, he or she must also be available to work with other executives of the campus, firm, organization, county, or city depending on the type of library. In some cases the director will also be responsible for working with agencies such as the Federal Emergency Management Agency (FEMA) and insurance. If the disaster team is not led by the director, the team leader should inform the director of all actions so that he or she can make decisions regarding recovery, resumption of services, etc. Additionally, in some cases such as a university library, some of these members might not be actual library staff members. The security officer and facilities manager might work for the university, but service the library as a separate department. Or in the case of a large institution, the library's disaster team might be a subcommittee of a larger disaster team.

DUTIES OF THE DISASTER TEAM MEMBERS

Director or Deputy Director

The director or deputy director should act as chair or leader of the library's disaster team. As chair, this person will ensure that disaster preparedness remains an important part of library planning.

Regular Duties

- Calls regular meetings of the disaster team throughout the year.
- Ensures the disaster plan is updated annually or as needed.
- Creates and maintains a telephone tree so that employees and other important people are notified quickly, should disaster strike.
- Ensures that items on the disaster supply list are available and up-to-date.
- Initiates a relationship with recovery firms and agencies who might be able to assist if disaster strikes.
- Works with campus, hospital, city, county or company-wide disaster teams to ensure compliance with the bigger picture.

During and After a Disaster:

- Serves as recovery director.
- Maintains direct communication with campus, hospital, city, state, organizational, or corporate officials.

- Notifies the disaster team members of immanent danger (begins the telephone tree process).
- Establishes a command center.
- Ensures methods of communication both inside and outside the library.
- Delegates duties.
- Begins salvage operations after the building is deemed safe by facilities management or local safety officials.
- Oversees overall management of recovery and salvage operations.
- Supervises delivery and installation of equipment.
- Assesses and records damage with other disaster team members.
- Identifies storage space for priority recovery list items.
- Determines if a mold assessment of the affected collections is necessary.
- Receives reports from disaster team members.
- Prepares a post-disaster report.
- Works with facilities and accounting on the restoration of the Library.[1]

Collections Manager

Regular Duties

- Maintains an inventory of the library collections (primarily using the OPAC).
- Identifies specific priority collections to be saved or recovered first.
- Mitigates possible damage to priority collections.

***During** and **After** a Disaster:*

- Supervises the staff, volunteers, and vendors during collection recovery efforts.[2]
- Assesses damage to the collections.

---

[1] This step can include everything from having furniture refinished, purchasing new furniture, selecting carpet and tile, etc.
[2] For liability sake, all volunteers should sign a waiver form before doing any work. Most institutions have volunteer waiver forms in place.

- Advises director and accountant on the extent of the damage to the collections.
- Locates specific priority collections to be saved or recovered first.
- Determines which items can be recovered in-house and which need to be sent out for recovery.
- Determines which parts of the damaged collection are not worth recovery efforts.
- Advises director and accountant on the need of a recovery company if collections need to be dried.
- Maintains contact with recovery company until the materials are returned.
- Supervises in-house cleaning and drying.
- Supervises the processing of all damaged materials.
- Trains staff and volunteers.
- Prepares a written report of the recovery and/or relocation activities.

Accountant

Regular Duties

- Establishes and maintains an inventory of library possessions.
- Ensures insurance coverage is up-to-date.

During and *After* a Disaster:

- Tracks and coordinates expenditures.
- Authorizes temporary staff assignments if needed.
- Authorizes payment for supplies and services needed.
- Contacts recovery vendors and services at the request of the disaster team or collections manager.
- Acts as financial liaison with FEMA, if appropriate.
- Maintains list of materials sent out for restoration (including collections and furnishings).
- Updates the inventory of library possessions as damaged items are discarded.
- Maintains a list of possessions sent out for refurbishing, if applicable.
- Submits insurance claims.

Security/Safety Officer

Regular Duties

- Creates an evacuation team with representatives from every area of the library.
- Creates, with the evacuation team, evacuation procedures for the building.
- Conducts periodic drills, with the disaster team leader.
- Stocks and maintains the disaster supplies.

***During** and **After** a Disaster:*

- Maintains communication with campus, city, county, state, federal, or other security agencies.
- Works with outside agencies to ensure the safety of the building, including reentry following the disaster.
- Maintains internal library security.
- Maintains security of all exterior doors.
- Keeps first aid supply stocked.

Human Resources Representative

***During** and **After** a Disaster:*

- Relocates employees displaced from offices or work spaces.
- Arranges for food and drink for recovery workers.
- Assists any employee injured in the disaster or during recovery with workman's compensation or insurance claims.
- Prepares compensation plan for employees involved in the recovery, if applicable.
- Recruits volunteers and ensures they all sign a waiver form.
- Enrolls the assistance of the Employee Assistance Program if necessary or available.
- Maintains current list of all staff phone numbers for updating the telephone tree.

Systems/Automation Head

Before a Disaster:

- Ensures all computers and servers have a reliable back-up system.
- Stores back-up tapes and discs at an off-site facility.
- Creates a mirror site for electronic resources, if feasible.

During and *After* a Disaster:

- Secures and reestablishes computer network and systems.
- Reestablishes telephone connections.
- Reestablishes security system.
- Removes damaged or destroyed equipment.
- Identifies appropriate means for disposal of destroyed equipment (there are EPA guidelines for disposal of many types of equipment including printers and photocopiers).
- Works with accountant in replacement of destroyed equipment.

Public Relations Representative

Before a Disaster:

- Establishes a relationship with major media outlets.
- Maintains a list of key media contacts.
- Keeps an updated file of information and statistics pertaining to the library.

During and *After* a Disaster:

- Keeps the director, disaster team, and library staff informed of latest news from outside the library.
- Acts as the conduit for public information on the disaster.
- Contacts media with library-related announcements, including library closure and reopening, waiving of fines, return of library materials, etc.

- Photographs the damage to the collections and library contents, as well as damage to the building, if appropriate.[3]
- Maintains a photographic record of recovery efforts.

Facilities Manager

Before a Disaster:

- Improves the building to avoid possible damage from disaster (depending on types of disasters possible and depending on geographic location).

    build flood walls and gates

    strengthen walls and roofs

    install storm shutters

    install fire detection and alarm systems

    install sprinkler sytems

    keep bushes and trees around the building trimmed

    install a green roof

    waterproof the electrical system

    install porous concrete to parking lots and sidewalks

    increase the green space around the building

- Maintain contacts with disaster recovery firms, utility companies, and parent institution facilities departments.
- Ensure blueprints of the building are up-to-date.

During and After a Disaster:

- Determine when the building is safe for reentry with public safety officials and library safety officer.
- Test water supply for contamination.
- Restore all utilities (electricity, water, gas).
- Contract with construction companies for building restoration.

---

[3] Photographs will fill various needs including insurance claims, FEMA needs, and archiving the disaster for library records. Each need might have specific requirements, so check with the agencies involved.

- Contract with an architect for design of the building restoration.
- Make suggestions to library director on improvements that can be made while building restoration is taking place.
- Identify and purchase construction supplies for building restoration.
- Manage contracted recovery workers.

Depending on the library, other staff members might have duties after a disaster, such as circulation staff. Following a disaster, library clients might become concerned about overdue books and fines, and possibly destruction of library materials they have checked out if the disaster is widespread. For the first few days, or at least while the library is closed, a good public relations move is to have a circulation assistant stationed at the front door to inform clients on library policies for overdue and destroyed books. In most cases it is advisable to waive all fines immediately following a widespread disaster. Additionally, circulation staff should check book drops around the campus to retrieve books turned in before or during the disaster. In many cases these books could be ruined due to floodwater or other results of the disaster. If so, it is advisable to waive fines and fees.

Again, it should be noted that different types of libraries will have different responsibilities for members of a disaster team. In the survey sent out to the medical library listserv, a hospital librarian at a major Houston hospital responded that her institution does have a hospital-wide disaster team, but she is not part of it. Members of the team include only representatives from administration, information technology, facilities, pharmacy, and the emergency room. Sample 1.2 show examples of disaster team duties from three different libraries.

Sample 1.1

Disaster Team Duties from Brown University Library

Recovery Director/Coordinator—Primary responsibility is to oversee all aspects of the recovery activities. Serves as spokesperson for the recovery effort to all audiences. At the time of a disaster, assists the conservator in accessing damage and determining priorities for salvage.

Financial Liaison—responds to all financial and insurance requirements related to the recovery efforts, including the provision of purchase orders, emergency approval of expenditures, and notification to risk management office.

Supply Coordinator—provides access to stockpiles of supplies as well as any transportation required to pick up and deliver supplies. Reorders supplies as needed during recovery effort. Monitors contents of disaster kits and replenishes as necessary.

Training Instructor—maintains the understanding of duties among disaster team members and conducts regular refresher courses in emergency preparedness. Works with scheduler and training coordinator to ensure adequate levels of trained volunteers.

Scheduler—coordinates recovery activities to ensure proper flow of materials and elimination of bottlenecks. Works closely with volunteer coordinator to ensure adequate number of fresh workers assisting with recovery. Provides for breaks and other human needs during recovery activities.

Recovery Director/Coordinator—Oversees all aspects of the recovery activities. Serves as spokesperson for the recovery effort to all audiences. At the time of a disaster, assists the conservator in accessing damage and determining priorities for salvage.

Building Supervisor—assists recovery team, fire department, police and security, and other safety personnel in gaining access to all necessary areas. Working with plant operations, ensures the stabilization of the physical environment. Coordinates custodial activities during recovery including the regular removal of waste from the recovery site.

Conservator—assesses the extent of damage to materials and coordinates their sorting, preparing, packing, removal, and treatment. Establishes handling procedures for recovery effort, supervises in-house treatments, remains on call until recovery efforts are complete, manages long-term recovery treatments.

Photographer—documents damage to library materials and physical structure with well-framed photographs. Provides visual history of the disaster and recovery activities.

Volunteer Coordinator—estimates number of volunteers needed and provides the recovery team with workers necessary to accomplish recovery goals. Calls library staff and other potential volunteers to ask for help. Works closely with scheduler to coordinate maximum number of helping hands.

Alternates—assists in recovery operations. Serves in full capacity if first designate is unavailable.

Sample 1.2

Disaster Team Duties from the E. Lingle Craig Preservation Laboratory

Response Director—Head of Preservation

Recovery Specialist and Recorder—General Collections Conservator

Photographer—Designated by the Head of Preservation

Campus and Media Liaison—Executive Associate Dean

Logistics Coordinator—Head, Customer and Facilities Services

Administrative Services Coordinator—Budget Officer

Pack-Out and Relocation Supervisors—Stacks Supervisors

Collection Representative—Director of Collection Development

Campus Librarians will replace the Director of Collection Development for disaster response in campus libraries.

Duties:

Director:

- Responsible for overall management of recovery and salvage operation.
- Determines when to begin salvage after consulting with physical plant, building representative, and fire and safety.
- Notifies disaster response team members, establishes command center.

- Assesses and records damage with the photographer, recovery specialist, and risk manager.
- Determines the kind of salvage necessary.
- Determines the level of preservation response needed by consulting the collection representative and written priority lists, informs the administrative coordinator and campus and media liaison of needs.
- Directs logistics coordinator.
- Determines timetable for recovery.
- Requests volunteers, as needed, through media and campus liaison.
- Arranges training of crew team captains.
- Receives team reports.
- Prepares final report.

Recovery Specialist:
- Assesses damage in cooperation with the disaster response director and collection representative.
- Designates treatment area with the director.
- Advises budget officer and campus liaison on contacting outside agencies for assistance and supplies.
- Consults with logistics coordinator for the transport of supplies and materials and the movement of damaged collections.
- Is responsible for handling and treatment of materials from the time they are removed from the disaster site until the materials are reshelved.
- Supervises in-house cleaning and drying.
- Trains volunteers.
- Prepares report, including a photographic record on the rehabilitation process and unsalvageable materials, to the director.

Photographer:
- Photographs the extent of damage to the building, the furniture, and the collections as part of the initial disaster assessment.
- Provides a photographic record of the recovery, salvage, rehabilitation, and restoration processes, with attention to recording unsalvageable materials, under the direction of the recovery specialist.
- Tracks the dates and times of the photographs or film for the reports.

Campus and Media Liaison:
- Works with campus administration to establish, in advance, work space for recovery.
- Issues the approved authorization for the disaster recovery team to do its work.
- Acts as liaison with campus administration and coordinates with them.
- Serves as source of all public information on the disaster.
- Deals with media inquiries.
- Arranges media announcements.
- Issues information to the staff and to the university administration.
- Keeps the dean of the libraries informed.
- Authorizes temporary staff reassignments as needed.

- Receives reports from the disaster response director.
- Solicits volunteers as requested by the disaster response director.
- Thanks and acknowledges people who have participated in the recovery.
- Decides on restoration of services.

Logistics Coordinator:
- Sets up the command post.
- Tells library staff and volunteers where to report on the advice of the disaster response director.
- Delegates functions as appropriate.
- Makes sure any volunteers sign waiver forms.
- Issues name tags.
- Arranges for food and drink and sets up food area.
- Is responsible for all transportation and relocation activities.
- Makes any necessary arrangements to remove books from the disaster site.
- Arranges for transportation and moving equipment.
- Supervises loading and unloading.
- Oversees shipping of boxes to freezers or other sites.
- Supervises delivery and installation of needed equipment.
- Supervises crews which set up the established recovery work place.
- Arranges the return of books to their original location.
- Coordinates with the appropriate building services and library staff.

Administrative Services Coordinator:
- Coordinates budget and supplies.
- Is present at the command post.
- Authorizes payment and signs vouchers for supplies and services needed, for on-campus and outside vendors.
- Contacts vendors at the request of the disaster response director.
- Works closely with the logistics coordinator to arrange transport and delivery of needed supplies and services.
- Is responsible for submitting insurance claims with the preservation librarian.

Pack-Out and Relocation Supervisors:
- Performs regular safety inspections of library facilities.
- Supervises the training of volunteers in making and packing boxes.
- Keeps count of boxes sent to other sites.
- Works with collection representative and keeps general records of sections moved to other sites (depending on the size of the disaster).
- Prepares a written report of the pack-out activities.
- Monitors the progress and orderly restoration of the stack area, including clean-up and resetting shelving.

- Organizes and supervises the orderly return of library materials to approved shelving.
- Keeps records of the number of boxes and sections returned to the stacks.
- Prepares a report on relocation activities, including a photographic record.

Collection Representative:

- Develops a pre-disaster priority list to be used during salvage operations in consultation with the bibliographers.
- Reviews priorities and floor plans at least annually.
- Advises on priorities for action and salvage on the basis of the written guidelines at the disaster site (in consultation with the relevant bibliographers, if possible).
- Acts as recorder in damage assessment.
- Consults with the recovery specialist, as needed, during the recovery process.
- Works with appropriate bibliographers and serves as liaison to the cataloging and acquisitions departments to record destroyed items and to arrange for replacement copies.
- Maintains list of bibliographers and department heads with their telephone numbers.

Once identified, the first thing the disaster team should do is to identify what types of disasters and emergencies might occur in a particular geographic area. Figure 1.2 illustrates three potential groups of exposure, according to an article in the *Information Management Journal*, with various types of disasters and emergencies in each (Rike, 2002):

Natural Threats & Hazards	Technical/Mechanical Hazards	Human Activities & Threats
• Fire	• Power outage or failure	• Computer error
• Flood	• Gas leak	• Lost or misfiled documents and records
• Hurricane	• Software failure or malfunction	• Vandalism
• Earthquake	• Sewage failure or backup	• Theft
• Lightning strike	• Building structural failure	• Bomb threat
• Tornado, wind storm	• Electrical shortage or faulty wiring	• Civil disorder
• Snow and ice storms	• Toxic spill	• Strikes
• Wind	• Radiation contamination	• Kidnapping

Figure 1-2. Potential Types of Exposure

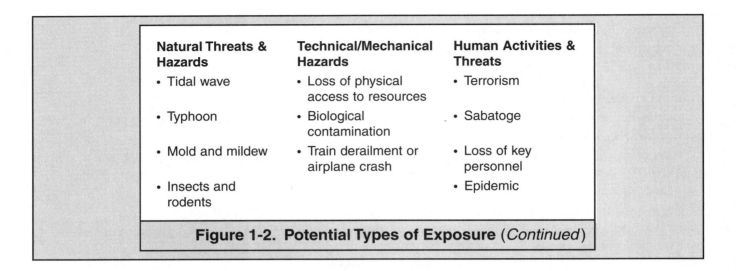

Natural Threats & Hazards	Technical/Mechanical Hazards	Human Activities & Threats
• Tidal wave	• Loss of physical access to resources	• Terrorism
• Typhoon	• Biological contamination	• Sabatoge
• Mold and mildew	• Train derailment or airplane crash	• Loss of key personnel
• Insects and rodents		• Epidemic

Figure 1-2. Potential Types of Exposure (*Continued*)

Not all of these hazards are applicable to libraries, but they might affect staff members, which can create a different sort of emergency if key staff members are out for lengthy periods of time.

1.2 STEP 2: RISK ASSESSMENT

Before writing a disaster plan, the team should perform a risk assessment of possible disasters. Information on possible natural disasters that can occur in your area can be obtained from local offices (city, county, or state) emergency management offices, the local chapter of the American Red Cross or from the U.S. Federal Emergency Management Agency (FEMA). Risk is not limited to natural disasters, though. Consideration should be given to the presence of hazardous materials in the area, whether they are produced locally or transported through the area on local roads. Don't forget the possibility of terrorist threats to high-profile sites in your area.

This risk assessment should include:

- Identification of and likelihood of various types of disasters (natural, human, and technical).
- Consequences and impact on the entire library of each disaster scenario.
- Estimated costs of loss and damage of collections.
- Estimated costs to replace and restore records, equipment, and facilities.
- Risk of the worst-case scenario striking the library.

Sample 1.3

Work Site Security Advisory System from Fairfax County (VA) Public Library

Threat Level Green (Low Risk, Business As Usual)

1. Review site-specific emergency response plan and general security procedures on an annual basis; conduct annual evacuation drill.
2. Ensure that all personnel receive proper training on emergency response plan, general security procedures, and agency protective measures for each threat level.
3. Assess facilities for vulnerabilities on an ongoing basis, and take appropriate measures to mitigate these vulnerabilities.
4. Ensure that emergency response and incident response teams are identified for each work site.
5. Enforce wearing of picture ID badges by all employees and volunteers so they are readily visible.
6. Verify identity of all county or contract personnel before providing access to non-public areas.
7. Ensure that all non-public entrances are kept locked at all times.
8. Log off all public and staff PCs at closing; personal desktop PCs should be logged off when not in use by designated individual.

Threat Level Blue (Guarded, General Risk)

1. Communicate threat level change to employees.
2. Review and update emergency response plan upon threat level change.
3. Update emergency contact lists.
4. Check and restock emergency supplies and equipment.

Threat Level Yellow (Elevated, Significant Risk)

1. Communicate threat level change to employees.
2. Review and update emergency response plan upon threat level change, increase the frequency of reviews to semi-annual, and continue drills.
3. Increase employee awareness by reviewing and retraining in emergency response plan, general security procedures, and agency protective measures for each threat level.
4. Increase security vigilance to include frequent perimeter observations. Report all suspicious persons, vehicles, items, and activities to supervisor and police at the non-emergency number (703) 691-2131.
5. Test alternate communications systems (e.g., walkie talkies, branch cell phones).

Threat Level Orange (High Risk)

1. Communicate threat level change to employees.
2. Post "Threat Level Orange" signs on front entrances*.
3. Review and update emergency response plan upon threat level change.
4. Verify all deliveries and check driver ID before allowing access to loading dock.
5. Restrict and/or monitor parking at entrances or areas close to facilities, if warranted by nature of specific threat.
6. Consider limiting access points to staff work areas.

7. Assess possible need for contract security personnel at certain public programs or events (administration).
8. Check function and status of internal security devices and emergency alarm panels.

Threat Level Red (Severe, Significant Risk)

1. Communicate threat level change to employees.
2. Review emergency response plan daily.
3. Review known threats and address possible security response (administration).
4. Consider canceling public meetings and events (administration).
5. Activate county closing plan when notified by county executive (administration).

Below is an example of security alert text employed by the library:

Orange Security Alert

Fairfax County has declared an orange (high) level security alert for county buildings.

- ***Please keep your belongings with you at all times.***
- ***Do not leave packages unattended.***
- ***Parking in certain areas may be temporarily restricted.***

We may take other temporary precautions to protect your safety and the security of this branch.

1.3 STEP 3: ESTABLISH DISASTER COMMUNICATIONS

One of the most important aspects of a disaster plan is the ability to communicate if a disaster should strike. Without communication, efforts to seek assistance, organize, mobilize, coordinate activities, and delegate assignments become impossible (Avery, 2002). There are many types of communications before (if possible), during, and after a disaster including internal within the library, communication with parent institution (campus in the case of a university library, city or county government in the case of a public library), and communication with the media on the status of the disaster.

First and foremost, there must be an effective system for communicating with all areas of the library in the event the building must be evacuated. Evacuation can occur if the fire alarm goes off, for a drill, for a bomb threat, or even if the building is in the path of a severe storm such as a hurricane and public safety officials have issued evacuation warnings. If the electricity is operational, an in-house intercom or public address system can be very effective in mass communication. Modern systems work through the library's phone system and allow for zoning, so that one or all areas can be contacted at one time. Sophisticated (meaning more expensive) systems allow for communication back to the command center. It is recommended that the circulation desk be the central point for notification of an emergency, since in most libraries this area is staffed any time the library is open. As always, there must be back-up, especially if the disaster cuts off the electricity and the intercom system with it. A bullhorn can be a very effective mass communication tool.

Every disaster plan should include a phone tree which lists who will call whom in the case of an emergency. The phone tree should include a back-up in case the first call person is not available or if that position is vacant when disaster strikes. For example, if the library director is the first call person, the deputy director or disaster team captain should be the back-up. Disaster team members should have a list of staff to be called, and departmental managers should be responsible for calling their own staff. Although this plan sounds easy, ensuring that everyone has current phone numbers can be a challenge. Human resources, if applicable, should be responsible for keeping a current phone numbers for all staff. For small libraries without their own human resources department, the library director should work with the parent institution to maintain an up-to-date phone list.

A secondary challenge is making sure the phone numbers are available at all times. Actually, the more recent technology of personal digital assistants (PDAs) makes this step easier. Instead of regularly updating paper lists, each member of the disaster team can update names and phone numbers on electronic contact lists and sync them to a PDA, which is very portable. If the PDA is charged regularly, the information should always be available. Alternate paper copies of the list should be kept at the office and at home. The disaster team leader should keep current the list of emergency numbers such as police, fire, or campus security, which should not change much. Keeping a current list of disaster recovery experts, such as moisture control, will be more challenging.

Often in disasters, the disaster team members find the library without electricity, which causes phone and e-mail services, our normal means of communication, to be disrupted. Therefore, the library should have institutional cell phones on hand or be prepared to reimburse staff for personal cell phone usage. Remember, though, that following a disaster some cellular telephone companies might not be operational.

Other wireless communication can also be helpful. If the library is without electricity for long, battery-operated walkie-talkies are helpful for communication during recovery efforts.

1.4 STEP 4: GAIN ACCESS TO FINANCES

In planning for a disaster, the most important step is insuring the library prior to a tragic event. As part of larger institutions, few libraries will do the negotiating for their own insurance, but an understanding of the principles is important.

The first step in insuring a library is a risk assessment. As you will read in Part II, different geographic areas are susceptible to different types of natural risk, but all libraries are at risk for fire, water damage, mold, and computer viruses. Insurance policies allow a library to reduce the risk of material or financial loss due to a disaster. There is a delicate balance between over-insuring and under-insuring. By over-insuring, you pay more than you need in premiums. By under-insuring, you would not have enough money to recover completely from a disaster. It is important to consult with risk managers, insurance brokers and agents, or insurance consultants before signing any contract.

There are two types of insurance—self-insurance and insurance contracts. Larger institutions such as universities or city and county governments often opt to self-insure, rather than contract with a company. In the case of self-insurance, the entity must have sum of money invested in a separate account to cover possible loss due to a disaster. This type of insurance requires careful money management, with strict guidelines for when the money can be used. The collection and facility should both be assessed annually to ensure there is enough money invested to recover in the case of a disaster. More common are contracts with major insurance companies. Provisions found in most insurance contracts include replacement value, actual cash value, average replacement cost, valuable papers and records policy, coinsurance, blanket coverage, specific coverage, all risk, named perils, and endorsement.

Having an adequate insurance policy is only half of the picture. In order to collect insurance money, you have to have proof of what you lost. For that reason it is a good idea to keep an up-to-date inventory of collections, furnishings, equipment, and supplies. Your online catalog records can be used as inventory of the collection. For the material items over a certain dollar level (furnishings, equipment, etc.) a staff member should be charged with updating an inventory on an annual basis. Remember that many items, especially computer equipment, devaluate annually.

Access to money following a disaster can be difficult. If the entire geographic area is without electricity, regular online bank transactions might not be possible and many ATM facilities may become inoperable. Many vendors will be unable to accept credit cards, though the need for supplies will be great. For this reason, it is advisable to have some back-up plans for getting your hands on money.

- The library, or parent institution, should have a real checkbook or the ability to manually write checks that can be used to purchase items or take to the bank to get cash. On business accounts, most large checks over $1,000 require two signatures, so keep signature cards up-to-date. In the case of a large university, city or county government, or a large corporation, the library director or accountant should know the key people with access to money.

- If possible, a few key library staff members should hold library-issued credit cards. These cards can be used to purchase disaster supplies to supplement those on hand, purchase food (breakfast, lunch, and possibly dinner) for recovery workers, and pay for recovery companies to help with clean-up.

- An on-hand source of cash is the money the library keeps for business purposes such as petty cash, service fees (fines, interlibrary loan, or mediated search charges) in the cash register or safe, and finally, the library's public photocopiers and photocopy card vending machines.

- Finally, often after a disaster, library staff in a sense of duty will spend their own money on disaster recovery. These staff members should be reimbursed as quickly as possible. With all the chaos after a disaster, it might be easy to push this step to the side while struggling with "bigger" issues.

There are many larger issues concerning finances in the wake of a disaster. While most libraries have an accounting department, most are also part of a larger system, such as a university, city, county, state, or business. These parent institutions will most likely control the finances following a disaster, but the library's accountant or the director should be familiar with many issues such as the specifics of the insurance policy, insurance company representatives, bank representatives, and auditors. Insurance policies should be written to cover library-owned items, but concessions should be made for personal items. Since we all spend so much time at work, we bring things in that make our work environment more appealing.

1.5 STEP 5: SECURE THE BUILDING

Every library faces security issues during normal operation but these issues escalate after a disaster. During the disaster emphasis must be placed on the safety of staff and clients, but during recovery efforts, many or all of the doors, usually secured by security systems, are wide open, including the front door, loading dock, departmental doors, and so forth. Many unknown people, including day laborers[4] and volunteers, have access to any area of the library. With exterior doors open, it is simple for total strangers to walk in and take anything they might fancy. Immediately after a disaster, chaos seems to reign, and it is difficult to monitor all doors. After the 2001 Houston flood, recovery work in the library progressed at a very quick pace, and many of the wet items were being discarded, while salvageable items were being shuffled from place to place. Unfortunately, since we had few secure locations, we lost a number of valuable items such as an undamaged computer, a possibly salvageable big-screen television, and a futon from the staff sick room. It was never determined if some salvageable items were accidentally mixed with items not to be saved or stolen. In the case of the computer and the television, we were quite sure they were stolen, but whether they were stolen by staff, laborers, or strangers off the street will never be known. The disaster team should indicate in the disaster plan specific employees who will be assigned to monitor entrance and exit points during recovery efforts. Or, if insurance or the library budget allows, the library can hire security guards, if available.

Following a disaster, not only are all the entrance and exit points accessible, but often staff areas are also susceptible to access by strangers. Doors normally secured by an electronic lock will be unlocked. Usually, these types of doors do not have a key back-up system. Staff should be briefed in advance to have locked cabinets or desks in their offices or work spaces to secure personal valuables (such as purses) in the event of a disaster. Recovery workers will also need areas where they can secure personal items. Even lunches can become targets when stored in a public area.

The bottom line—decisions, whether in advance or on the spot, must be made in regard to security. While staff members can be used to help secure doors, keep in mind that if the disaster is widespread, not all staff members will be able to help with recovery since they could have received damage at home. This can severely reduce the staffing level. Sometimes, the campus, city, county, or company can provide security agents to help monitor doors, if they are not needed elsewhere. If not, the disaster team

---

[4]Not to belittle hard-working day laborers, the Houston disaster was so wide-spread that Munters, our recovery firm, was forced to hire people off the street to help with clean-up efforts. These people came with little or no screening. Many were migrant workers from other countries who didn't speak English.

leader should investigate the cost of hiring a security firm to help. Depending on the circumstances, FEMA or insurance dollars might reimburse this expense. Even if they don't, not having to replace valuable items might defray some of the cost.

As we all know, library users imagine (or wish) that the library is always open, and all materials available. Immediately following the 2001 flood, people displaced from their offices in other buildings in the Texas Medical Center came to the library "just to photocopy some articles." It never occurred to them that the library suffered damage and might be closed. We had to keep either a staff member or a Texas Medical Center security guard at the front door to keep them out.[5] Securing affected areas does not end when the library reopens. Often, the damaged areas will not be fully repaired for weeks or months following the event, depending on the extent of the damage. Clients do not understand that some areas might be off-limits, even though other areas are open. In the weeks following our recovery, it became evident that clients had no idea that the library had suffered total destruction of the lower level. While we roped off stairwell access to the lower level, individual floor access via elevator could not be disabled. Construction workers often found clients wandering around the "hard hat" area trying to reach the now non-existent computer lab. The building manager was forced to build a doorframe with a locked door around the elevator exit on the lower level. Only staff with a key could exit through the door into the construction area. The elevator itself could not be disabled, since it provides access to the second floor of the library and was used by staff and construction crews to access the street level. Additionally, it was equally difficult to keep staff out of the area. Despite numerous verbal and written instructions not to enter the construction area, those who used the loading dock for normal access to the library found it difficult to change habits. Fortunately, we had no injuries, staff or client, during reconstruction.

1.6 STEP 6: FORMULATE A LIST OF STOCK DISASTER SUPPLIES

After a disaster hits is not the time to be thinking about purchasing disaster supplies! Having supplies on hand can help minimize damage and speed recovery. (Guide 2 provides a detailed list of agencies and consultants, many of whom offer emergency items not readily available elsewhere.) For

---

[5]An interesting note is that many folks just wanted to return items before they became overdue. The person at the door graciously took the books and explained that we would not be assessing fines for the time the library was closed.

example, if you have large plastic sheets on hand, materials underneath a broken pipe can be protected from water until the water can be turned off or the leak fixed. Supplies should be kept in a central area, ideally away from windows and in a fairly secluded area. Some libraries keep smaller disaster supplies in a large plastic trashcan with plastic trash bag liners. Other libraries keep these supplies in locked a cabinet in secure areas such as administration or a department manager's office to minimize the possibility of theft or "borrowing" items in lieu of ordering them for regular usage. Disaster team leaders might want to consider having individual supply cabinets on each floor of the library, and most definitely in each branch library. When disaster strikes, disaster team members will need access to the supplies as quickly as possible.

A suggested list of disaster supplies:

- Aprons—To protect clothing, especially if the disaster occurs during business hours and recovery staff are in business attire.
- Barricade Tape—To rope off affected areas.
- Batteries—For flashlights, walkie-talkies, and portable and weather radios.
- Book Trucks—While not in the disaster supply closet, these will be needed to remove damaged items of all sorts.
- Bottled Water—Water can be purchased in individual bottles or the larger one or five gallon variety.[6]
- Boxes—Collapsed cardboard boxes are needed for many events, but especially in packing damaged books and journals to be sent for drying.
- Brooms—Push brooms are especially helpful in cleaning large damaged areas.
- Camera—For documentation immediately after the disaster.
- Can Opener—For non-perishable food in the supply closet.
- Canned Food—To feed recovery staff or even clients if unable to leave the building.
- Caution Wet Floor Signs—For placement in recently flooded or cleaned area.
- Clipboards—To ease recovery staff in writing notes and inventory.

---

[6]The body can survive without food for days. However, water requirements must be maintained daily. Emergencies requiring greater expenditure of energy necessitate greater water consumption. Light work requires 16 ounces daily, while heavy work levels necessitate 64 ounces per day (Durham, 2002).

- Disinfectant—To minimize contamination.
- Duct/Masking Tape—To tape the boxes and a million other uses.
- Extension Cords—For many electrical items such as vacuum cleaners, shop vacuums, and drying fans.
- Face Masks (Disposable)—To protect recovery staff from dust, mold, and other contaminants.
- First Aid Kit—To treat minor injuries.
- Flashlights (Including Spare Batteries and Bulbs)—Often in a disaster there is no electricity.
- Freezer (Wax) Paper—For wrapping books and other materials before sending for freeze drying.
- Gloves (Work and Rubber)—To protect recovery workers' hands.
- Granola/Candy Bars/Chips—Sealed food items to go with canned food.
- Hard Hats—For head protection in damaged areas.
- Keep Out Signs—To work with barricade tape to keep all but recovery staff out of affected areas.
- Mops—For cleanup.
- Paper Towels—To help with cleanup.
- Pens/Pencils—For taking notes and inventory.
- Permanent Markers—For marking boxes and items to be discarded.
- Plastic Sheeting—To cover shelves and furniture in case of a water pipe leak.
- Plastic Trash Cans—For collecting refuse.
- Rags (Clean)—For cleanup.
- Rubber Boots—To protect feet and shoes.
- Rubber Buckets—For cleanup.
- Safety Glasses—To protect recovery staff's eyes from contaminantion.
- Sponges—For cleanup.
- Toilet Paper—In case supply in restrooms have been contaminated.
- Tool Kit—To dismantle furniture and computers.
- Trash Bags—For disposal of ruined materials.
- Writing Paper or Note Pads—For taking notes and inventory.

Since some items have a short shelf life, perishable items and batteries should be checked twice a year. A convenient time to check these items is when the switch to or from Daylight Savings Time occurs.

In planning for the probability (even possibility) that acts of terrorism will occur in the future, many government officials have rejected the feasibility of evacuating large populations from dense urban settings. One computer model estimated that in the Washington D.C. metropolitan area it would take 4 to 6 hours to evacuate the city's working population of 1 million people, assuming there were no accidents, construction, or illegally parked vehicles. For this reason, the idea of "sheltering-in-place" within one's home or community has garnered increasing attention and support. Libraries, as public spaces, could be called upon to serve as shelters (Gursky, 2004). Additionally, in the case of biological agents let loose in the air, governments might require everyone to stay put. For these reasons, the library disaster team should consider stocking disaster supplies for library clients as well as staff. This might mean having additional food, water, and facemasks on hand.

Finally, all staff members should be encouraged to keep a three-day supply of medications, a change of clothes, and a small supply of personal food items in the library during times when disaster is more likely. This would include hurricane season in the Gulf and Atlantic coasts, tornado season in the Midwest, and during the winter in the northern areas of the United States. These personal supplies might become very vital in the case of sheltering-in-place.

1.7 STEP 7: UNDERSTAND THE VULNERABILITIES

As we all know, the best offense is a good defense. In the case of disaster planning, one of the most valuable aspects is to know and understand your vulnerabilities and, if possible, be proactive. This proactiveness will often cost money, lots of money. Therefore, a library director must be prepared to defend the expense. Often, the money is made available only after disaster strikes through insurance or FEMA as mitigation.

The first step in knowing your vulnerabilities is to do a site survey or a physical examination of the facilities. (Guide 4, the "Solinet Disaster Prevention and Protection Checklist," serves as a useful guide for conducting such a survey.) Keeping local potential disasters in mind, consider what is housed in the lower level in the case of flooding, exposed windows for wind damage in areas affected by hurricanes or tornadoes, combustible materials verses non-combustible along with fire/smoke detectors and sprinkler systems. Suggested actions to minimize potential damage include:

- Move as much as possible off the ground floor in case of flood.
- Install flood gates.
- Keep plastic sheeting on hand for pipe leaks.
- Shutter windows.
- Create a green roof.[7]
- Do not shelve books on top shelves as they tend to topple easier.
- Do not situate shelves near seating areas.
- Maintain constant heat and humidity rates to avoid mold and mildew.
- Keep portable fire extinguishers on hand and train staff when to use them.
- Use a dry pipe or Halon fire system.
- Install zoned fire/smoke detection systems.
- Install fire doors in open stairwells.
- Institute a building-wide "no open flame" rule.
- Restrict food and drink to specific areas.
- Install firewalls and run virus protection regularly on all computers.
- Back up all servers regularly and store backups off site.
- Keep trees and bushes trimmed away from the building.

Part 2 will discuss more specifically things that can be done for different types of distasters to minimize damage.

Sample 1.4

Continuity of Operations Plan from Fairfax County (VA) Public Library

Fairfax County Public Library (FCPL) has developed the plan outlined below to facilitate the continuity of its operations, the protection of its assets, and the eventual orderly resumption of full service to residents in the event of a significant emergency event, act of war, or disaster. The plan will be included as an appendix to the Fairfax County emergency operations plan.

---

[7]A new concept for buildings in flood-prone areas is that of a green roof, or a contained green space on top of buildings. Benefits of a green roof are expanded roof life, storm water retention reducing the possibility of leaks, decreased utility bills, sound insulation and they also have positive effects on the environment.

Mission Essential Functions

Protection of assets (libraries and contents).

Protection of information and databases (customer, inventory, transactions, and information found on library Web site).

Protection of Assets

FCPL operates twenty-one remote locations (library branches and technical operations), which contain significant inventories of valuable equipment, furniture, and library materials. Each of these locations has standard operating policies and procedures for clearing and securing the building at the end of each day's normal operating hours. These same procedures are followed whenever the library branch is required to evacuate for an unusual event, or when weather or other conditions cause an early closing.

In addition, each remote location has developed an emergency response plan, which is regularly updated and practiced. The emergency response plans contain additional guidance regarding procedures to be followed in specific emergency situations. The emergency response plans are the library's on-site blueprint for the protection of both human life and county assets.

Library administration and access services are both located within the government center, and are included in the government center emergency response plan.

Protection of Information and Databases

The Department of Information Technology provides custodial care of the library's servers, information, and databases, which reside in the enterprise operations center. As custodians, DIT staff ensure that mission-critical information and data are safeguarded by:

- Implementing back-up plans and procedures, including off-site storage of back-ups.
- Planning and practicing recovery procedures for rapid restoration of data for the resumption of normal operations.
- Maintaining relationships with applications vendors for the administration of the software used by the library.
- Maintaining networks and servers according to county standards and guidelines.

The library's business system, Sirsi Unicorn, is a turn-key, off-the-shelf application, which can be restored by the vendor, if necessary. The library also provides access to several subscription electronic information sources through links on the library Web site. Since these resources do not reside on the county network, they can quickly be available if the county's network resources are available to make the links.

Line of Succession

There are four key FCPL administrators, for whom the following interim successors have been identified:

Library Director
Deputy Director
Associate Director, Support Services
Associate Director, Library Administration
Branch Coordinator
Branch Coordinator

Deputy Director
Associate Director, Support Services
Associate Director, Library Administration
Branch Coordinator
Branch Coordinator

Associate Director, Support Services
Cataloging Coordinator
Coordinator, Collection Management & Acquisitions
Assistant Coordinator, Collection Management & Acquisitions

Associate Director, Library Administration
Deputy Director
Human Resource Manager
Financial Management Officer

1.8 STEP 8: ESTABLISH EVACUATION PLANS

According to the U.S. Occupational Safety and Health Administration (OSHA), all employers should have an established emergency evacuation plan. Most commonly, buildings are evacuated because of fire, but in recent times other factors can cause an evacuation. As the threat of terrorism elevates, bomb threats and bioterroristic threats have become more common. In libraries in high elevations, or at the bottom of a mountain, the threat of an avalanche could necessitate quick evacuation.

At minimum, emergency evacuation plans should include:

- A preferred method for reporting fires and other emergencies.
- An evacuation policy and procedure.
- Emergency escape procedures and route assignments, such as floor plans, workplace maps, and safe or refuge areas.
- Names, titles, departments, and telephone numbers of individuals both within and outside your company to contact for additional information or explanation of duties and responsibilities under the emergency plan.
- Procedures for employees, who remain to perform or shut down critical plant operations, operate fire extinguishers,

or perform other essential services that cannot be shut down for every emergency alarm before evacuating.
- Rescue and medical duties for any workers designated to perform them (U.S. OSHA, 2001).

A subcommittee of the disaster team should be a team of staff members who are charged with evacuating certain areas of the building. There should be representatives from every department to serve as floor wardens, each responsible for evacuation of specific public and private areas. Floor wardens often wear a special badge identifying them as such. Progressive institutions will issue floor wardens special vests and hard hats to be worn during a drill or an actual evacuation. These items will help identify the officials, and in the case of hard hats, help with personal protection since they will be the last to evacuate. Floor wardens usually keep a flashlight nearby, in case of power outage. If possible, it is important to have alternate floor wardens for every area.

All floor wardens and alternates, and possibly all disaster team members should receive training on the use of fire extinguishers, which includes when NOT to use the extinguisher but call the fire department. According to the U.S. Fire Administration, fight or flight is the most important decision to make when facing a fire. If trained to use a fire extinguisher, staff should size up the fire and determine if it is small enough to be put out with a fire extinguisher.

Additionally, every type of library should have evacuation plans posted in all areas, including public and private, with the name of the floor warden and alternate listed. (Appendices 6–10 provide examples of evacuation plans employed by a variety of libraries.) Of course, the floor wardens are not in the library 24 hours a day, so a back-up plan should also be in place for the evening and weekend staff. While floor wardens bear the bulk of the

---

- Make sure everyone is out of danger.
- Notify the fire department.
- Size up the fire—is it small enough to be handled by a fire extinguisher?
- Make sure the fire is not between you and the exit.
- Is your extinguisher the right extinguisher for the job?
- Is the fire extinguisher fully charged? You can tell by looking at the pressure gauge.
- Do you know how to use the fire extinguisher? www.usfa.fema.gov/public/cfs/cfs-03

Figure 1-3. Basic Steps before Fighting a Fire

responsibility, all employees must become familiar with the location of exits, fire alarms, and fire extinguishers in the building where they work.

An important part of an evacuation plan is the designation of the assembly area for staff and clients. This area might be designated by the campus, city, county, or by the library itself. It is important to have an alternate assembly area in case the primary area is deemed unsafe. If everyone is assembled in one place, communication is easier.

Planning—Pre-Emergency Responsibilities for Floor Wardens:

- Know at least two exits (elevators are not exits during evacuations).
- Know the location and operation of the fire alarm system.
- Keep emergency phone numbers conspicuously posted.
- Participate in all evacuation drills and take them seriously, knowing area-specific evacuation procedures.
- Become familiar with the locations and types of fire extinguishers, and know how to use them.
- Know where the members of your department are expected to assemble upon exiting.
- Be aware of neighboring departments in case they need assistance in evacuation.
- Advise personnel to evacuate at the first sign of an alarm.
- Assign one person and a back-up to assist in evacuating disabled individuals.

Duties During an Emergency

- Unless you are sure that someone has already done so, activate the alarms and call 911. In some institutions alarms automatically notify emergency agencies, but a back-up call ensures contact has been made.
- If the alarm is because of a fire, confine it, if possible, by closing all doors and windows.
- Alert everyone in the building so they can begin evacuating.
- Double check neighboring departments to make sure that they are aware of the evacuation.
- If anyone refuses to leave the building, note their location and continue to evacuate the building.

- Report the last known location of anyone refusing to evacuate to emergency officials.
- Take small personal belongings and exit the building.
- Meet at the pre-designated location outside the building so that a headcount of the department may be taken.
- Do not re-enter the building until allowed by the emergency officials.

Emergency Procedures for Disabled Personnel

- One pre-designated person should stay with the disabled individual while another person reports his/her location to emergency officials who are trained in evacuation of the disabled.
- Close all doors and wait for emergency officials.
- Hearing-impaired and visually impaired persons need only one person assigned to notify them of the evacuation and guide them to safe escape routes.

Sample 1.5

Departmental Evacuation Plan from the HAM-TMC Library

Fire Captain: Name of Staff Member

Alternate: Name of Staff Member

All alarms will be treated as an actual fire alarm and the following procedures will be followed in evacuating the lab, classroom, and street-level public areas.

When the alarm sounds, staff members assemble in the reception area, closing their office doors as they leave.

Gather essential personal belongings.

Captain or alternate brings a flashlight in case lights are out.

Walk through personal offices, computer lab, classroom, and street-level conference room and direct patrons and staff to nearest emergency exit.

Check that operations and RML offices are aware of the evacuation.

Close all doors and turn off lights in each office and room.

Congregate at the UT Medical School breezeway and wait there until the all clear is given.

The departmental fire marshal or alternate will then account for all department personnel and report to the team leader.

Directions to Assembly Area:

Take the short flight of concrete steps up and cross the paved area to the sidewalk and turn left.

Follow sidewalk to Ross Sterling; turn left toward patio area and go to the breezeway under the UT Medical School.

Alternate Directions to Assembly Area:

Take short concrete stairs to loading dock then to sidewalk and make a left along East Cullen then left along Ross Sterling to the UT Medical School breezeway.

If the fire is small and contained, use the fire extinguisher across from the elevator, inside the HIEC lab to the right of the main door and to the right of the emergency exit next to the ladies room.

1.9 STEP 9: WRITE THE DISASTER PLAN

The writing of a disaster plan is the most important step in planning for a disaster since it serves as a blueprint for recovery efforts, which helps to minimize loss. The plan incorporates many of the steps listed above and is the culmination of much planning and work. As noted in the introduction, of the librarians responding to a survey sent out on the Medlib-l listserv, many indicated that their libraries did not have an up-to-date disaster plan. Rather than completing the survey, most responded by asking for information on writing a plan.

The first thing to do when writing a plan is covered in Step 2, the risk assessment of the types of disasters that might occur in a specific geographic area. (See Part II of this book for discussions on many of the types of disasters libraries might encounter with suggestions on how to plan and recover from specific events.) This list could include natural disasters such as floods, tornadoes, wild fires, earthquakes, and hurricanes. (Appendices 3, 14, and 15 provide first-hand accounts of specific library disasters.) There are also man-made disasters such as electrical fires, plumbing leaks, vandalism, and the use of water to extinguish a fire. Also to be considered are disasters of different scales such as mold or insect infestation. Finally, there are the truly tragic disasters that are cause by acts of terrorism, which include computer viruses, tainted mail, or even destruction of buildings. No plan can cover every eventuality, but having a plan in place can provide valuable information such as chain of command, duties of specific staff members, lists of disaster supplies and recovery firms, and emergency phone numbers. "New" types of disasters, such as massive blackouts, can be added as the plan is updated annually.

Certain elements are essential to a disaster plan and a sample plan is included in the appended CD-ROM. (Likewise, Guide 1 presents the Disaster Plan Template offered by Amigos Library Services, Inc.) Make sure the plan is a working document to be reviewed frequently and updated on a regular basis. Essential elements of a good plan should include:

General Introduction—This section includes the purpose of the disaster

Discussion of recovery for specific types of disasters is covered in Part II.

plan, disaster definitions, update schedule, and identify the main author and where the guide is stored both electronically and in hard copy. It is recommended that each disaster team member keep a paper copy of the plan at home and at the office. A .pdf version can also be downloaded to personal digital assistant (PDA), which are recommend for all disaster team members.

Disaster Team—The disaster team should be listed by position (e.g., deputy director, accountant) with a list of duties in case of a disaster.

Phone Numbers—There should be four lists of phone numbers, a list of emergency numbers such as police, fire, and sewer departments; a phone tree of who calls whom among the library staff in the case of a disaster; a list of recovery experts who can help after the disaster strikes; and a list of media contacts, including national library publications such as *American Libraries* and *Library Journal*. The phone-tree list of employees should include office, home, cellular, and pager numbers, where applicable. This section of the disaster plan is the most difficult to keep updated. To make the process easier and paperless, the all phone numbers can be maintained on disaster team members' electronic address book, which can be synced with their PDAs.

Library Closure Procedures—Depending on the library, closure may be at the discretion of the director, the mayor, the university or college president, the company CEO, or whoever has ultimate responsibility. The phone tree listed above should be used to inform staff of the decision as quickly as possible. The last thing anyone wants if for diligent employees to venture out in a dangerous situation to get to work. Closure procedures should include notification of the media so that library clients will be informed. Media can also be used to inform clients and staff when the library reopens.

Emergency Evacuation Procedures—These procedures should be specific to every section of the library. There should be staff from each department responsible for evacuation of that department as well as the public areas near the department. Evacuation procedures should include the assembly area outside the library, an alternate assembly area, what to do with evacuation of the physically disabled, communication with authorities, communication on successful evacuation, and communication on returning to the library once secured by authorities.

Communication—As seen above, communication is vital during a disaster and includes communication between the disaster team, staff, clients, campus/city/county officials, and media. Various forms of communication can be used including cellular phones, walkie-talkies, hand-held radios, and e-mail (if the library has not lost electricity).

Disaster Supplies—The library should keep on hand supplies to be used in the case of a disaster such as flashlights with good batteries and bulbs, bottled water, mops, buckets, and plastic sheeting. It is also recommended that staff members keep a basic supply of things they might need if disaster strikes. For example, during hurricane season, we remind staff to keep a small supply of medications in their desk drawers and some non-perishable food items, just in case we get stranded in the building.

Specific Disasters—The plan should include how staff should react to disasters specific to the geographic area. For example, coastal areas should include tropical storms and hurricanes, but not earthquakes except for areas like California, which suffers both types of events. The Midwestern area of the United States would definitely include tornadoes, but not hurricanes. Unfortunately, due to recent events, the disaster list should include those caused by terrorism including bomb threats, anthrax, and computer viruses. Finally, we learned in the summer of 2003 that large geographic areas could also suffer from electrical blackouts, which also have implications for libraries, especially those located in health institutions such as hospitals.

Opening Procedures—Every plan should include procedures on opening the library, first to the staff for recovery effort, and then to the public. In most instances the library will be part of a larger institution which will, most likely, be responsible for the initial safety inspection prior to anyone entering the facility. If not, local authorities should be called in to inspect the premises before anyone enters. The decision of when to open the library to the public is usually the discretion of the library director.

Priority List of Collections, Administrative Records, and Equipment—While everything in a library is considered valuable, there are some items that are more valuable such as payroll, servers, and certain collections. Each library must assess their own collections and determine what are priority items.

Inventories—For insurance and replacement purposes, the plan should include an inventory, including photographs or videos, of furniture and equipment. Hopefully, for computer files and electronic catalogs, the servers are backed up regularly with the tapes being stored off site.

Security—The plan should include names and numbers of in-house security, local or campus security, city or county security, and even state or federal security such as FBI, ATF, and the National Guard.

Library Floor Plans—Every disaster plan should include detailed floor plans of the entire building. While library, university, city, and company staff might be involved in recovery of a disaster, most likely, outside people will also be involved. Having an accurate floor plan can provide identification of damaged areas and collections, facilitate disposal and recovery, and can especially help with reconstruction.

Glossary of Acronyms (e.g., FEMA, OSHA)—Every plan will include the usage of various acronyms. A glossary appended to the end of the document will help define these acronyms.

Once written, the disaster plan must be reviewed and updated regularly. Each member of the disaster team should keep an updated paper copy of the plan at work and at home. It is advisable to also load the plan onto personal PDAs. The plan should also be loaded onto the library's intranet so others can have access, which should not only be housed locally but should have a mirror site somewhere geographically distant from the library.

1.10 STEP 10: CONDUCT DISASTER DRILLS

One of the most proactive things any disaster team can do to lessen the effects of a disaster is to be prepared, including conducting regular disaster drills. There can be many kinds of drills: fire, inclement weather, or a bomb threat, for instance. It is essential that all library staff be prepared to respond appropriately in the face of emergencies such as fires, explosions, and chemical releases, but floor wardens from each department should facilitate evacuation. It can also be helpful to time drills, to see if there are ways to improve evacuation time.

All institutions should schedule fire/evacuation drills at least once a year. Often the parent institution schedules these drills, but if not library management can make the decision to conduct a drill. Drills serve to inform staff and clients what to do in the event of an actual evacuation, and also reveal problems in those plans. For example, does the intercom system really work in all areas, do floor wardens know to check other departments, and do all staff members know the official assembly area?

Sometimes an impromptu drill can help illustrate where planning needs to be tightened. On January 9, 2003 the University of Texas at Houston Health Science Center received a bomb threat via a phone call at approximately 12:30 P.M. Since many UT-H offices are housed on the third and fourth floor of the library building, the decision to evacuate the library was made. While evacuation interrupted daily activities, it served to show flaws in current evacuation plans that would not be revealed in a scheduled fire drill. For example, building officials opted to not pull the fire alarm, but to call officials by phone. Therefore, fire alarms did not go off and library staff relied on the internal paging for notification of clients and staff. While this paging system is broadcast in most public areas, it does not broadcast in all office areas. Thus, two departments were oblivious to the alarm. Additionally, library staff are instructed in the evacuation plans to assemble next to the UT-H building, which in this case was a very bad idea, since the threat was against the University of Texas. When staff were told to go to areas away from the UT building, another problem arose, that of reassembling staff once the all clear was given, since they were no longer in a central area. The disaster team has since implemented plans of communicating by cell phone in the case that staff need to leave the designated meeting area.

Since the flood caused by Tropical Storm Allison, the Texas Medical Center (TMC) has conducted emergency weather drills. These drills have emulated an actual hurricane hitting the Houston area and take place over an extended period of time. During the first drill, TMC staff sent faxes and e-mails about a fictional storm in the Gulf of Mexico, its approach to the

Texas Gulf Coast, its eventual landfall, and the resulting damage. All TMC were encouraged to initiate emergency plans such as activating floodgates, evacuation of low-lying areas, and the dismissal (in theory) of non-essential personnel.

Sample 1.6

Disaster Drill Memos from the Texas Medical Center

Since the tragic events of September 11, 2001, many communities are conducting emergency drills. On September 25, approximately 1,700 emergency responders and health care professionals from twenty government agencies gathered to participate in a full-scale terrorism exercise. The event was the largest multi-agency terrorism preparedness drill to take place in Houston. In the scenario, a large fall festival at a local sports stadium with 100,000 attendees was attacked by a suicide bomber aboard a city bus. This bomb was not only explosive, but included a biological agent. Unfortunately, the local libraries were not invited to participate in this drill, but there are areas where librarians could be helpful.

Finally, drills cannot take place in a vacuum, but must involve people outside the library proper. First, building or campus facilities management as well as security must be involved. In the case of a building evacuation, someone must be posted at all doors to keep anyone from reentering before the building is deemed safe. City and county fire departments must also be notified in the case of a drill for two reasons. First, to conduct an effective drill, the fire alarm must be pulled. The fire department must be notified in advance so they know that the alarm is only a drill. Finally, many institutions like to have the campus or local fire department on hand to help assess the effectiveness of the drill and to make suggestions on improvements.

Sample 1.7

Fire Drill Policy from the Waupaca (WI) Area Public Library

In an attempt to provide a safe atmosphere during a crisis, the staff of Waupaca Area Public Library will, twice yearly, hold a fire drill. These drills should take place during the months of May and November. The drills will be coordinated with guidelines set by the Waupaca Area Fire Department. After each drill, a report sheet will be filled out so that staff and fire officials can see possible areas of safety violations and problems and monitor progress of staff training.

The fire drills will be activated in different ways so that the fire alarm system can be tested, as well as staff skills be tested. Canned smoke, heat and magnetic sources will be used to activate a fire alarm.

At no time will a library employee re-enter the building during a drill, false alarm, or actual fire until an all clear page has been issued. This is in compliance with Waupaca Area Fire Department regulations.

Approved by the Waupaca Area Public Library Board of Trustees March 8, 1994.

1.11 STEP 11: REVISE AND UPDATE THE PLAN

One of the most important steps in disaster planning, yet the easiest to forget, is to keep the plan updated. When Tropical Storm Allison flooded Houston, the HAM-TMC Library had a disaster plan that was ten years out of date. Most of the information in it was obsolete. For example, in the list of priority items to be saved was the shelf list. The library has not had a physical shelf list for many years. Additionally, there were no instructions on saving valuable servers and restoring data and the phone tree listed staff that no longer worked at the library. Therefore, the library's disaster team now meets quarterly to reread the plan and make updates. The disaster team leader and human resources update the phone tree anytime key staff leave and are replaced.

PUTTING IT ALL TOGETHER

The library's approach to emergency preparedness must be more than just a written plan, although a written plan is a core component of an preparedness effort. An effective library strategy considers emergency preparedness a process, not just a product, with the following steps:

> Step 1: Create a Disaster Team
>
> Step 2: Risk Assessment
>
> Step 3: Establish Disaster Communications
>
> Step 4: Gain Access to Finances
>
> Step 5: Secure the Building
>
> Step 6: Formulate a List of Stock Disaster Supplies
>
> Step 7: Understand the Vulnerabilities
>
> Step 8: Establish an Evacuation Plan
>
> Step 9: Write a Disaster Plan
>
> Step 10: Conduct Disaster Drills
>
> Step 11: Revise and Update the Plan

The California Preservation Program's Generic Disaster Plan workbook (http://cpc.stanford.edu/disasters/generic/index.html) workbook delineates the four key areas that any library's disaster plan should address:

- Disaster Preparedness and Prevention
- Disaster Response
- Disaster Recovery: Restoration Methods
- Disaster Recovery: Recovery and Completion

Each of these key areas is elaborated in further detail (see The Generic Disaster Plan) throughout the workbook.

Sample 1.8

The Generic Disaster Plan Workbook

Outline of Generic Disaster Plan

The Generic Disaster Plan Workbook is based on the IELDRN Generic Disaster plan and provides a framework to assist institutions in writing their own disaster plan. The document presented here is optimized for Web presentation. It is also available for *printing*. A final version is available for download as a Rich Text Format file (.rtf) and can be modified using a word processing program such as Microsoft Word or WordPerfect.

Introduction

Modules:

1. Disaster Preparedness and Prevention
    1. Guidelines
    2. Collection Salvage Priorities
    3. Insurance Coverage
    4. Security, Public Relations, Psychology
    5. General Housekeeping Guidelines
    6. Hazards Survey
    7. Building Safety Checklists

2. Disaster Response
    1. Contact Lists for Initial Response to an Emergency
    2. Disaster Response Activities
    3. Preliminary Disaster Recovery Planning
    4. Assessment of Damage
    5. Planning the Recovery
    6. Appendices

3. Disaster Recovery: Restoration Methods
    1. Freezing
    2. Drying
    3. Smoke, Soot and Char Damage
    4. Broken Books
    5. Biopredation

4. Disaster Recovery: Recovery and Completion
    1. Housekeeping
    2. Reshelving
    3. Assessment and Revision of the Plan

From http://cpc.stanford.edu/disasters/generic/index.html.

SUMMARY

Finally, it should be noted that disasters can also have a positive effect on the people affected by support offered by friends, colleagues, and strangers. While many TMC institutions worked together after the June 2001 flooding, there are examples from all over. Years ago, in a conversation with a minister of a predominantly African American church which was destroyed by arson, the minister said that the disaster helped to bring the community together. They received aid from all areas of the community and from churches of every denomination.

One account from a physician in New York City is very compelling.

> As a native New Yorker, I watched the Twin Towers go up. And then I marveled as, at their feet, a whole ecosystem blossomed—river front gardens, museums, esplanades, winter playgrounds, and Manhattan miracle, a softball field. Their destruction brought a stupendous outpouring of generosity and human feeling from all over the country—truckloads of Philly cheese steaks from Jefferson Hospital, mountains of teddy bears from Oklahoma City, and doctors and nurses from Alaska and every state in between to take the long shifts of the rescue effort. At the edges of the killing ground, a new spirit seemed to take root. Nothing would more honor our dead than to try to take that spirit, humbly, into the wider world. (Dejer, 2002)

BIBLIOGRAPHY

Avery, Bill. "Are You Ready?" *Parks and Recreation* 37, no. 9 (September 2002): 114–16.

D'Antoni, Helen. "Disaster Preparedness for the Unprepared." *Information Week* 879 (March 11, 2002): 74.

Dajer, Antonio. "The Lessons of September 11." *Topics in Emergency Medicine* 24, no. 4 (December 2002): 7–11.

Durham, Britt and Williams, Joanne. "Civilian Preparedness: Disaster Planning for Everyone." *Topics in Emergency Medicine* 24, no. 3 (September 2002): 66–70.

Forston, Judith. "Disaster Planning: Managing the Financial Risk." *The Bottom Line* 6, no.1 (Spring 1992): 26–33.

Gursky, Elin. "Schools as Shelters: Anticipating 21st-Century Terrorist Threats." *HPAC Engineering* 76, no. 2 (February 2004): 49–53.

Rike, Barb. "Prepared or Not . . . That is the Vital Question." *Information Management Journal* 37, no. 3 (May/June 2002): 25–33.

U.S. Code of Federal Regulations, Title 36, Volume 3, Part 12.36.14. (Available: www.access.gpo.gov/nara/cfr.waisidx_98/36cfr1236 _98.html.)

U.S. Occupational Safety and Health Administration. *How to Plan for Workplace Emergencies and Evacuations.* Washington, D.C.: OSHA, 2001.

Zablocki, Elaine. "Preparing for the Improbable: A New Dimension in Hospital Disaster Planning." *Medicine on the Net* 8, no. 2 (February 2002): 1–4.

PREPARE BY UNDERSTANDING THE MOST COMMON DISASTERS

Like death and taxes, natural and manmade disasters are a fact of life. In Part I, we focused on the organizational and planning tools that are available to libraries as they are developing disaster plans. In Part II, we will look at the various types of disasters, how to plan for them, and implications for libraries. Planning for disasters requires that we think about the unthinkable, taking into account both the characteristics of different types of disasters and the implications each type of disaster has for libraries. It is essential for library staff to consider this background information, when developing their local disaster plans.

One of the first known library disasters was the burning of the great Library of Alexandria in the First Century B.C. The cause of this disaster is still being debated today, but historical scholars still agree that this was one of the greatest losses of archival material in history. Another early disaster was the burning of the library in the Gall Monastery in Switzerland in 937 A.D., a disaster that was caused by an arsonist. In more contemporary times, the British destroyed the Library of Congress in Washington, D.C. in 1814. In the past decade alone libraries in North America have been struck by earthquakes, tornadoes, floods, fires (manmade and natural), and hurricanes, to name just a few varieties of misfortune.

We will look at the following types of disasters:

Natural Disasters

2.1	Building Fires
2.2	Wildfires
2.3	Hurricanes
2.4	Tsunamis/Tidal Waves/Tidal Surges
2.5	Floods
2.6	Tornadoes
2.7	Earthquakes
2.8	Landslides and Debris Flows
2.9	Winter Storms

NATURAL DISASTERS

The scope of most disasters is largely local. Many disasters lead to other disasters. For example, extinguishing a fire leads to water damage; hurricanes lead to floods, storm surge, wind damage and tornadoes; winter storms can lead to avalanches. We will not look at disasters (such as war or famine) that are primarily national or international in scope.

When appropriate, we will consider essential **Characteristics**, focusing on what to do *Before*, *During*, and *After* the disaster. While this section of the book is a brief summary of the most prevalent types of disasters, Part III contains a list of websites that can be of assistance with specific emergencies. The list of agencies and consultants in Guide 2 provides valuable information on folks who are available to help before, during and after a disaster. With each type of disaster, a section on putting it all together highlights the major considerations for library staff in the event of an emergency and provides detailed examples of disaster plans and/or disaster scenarios.

One thing must be emphasized when dealing with disasters. When disaster strikes, there are many levels in which the library will be affected. The most important issue is the safety of the library staff and patrons. Secondly, if the library has suffered a disaster, such as a hurricane, then some of the library staff have likely suffered similar effects at home. Not all staff will be readily available to assist with recovery. Finally, library staff are not normally safety experts. All recovery efforts must be done in conjunction with trained experts.

2.1 BUILDING FIRES

While many of the disasters discussed in this book are specific to particular geographic regions or at specific times of the year, building or structural fires can hit anywhere and during any season. In a quick search of the library literature, building fires were noted in the Minnetonka (MN) High School Media Center, the main branch of the Detroit (MN) Public Library, the Macedon (NY) Public Library, Bush Memorial Library at Hamline University in St. Paul (MN) and a branch of the Clearwater (FL) Public Library System in North Greenwood. Whether accidental or as the result of an arsonist, fires use library and archival materials (books, archives, photographs, furniture) as fuel. While a fire is bad enough on its own, the efforts by fire fighters to extinguish the fire contribute additional destructive measures.

CHARACTERISTICS

Fire burns because three elements are present—heat, fuel, and oxygen. In technical language, fire is a chemical reaction that happens when a material unites with oxygen so rapidly that it produces flame. Fire is like a triangle, if any one of three elements is taken away, the fire goes out. This principle is the basis for fire extinguishment. Heat can be taken away by cooling, oxygen can be taken away by excluding air, fuel can be removed to a place where there is no flame, chemical reaction can be stopped by inhibiting the oxidation of the fuel.

There are three types of fires that might occur in libraries:

- **CLASS A** fires occur in ordinary combustible materials such as wood, cloth and paper. The most commonly used extinguishing agent is water, which cools and quenches. Special dry chemicals also extinguish fires in these materials. These chemicals provide a rapid knock down of flame and form a fire retardant coating, which prevents reflash.

- **CLASS B** fires occur in the vapor-air mixture over the surface of flammable liquids such as grease, gasoline, and lubricating oils. A smothering or combustion inhibiting effect is necessary to extinguish Class B fires. Dry chemical, foam, vaporizing liquids, carbon dioxide and water fog all can be used as extinguishing agents depending on the circumstances of the fire.

- **CLASS C** fires occur in electrical equipment where non-conducting extinguishing agents must be used. Dry chemical, carbon dioxide, and vaporizing liquids are suitable. Because foam, water (except as a spray), and water-type extinguishing agents conduct electricity, their use can kill or injure the person operating the extinguisher, and severe damage to electrical equipment can result.[1]

Since structural fires can occur anywhere and at any time, the first step in preventing damage to a library is to install a commercial fire detection and alarm system. Early detection of fire can help evacuate clients and staff and minimize damage by sounding the alarm in a timely manner. Detection systems provide a means to identify a developing fire through either manual or automatic methods and second, they alert building occupants to a fire condition and the need to evacuate. Another common function is the transmission of an alarm notification signal to the fire department or other emergency response organization. Fire detection systems may also shut down electrical, air handling equipment or special process operations, and they may be used to initiate automatic suppression systems. There are a number of different types of detection systems used by libraries.

DETECTION SYSTEMS

Manual Fire Detection

Manual fire detection is the oldest method of detection. In the simplest form, a person yelling provides a fire warning. Since vocal notification of a fire might not be totally effective, manual alarm on emergency exit doors with loud buzzers should be installed. The advantage of manual alarm stations is that they provide staff and library users with a readily identifiable means to activate the building fire alarm system. Manual alarms are simple devices, and can be highly reliable when the building is occupied but they will not work when the building is unoccupied. Unfortunately, they can also be used for malicious alarm activations. Nonetheless, they are an important component in any fire alarm system.

Thermal Detectors

Thermal detectors are the oldest type of automatic detection device, having origin in the mid 1800's, with several styles still in production today. The most common units are fixed temperature devices that operate when the

[1] http://www.firefire.com/Products/glossary/glossary.htm

room reaches a predetermined temperature (usually in the 135°–165°F/ 57°–74°C). The second most common type of thermal sensor is the rate-of-rise detector, which identifies an abnormally fast temperature climb over a short time period. Both of these units are "spot type" detectors, which means that they are periodically spaced along a ceiling or high on a wall. The third detector type is the fixed temperature line type detector, which consists of two cables and an insulated sheathing that is designed to breakdown when exposed to heat. The advantage of line type over spot detection is that thermal sensing density can be increased at lower cost. Thermal detectors are very easy and inexpensive to maintain, but they do not function until room temperatures have reached a substantial temperature, at which point the fire is well underway and damage is imminent.

Smoke Detectors

Smoke detectors are a much newer technology, having gained wide usage during the 1970s and 1980s. These devices are designed to identify a fire while in its smoldering or early flame stages, replicating the human sense of smell. The most common smoke detectors are spot type units, which are placed along ceilings or high on walls in a manner similar to spot thermal units. For large open spaces such as galleries and atria, a frequently used smoke detector is a projected beam unit. This detector consists of two components, a light transmitter and a receiver, that are mounted at some distance (up to 300 ft/100m) apart. As smoke migrates between the two components, the transmitted light beam becomes obstructed and the receiver is no longer able to see the full beam intensity. This is interpreted as a smoke condition, and the alarm activation signal is transmitted to the fire alarm panel.

Another type of smoke detector is the air aspirating system. This device consists of two main components: a control unit that houses the detection chamber, an aspiration fan and operation circuitry; and a network of sampling tubes or pipes. Along the pipes are a series of ports that are designed to permit air to enter the tubes and be transported to the detector. Under normal conditions, the detector constantly draws an air sample into the detection chamber, via the pipe network. The sample is analyzed for the existence of smoke, and then returned to atmosphere. If smoke becomes present in the sample, it is detected and an alarm signal is transmitted to the main fire alarm control panel. Air aspirating detectors are extremely sensitive and are typically the fastest responding automatic detection method.

The key advantage of smoke detectors is their ability to identify a fire while it is still in early stages. They provide added opportunity for emergency personnel to respond and control the developing fire before severe damage occurs. They are usually the preferred detection method in life safety and high content value applications. The disadvantage of smoke detectors is that they are usually more expensive to install, when compared to thermal sensors, and are more resistant to inadvertent alarms. However, when properly selected and designed, they can be highly reliable with a very low probability of false alarm.

Flame Detectors

Flame detectors represent the third major type of automatic detection method, and imitate the human sense of sight. As "line of sight" devices, they operate on either an infrared, ultraviolet or combination principle. As radiant energy in the approximate 4,000 to 7,700 angstroms range occurs, indicative of a flaming condition, their sensing equipment recognizes the fire signature and sends a signal to the fire alarm panel.

ALARMS

Upon detection of a fire, somehow a message needs to be sent to both the occupants of the building and to the local fire department. Occupant signaling components include various audible and visual alerting components, and are the primary alarm output devices. Various systems use different types of sounds, including bells, horns, and chimes. Additionally, loud speakers can be used with either a live human voice or a recorded voice message. All alarms should also include a strobe or flashing light device for hearing impaired staff or clients. Standards such as the Americans with Disabilities Act (ADA) mandate visual devices in all public buildings.

Along with notifying occupants of the building of a fire, most alarms also notify local emergency officials. The most common arrangement is an automatic telephone or radio signal that is communicated to a constantly staffed monitoring center. Upon receiving the alert, the center will then contact the appropriate fire department, providing information about the location of alarm. In some instances, the monitoring station may be the police or fire department, or a 911 call center. In other instances alarms contact a private monitoring company that is under contract to the organization.

Other output functions include shutting down electrical equipment such as computers, shutting off air handling fans to prevent smoke migration, and shutting down operations such as chemical movement through piping in the alarmed area. They may also activate fans to extract smoke, which is a common function in large atria spaces. These systems can also activate discharge of gaseous fire extinguishing systems, or preaction sprinkler systems.[2]

---

[2] http://www.nedcc.org/plam3/tleaf32.htm

SPRINKLER SYSTEMS

Most libraries and archives have a sprinkler system, which is a series of water pipes that are supplied by a reliable water supply. At selected intervals along these pipes are independent, heat-activated valves known as sprinkler heads, which are responsible for water distribution onto the fire. Most sprinkler systems are integrated with the alarm and detection system, and can even be programmed to shut down equipment and/or seal off part of the building. As a rule, sprinkler systems only activate when the heat of a fire intensifies to 57–107°C (135–225°F), when the systems sensors become exposed to the increased heat. The system senses where the heat has increased, and only releases water in this area.

There are three basic types of sprinkler systems: wet pipe, dry pipe, and preaction, with each having applicability, depending on a variety of conditions such as potential fire severity, anticipated fire growth rates, content water sensitivity, ambient conditions, and desired response. In large multifunction facilities, such as a library, two or more system types may be employed.

Wet Pipe Sprinkler Systems

Wet pipe sprinkler systems are the most common sprinkler system used in libraries. As the name implies, a wet pipe system is one in which water is constantly maintained within the sprinkler piping. When a sprinkler activates this water is immediately discharged onto the fire. Wet pipe system advantages include system simplicity and reliability, relative low installation and maintenance expense, ease of modification, and short term down time following a fire. The main disadvantage of these systems is that they are not suited for subfreezing environments and can freeze or burst in unprotected conditions such as power outage or if installed in some warehouses.

Dry Pipe Sprinkler Systems

Dry pipe sprinkler systems contain pipes that are filled with pressurized air or nitrogen, rather than water. This air holds a remote valve, known as a dry pipe valve, in a closed position. The dry pipe valve is located in a heated area and prevents water from entering the pipe until a fire causes one or more sprinklers to operate. Once this happens, the air escapes and the dry pipe valve releases. Water then enters the pipe, flowing through open sprinklers onto the fire. Many libraries have dry pipe systems over water sensitive areas, so that the possibility of pipes leaking over valuable materials is eliminated. Dry pipe systems have some disadvantages that must be evaluated before selecting this equipment, which include increased complexity, higher installation and maintenance costs, lower design flexibility, increased fire response time, and increased corrosion potential.

Reaction Sprinkler Systems

Reaction sprinkler systems use the basic concept of a dry pipe, except water is held from piping by an electrically operated valve, known as a preaction valve. The operation of this valve is controlled by independent flame, heat, or smoke detection. Two separate events must happen to initiate sprinkler discharge. First, the detection system must identify a developing fire and then open the preaction valve. This allows water to flow into system piping, which effectively creates a wet pipe sprinkler system. Second, individual sprinkler heads must release to permit water flow onto the fire. The primary advantage of a preaction system is the dual action required for water release: the preaction valve must operate and sprinkler heads must fuse. This provides an added level of protection against inadvertent discharge, and for this reason, these systems are frequently employed in water sensitive environments such as archival vaults, fine art storage rooms, rare book libraries, and computer centers. The disadvantages to preaction systems include higher installation and maintenance costs, modification difficulties, and potential decreased reliability with the higher level of complexity.

While there are always concerns about sprinkler systems causing undue water damage, one must consider that water damage can usually be repaired or restored, burned materials, are often beyond repair.[3]

Before *a fire:*

- Install detectors and alarms.
- Begin a system of checking detectors and alarms on a regular basis.
- Install fire extinguishers in every department.
- Conduct fire extinguisher training, led by local fire experts.
- Name floor marshals from each department.
- Develop two escape plans each area of the building.
- Choose a safe meeting place outside the library.
- Conduct fire drills.
- Post-emergency numbers near telephones. However, be aware that if a fire threatens your library, you should not place the call to your emergency services from inside the building. It is better to get out first and place the call from somewhere else.
- Do not store combustible materials in closed areas or near a heat source.

[3] http://www.nedcc.org/plam3/tleaf32.htm

- Check electrical wiring regularly.

    Replace wiring if frayed or cracked.

    Make sure wiring is not under rugs, over nails, or in high traffic areas.

    Do not overload outlets or extension cords.

    Outlets should have cover plates and no exposed wiring.

    Only purchase appliances and electrical devices that have a label indicating that they have been inspected by a testing laboratory such as Underwriter's Laboratories (UL) or Factory Mutual (FM).

During *a fire:*

- Floor marshals evacuate offices and public areas of the building, using the stairs to escape.
- Floor marshals stay with handicapped individuals until authorities arrive to help evacuate.
- Floor marshals note the presence of any individual refusing to evacuate and report this position to authorities.
- When evacuating, stay low to the ground.
- If possible, cover mouth with a cloth to avoid inhaling smoke and gases.
- Close doors in each room after escaping to delay the spread of the fire.
- If in a room with a closed door:

    If smoke is pouring in around the bottom of the door or it feels hot, keep the door closed.

    Open a window to escape or for fresh air while awaiting rescue.

    If there is no smoke at the bottom or top and the door is not hot, then open the door slowly.

    If there is too much smoke or fire in the hall, slam the door shut.

After *a fire:*

- Refer serious first aid emergencies to authorities.
- Stay out of damaged buildings. Return to the library only when local fire authorities say it is safe.

- Contact insurance agent.
- Do not discard damaged goods until after an inventory has been taken.
- Save receipts for money relating to fire loss.[4]

Finally, while all public buildings are required to have fire extinguishers installed, possession does not necessarily mean that staff should automatically use them. Staff must be trained to recognize what type or size of fire can be fought in-house, when they should concentrate on contacting the authorities and evacuation. Your local fire department can provide instructions of fire extinguisher usage.

PUTTING IT ALL TOGETHER

In a fire situation the chief goal is to evacuate the building as quickly and safely as possible. Any fire-specific disaster plan should address the following issues:

- Who's responsible.
- Designated evacuation routes for specific locations.
- Alternate exits.
- Meeting places.
- Floor sweeps.
- Dealing with patrons who are non-ambulatory, visually impaired, or hearing impaired.

The following pages contain fire-related evacuation plans from several different libraries located in the United States.

Sample 2.1

Central Washington University Library's Evacuation Plan

   Who's Responsible: Each on duty Department Supervisor will be responsible for the evacuation of departmental staff. To assure the safety of patrons and staff, Supervisors from the following departments will be responsible to sweep each floor as follows:

First Floor—Reference

Second Floor—Serials

---

[4] http://www.fema.org/hazards/fires/housef.shtm

Third Floor—Documents

Fourth Floor—Music

Alternate Exits: If the designated exit is blocked, proceed to the nearest alternative stairwell or exit as necessary. In case of fire **do not** use elevators.

Meeting Place: The East end of the parking lot that is North of the building (along Dean Nicholson Avenue across from the Psychology Building).

First Floor

Location	How to Exit
• Circulation Department	**EAST, OUT THE MAIN DOOR** • Alternate Route: out the East or South emergency doors
• Media Circulation Department	**OUT THE WEST DOOR** • Alternate Route: out the East or South emergency doors
• Technical Services and Media Services Areas	**OUT THE WEST DOOR** • Alternate Route: out the East or South emergency doors
• Media & Distance Education Classrooms	**OUT THE WEST DOOR** • Alternate Route: out the East or South emergency doors
• Reference Department & Public Areas	**EAST, OUT THE MAIN DOOR** • Alternate Route: out the South emergency door

Second Floor

Location	How to Exit
• Periodicals Room	**DOWN THE EAST STAIRS & OUT THE MAIN EXIT** • Alternate Route: take the West or South stairs & exit
• Fishbowl	**DOWN THE WEST STAIRS & OUT THE WEST EXIT** • Alternate Route: West or South stairs & exit
• Academic Computing	**DOWN THE EAST STAIRS & OUT THE MAIN EXIT** • Alternate Route: take the South stairs & exit
• Dean's Office	**DOWN THE WEST STAIRS & OUT THE WEST EXIT** • Alternate Route: South stairs & exit
• Staff Lounge	**DOWN THE WEST STAIRS & OUT THE WEST EXIT** • Alternate Route: South stairs & exit
• Second Floor Stacks & Study Areas	**EXIT via THE NEAREST STAIRWELL & DOOR**

Third Floor

Location	How to Exit
	EXIT THE EAST OR WEST STAIRWELL & DOOR
• Docs, Maps & Microforms	• Alternate Route: South stairs & door
	EXIT THE WEST STAIRWELL & DOOR
• Computer Lab	• Alternate Route: South stairs & door
• Third Floor Stacks & Study Areas	**EXIT NEAREST STAIRWELL & DOOR**

Fourth Floor

Location	How to Exit
• Music Library	**DOWN THE EAST STAIRS, OUT THE EAST EXIT**
• Fourth floor stacks & study areas	**EXIT NEAREST STAIRWELL & DOOR**

From http://www.lib.cwu.edu/info/policies/emergency.html

Sample 2.2

Evacuation Plan for California State University, San Marcos

Library marshals' responsibilities will be to ensure the following steps are carried out:

• Call "911" and inform University Police of situation.
• Evacuate all occupants through designated exit routes giving special attention to the disabled and elevator occupants. Spotters will be designated by Floor Marshals to assist trapped elevator occupants, obtain their names and maintain contact until University Police are notified. Never try to force elevator doors open.

 In case of non-life threatening emergency follow normal closing procedures.

• (3rd floor) Exit library through the closest most accessible evacuation route and gather in the area in front of the cashier's office of Craven Hall.
• (4th floor) Exit library through the closest most accessible evacuation route and gather in the parking area in front of the Dome.

 A headcount needs to conducted by the Floor Marshal or Assistant Floor Marshal of all members from each department at designated gathering place.
 Note: Fourth floor evening and weekend staff and student assistants should evacuate down the most accessible stairs and meet third floor personnel in front of the cashier's office of Craven Hall to be included in headcount. Marshals may request the assistance of staff and student assistants to assist with evacuation and closing procedures.

• Make brief reports at quarterly staff meetings and communicate all matters regarding safety such as reminding staff of where emergency exits, fire extinguishers and alarm pulls are located.
• Conduct walkthroughs for those who need to familiarize themselves with evacuation routes.

- Work with LIS dean and other relevant campus departments to stage evacuation drills.
- Meet quarterly or as needed with other marshals and assistants to review and/or update procedures, etc.
- Keep Intranet site updated on safety and evacuation issues.
- Maintain updated copies of names of current staff and student assistants and updated student schedules from each unit.
- Conduct periodical 2–way radio training for staff and students who are not yet familiar with them.
- Be familiar with procedure to evacuate a disabled person.

Non-ambulatory persons: There are many considerations when moving a person in a wheelchair. Wheelchairs have many moving parts; some are not designed to withstand stress or lifting. You may have to remove the chair batteries. Life support equipment may be attached. Lifting a person with minimal ability to move may be dangerous to their well being. *Always consult with the person in the chair regarding how best to assist them.*
   Always consult with the person with regard to:

- Ways of being removed from the wheelchair. Wheelchairs should not be used in stairwells, if at all possible.
- The number of people necessary for assistance.
- Whether to extend or move extremities when lifting because of pain, catheter leg bags, spacticity, braces.
- Whether a seat cushion or pad should be brought along if they are removed from the chair.
- Whether to carry forward or backward on a flight of stairs.
- Assist as needed if removed from the wheelchair (ask whether they prefer a stretcher, chair with cushion pad, car seat, or if paramedic assistance is necessary).

Visually Impaired Persons: Most visually impaired persons will be familiar with the immediate area they are in. In the event of an emergency, tell the person the nature of the emergency and offer to guide them by having the person take your elbow and escorting them (this is the preferred method when acting as a "sighted guide"). As you walk, tell the person where you are and advise of any obstacles. When you have reached safety, orient the person to where they are and ask if any further assistance is needed.
Hearing Impaired Persons: Persons with impaired hearing may not perceive emergency alarms and an alternative warning technique is required. Two methods of warning are:
   Writing a note telling what the emergency is and the nearest evacuation route ("Fire—go out rear door to the right and down, NOW!").
   Turning the light switch on and off to gain attention, then indicating through gestures or in writing what is happening and what to do.

Sample 2.3

Angelo and Jennette Volpe Library and Media Center Evacuation Plan, Tennessee Technological University (Cookeville, TN)

Recommendations and Evacuation Plans

- Re-evaluate Extended Hours Room (Room 248) and the Educational Technologies Center (Room 130) for appropriate fire extinguishers and alarm system.

- Install **Emergency Evacuation Route** signs for study rooms and faculty rooms.
- Provide **hang tags** for all office doors for fire evacuation procedure.
- Letter pillars for **evacuation procedures**.
- Test to see if an **NOAA (National Oceanic and Atmospheric Administration) weather radio** works in the Library. If so, purchase one.
- Purchase **plastic sheeting** to cover equipment and materials. (Recommended: 4 mm thick.)
- Have basic **library emergency procedures** taught in all English 101 classes and have library emergency procedures put in student handbook.
- **Distribute** copy of *Disaster Preparedness and Training Plan* to Disability Services.
- Set **library fire alarm system** to automatically call a monitoring agency, especially at night and on weekends.
- Install more **safety lights** at back of building and next to Extended Hours Room (Room 248) exit.
- Remove **plants** from center front door exit, because the American Disabilities Act (ADA) requires that handicap exits be cleared at all times.
- Test **emergency lighting system** and **alarms** between each semester.
- Check **flashlights** every month to see if they are in good working condition. Have extra batteries and bulbs.
- Obtain **dehumidifiers and fans**.
- Mark **area in center** on each level for handicap patrons to meet to receive assistance in an emergency.
- Purchase **thermometers and humidity gauges**.
- Provide **first aid and CPR training** for library staff.
- Use warm, **white fluorescent lights, with filters**, for light-sensitive materials.
- Use **air filters** of activated microporous alumina impregnated with potassium permanganate.
- **Post locations of emergency and recovery supplies.**
- Test for **radon**.
- Purchase and mount a **knox box** outside library with essential keys for emergency personnel.
- Purchase and install **power-operated interior entrance/exit center doors** to accommodate ADA patrons.
- Have one **master key** available for emergency use.
- Purchase a **shop vac** adequate for water removal.

2.2 WILDFIRES

In the fall of 2003, wildfires in Southern California had an impact on numerous libraries, whether from the threat of being in the path of the fires, to poor air quality or even by the libraries themselves becoming a refuge for individuals affected by the fires. Four branch libraries of the San Bernardino County Library were closed for weeks while the fires raged, but after a three-day shutdown due to smoke of the Escondido Public, the library opened its doors to local residents, especially children, needing some normalcy. Librarians from this library also drove a bookmobile to the local evacuation center located at a local church. While there, they read stories, entertained children, and distributed books. Sample 2.4 gives a firsthand account of the impact of the fires on the San Diego County Public Library.

Sample 2.4

Wildfires, San Diego County (CA) Library

Wildfires that raged in California in October 2003 have been ranked as among the worst disasters to hit a state that has had its share of tragedies. Calculations show that about seventy staff members of the San Diego County Library either directly or indirectly helped in a hands-on way during and after the fires. Some staff from libraries and other County departments were deployed to hastily set up local assistance centers housed together with FEMA Centers and Red Cross emergency centers. Staff also worked County hotlines to receive the deluge of calls from victims responding to the County's offer of a week's loan of free dumpsters for clearing off the burned remains of their home and possessions. I, too, spent four days doing these jobs.

While the fires were raging, all libraries were officially closed for two days, as were most businesses and organizations in this county. The atmosphere throughout our region, all the way out to the Pacific Ocean, was thick with dark, toxic fumes (even resembling an eclipse at times) and people were told to stay indoors at home with all the windows closed, to wear masks, and turn on their air conditioning with filters, if they had air conditioning. The fires were jumping across major multi-lane highways that had previously been assumed to be natural fire breaks. People were glued to their televisions, trying to get a sense of where the fires were headed. With three major fire areas, the media had a Herculean task to try to cover this news, since they were themselves often in danger trying to do so. Winds made the fire unpredictable and swift. Fires came within a block of two of our branches—Crest and Julian. Learning from reports of how many people had no time or warning to pack up anything before being evacuated, others did start to focus on what they cared about among their personal possessions and packed them up in anticipation of having to leave.

Though our back country branches are usually closed on Mondays, once we were instructed by the County Board of Supervisors that the libraries should reopen, as was possible, the executive team of the library met every morning for a week to gather information on the current status of the fire, what staff members were available, and which facilities had electricity, computers, and water. A master wall white board was revised daily, as new information came in. The back country branches were open for three consecutive Mondays, so that the public would have a place to get information and a place to connect with community. We did out best to have these libraries open as soon as we could, a couple even when there was no electricity (they closed at dusk).

Our staff was terrific, some showing up for work even during the period when they were evacuated from their homes and didn't know whether they would have a home to which they could return. Four of our staff members did lose their homes. Some of the personal stories appeared in our weekly online newsletter.

The most recent aftermath is "Fire Writing Workshops." A local citizen thought of this program and has conducted the first session at our Lakewide Branch, which drew 29 people. She had published a book about sites of interest in some of the areas that had burned and, of course, was overwhelmed to find some of these areas destroyed. A parks ranger, I believe, said "We should not lose these stories," and so she embarked on this project. A local historian in another of the communities hardest hit (Julian), has now scheduled a similar program for her community.

Ellen Zyroff
Library Director

The treat of wildfires is not limited to rural libraries, but can also affect urban areas. Advance planning and knowing how to protect buildings in these areas can lessen the devastation of a wildfire. The discussion of fire detection systems, alarms and sprinklers in 2.1 also applies in the case of a wildfire. The main difference between building fires and wildfires is that usually, in the case of a wildfire, there is advance notice that the fire will strike.

Before a Wildfire:

- Learn and teach safe fire practices.
- Install the fire detection, alarm and sprinkler systems discussed in 2.1.
- Obtain local building codes and weed abatement ordinances for structures built near wooded areas.
- Use fire-resistant materials such as stone when building, renovating, or retrofitting structures.
- Use only thick, tempered safety glass in large windows and sliding glass doors.
- Create a safety zone such as a fountain, pond, or patio to separate the library from combustible plants and vegetation.
- Check for fire hazards around library building.
- Install electrical lines underground, if possible.
- Keep all tree and shrub limbs trimmed so they don't come in contact with the wires.
- Prune all branches around the building to a height of 8 to 10 feet.
- Keep trees adjacent to buildings free of dead or dying wood and moss.
- Remove all dead limbs, needles, and debris from rain gutters.
- Store combustible or flammable materials in approved safety containers and off site, if possible.
- Make evacuation plans from the library building and the neighborhood in which it is located.
- Conduct evacuation drills.
- Have disaster supplies on hand.

During a Wildfire:

- Turn on a battery-operated radio to get the latest emergency information.

- Remove combustible items from around the library building.
- Take down flammable drapes and curtains and close all venetian blinds or noncombustible window coverings.
- Close all doors and windows to prevent draft.
- Close gas valves and turn off all pilot lights.
- Turn on a light in each room for visibility in heavy smoke.
- If hoses and adequate water are available, leave sprinklers on roofs and anything that might be damaged by fire.
- Be ready to evacuate all patrons and staff when fire nears or when instructed to do so by local officials.

If trapped in a wildfire, remember, you cannot outrun a wildfire:

- Crouch in a pond or river.
- Cover head and upper body with wet clothing.
- If water is not around, look for shelter in a cleared area or among a bed of rocks.
- Lie flat and cover body with wet clothing or soil.
- Breathe the air close to the ground through a wet cloth to avoid scorching lungs or inhaling smoke.

After a Wildfire:

- Only reenter the area and the library when instructed by safety officials.
- Take care when re-entering the building.
- Remember, hot spots can flare up without warning.
- Check the roof immediately and extinguish any sparks or embers.
- For several hours afterward, re-check for smoke and sparks throughout the library building.[5]

[5] http://www.fema.gov/hazards/fires/wildlanf.shtm

PUTTING IT ALL TOGETHER

The FEMA Web site makes it clear that there are many actions we can take to reduce the risk to library buildings. Even so, the fact remains that wildfires, like tornadoes, hurricanes, and other natural phenomena, are beyond our control. The response to a wildfire situation is necessarily a community response and any library disaster plan must be coordinated with local firefighting and law enforcement agencies.

Firewise (http://www.firewise.org) is the Web site of the National Wildfire Coordinating Group, a consortium of wildland fire agencies that includes the USDA-Forest Service, the Department of Interior, the National Association of State Foresters, the U.S. Fire Administration and the National Fire Protection Association. *Firewise* indicates that there are six steps to developing a cooperative approach to wildfire protection. They are:

- Identify partners and get commitment.
- Define the current situation.
- Define roles and responsibilities.
- Set goals and objectives.
- Document and implement.
- Evaluate and revise.

While these steps are primarily written for firefighting agencies, the recommendations under *Identify partners and get commitment* are particularly germane to would-be partners such as libraries:

A partnership is not itself a goal but rather a means of achieving a goal. Partnerships are voluntary, mutually beneficial, desired arrangements between groups. They are established to accomplish mutual objectives that are consistent with the mission of each group. It is important that the interests of each agency, organization, or group be carefully acknowledged in the process.

A partnership should include:

- Appropriate legal authority.
- Consistency with agency plans, policies, and priorities.
- Evident public benefit.
- Mutual interest in and benefits from a common objective.
- Realistic time frames.
- Voluntary participation.
- Written agreement(s) between parties.

Establish a dialogue among the agencies and organizations that can increase the level of fire protection. Concentrate on those agencies you know that may be asking the same questions and seeking similar solutions.

In effect, the library disaster plan becomes a component of the community's *Cooperative Fire Protection Agreement* (the *Firewise* model appears on the following page). In the previous section we discussed various issues that the library disaster plan needs to address with respect to a building fire. With respect to wildfires, plan should also specifically focus on the following issues:

- Risk assessment.
- Communication with local firefighting and law enforcement agencies.
- Communication with library staff and patrons.
- Multiple evacuation routes from the area in which the library is situated.
- Transportation issues.

In addition to the Model Cooperative Fire Protection Agreement, we have provided a sample wildfire plan for a hypothetical library in South Florida.

Sample 2.5

La Fantasia Public Library Disaster Plan

Section W: Wildfire

Introduction

In drought conditions La Fantasia County has been known to experience wildfires, often the result of lightning strikes but frequently resulting from human carelessness. Given La Fantasia County's dense foliage, these fires can spread quickly and dangerously. Per the order of the La Fantasia County Commission, all government buildings—including the La Fantasia main library and its six branch locations—are required to maintain a safety zone such as a fountain, pond, or patio to separate them from combustible plants and vegetation. Even so, we cannot depend on the safety zone to prevent our library buidings from being overtaken by wildfires. The following plan addresses key issues we must face in a wildfire situation:

1. Who's Responsible?

The director of the library or her designee is responsible for maintaining communication with the LFCFD and making decisions regarding whether to close/evacuate the branches.

The deputy director for library operations or his designee is responsible for maintaining communication with the branch managers.

The branch managers are responsible for making sure that the branches are closed/evacuated quickly and safely. They are also responsible for coordinating emergency transportation.

The library emergency team members in each branch are responsible for assisting the branch managers in carrying out close/evacuation procedures.

2. Assessing Risk

La Fantasia County Fire Department notifies local media outlets when the risk of wildfires is high and likewise maintains a "wildfire conditions" Web site, http://www.lfcfd.gov. Moreover, the La Fantasia County Cooperative Fire Protection Agreement mandates communication between LFCFD and all public agencies in La Fantasia County when wildfire conditions exist.

3. Communicating with Public Safety Agencies

If wildfire breaks out in La Fantasia County, all public agencies, including the library system, will be notified by the LFCFD. The library system administrative office will maintain communication with the LFCFD.

4. Communicating with Library Staff and Patrons

If notified by LFCFD that a wildfire exists in La Fantasia County, the library administrative office will contact each of the five branch managers (including the Main Branch) by phone to indicate that an area emergency exists. Branch managers will contact their branch disaster team members and activate the emergency walkie-talkie system.

5. Deciding to Evacuate

The library system administrative staff will maintain close contact with the LFCFD regarding the size, extent, and location of the wildfire. Any wildfire approaching within 2 miles of a branch will be deemed sufficient reason to close/evacuate the library building.

6. Carrying out Closing/Evacuation

Once the library director or her designee has decided to close/evacuate a branch in response to a wildfire threat, the deputy director or his designee will communicate that decision to the local branch manager. Working with the branch's library emergency team, the branch manager will:

a. Announce that the library is closing due to the existence of wildfire conditions in La Fantasia County.
b. Indicate that there is no immediate threat to the library.
c. Indicate where the wildfire is located.
d. Ask patrons to evacuate the building.
e. Indicate the route leading away from the wildfire.
f. Arrange for emergency transportation, if necessary.

7. Evacuation Routes

Most branches in La Fantasia County are situated in locations for which there are multiple evacuation routes. The Mirador Branch, located within Mirador Estates subdivision, is the exception. The only exit from the subdivision is Mirador Drive, which connects directly with U.S. Highway 47, providing north and south egress from the area.

8. Transportation Issues

The Cooperative Fire Protection Agreement among public agencies in La Fantasia County provides that the La Fantasia Transit Authority will provide emergency transportation to affected public agencies (e.g., the library system) that do not have their own transportation abilities.

9. Dealing with mobility, vision, and hearing-impaired patrons

See Section F., *Building Fires.*

Model Cooperative Fire Protection Agreement
Suggested Items for Consideration During Development

I. Title

II. Authorities

Reference applicable laws or higher level agreements.

III. Purpose/Recitals

Describe why Agreement is necessary.
Describe who is involved.
Describe mutual benefit.

IV. Defintions

The key definitions in this section will standardize usage in the context of the agreement, thereby simplifying and improving communications. Include as appropriate key definitions such as:

Reciprocal (Mutual Aid) Fire Protection: Reciprocal initial attack zones for lands of intermingled or adjoining protection responsibility may be established. Within such zones a supporting party will, upon request or voluntarily, take initial attack action in support of the protecting party as they are in a position to provide. The protecting party will not be required to reimburse the supporting party for costs incurred. The reciprocal assistance period, defined in Annual Operating Plans, does not usually exceed 24 hours.

Reimbursable (Cooperative) Fire Protection: The protecting party may request fire suppression resources from supporting parties, per conditions set in the agreement, (and Annual Operating Plans). Such resources are to be paid for by the protecting party.

Offset (Exchange) Fire Protection: The parties may exchange responsibility for fire protection for lands under their jurisdiction. The rate of exchange will be based upon comparable cost, acreage involved, complexity, and other factors as may be appropriate and mutually agreed to by the parties. The exchange zones are often documented in Annual Operating Plans. The goal is to gain an equal exchange that provides greater overall fire protection.

Fee Basis (Contract) Fire Protection: For an agreed upon fee, one party may assume fire protection responsibilities on lands under the jurisdiction of another. The terms and conditions of such arrangements are generally outlined in a contract agreement.

Annual Operating Plan: An annually updated document that outlines operational procedures in support of a multiyear Cooperative Fire Protection Agreement. Annual Operating Plans are normally developed locally, and must be authorized by appropriate officials.

V. Interagency Cooperation

Identify sources of oversight and direction as needed to cover specific actions. Require local annual operating plans. Enable and direct cooperative efforts, such as:

• Area Coordinating Group
• Local Cooperative Initiatives
• Joint Projects and Local Agreements

- Incident Command System
- Interagency Dispatch Centers/Service Centers
- MultiAgency Coordination (MAC) Groups
- Fire Prevention
- Prescribed Fire and Fuels Management
- Licensing Training
- Communication Systems
- Weather Data Processing System
- Automatic Weather Stations
- Aviation Operations
- Joint Facilities
- Inmate Use
- Military Resources

VI. Fire Protection

Define jurisdictional responsibilities and limitations. Include protection area and boundaries. Methods of fire protection assistance pursuant to agreement.

- Reciprocal
- Reimbursable
- Offset
- Fee Basis or Contract

VII. Fire Suppression

- Closest Forces Concept
- Shared Resources
- Joint Resources
- Fire Notifications
- Protection Priorities
- Boundary Fires
- Independent Action on Lands Protected by Another Agency
- Appropriate Suppression Response Policies
- Escaped Fire Situation Analysis (EFSA)
- Determination of Cause and Preservation of Evidence
- Fire Reports and Documentation
- Post Fire Analysis
- Law Enforcement Actions
- Fire Disasters and Relief

VIII. Reimbursements

Appropriated Fund Limitation: "Nothing herein shall be interpreted as obligating the parties to this agreement to expend funds, or as involving them in any contract or other obligation for the future payment of money in excess of appropriations authorized by law and administratively allocated for the work contemplated in this Agreement."

- Specific Reimbursable Services and Procedures
- Cost-sharing (for incidents affecting more than one agency)
- Procurement
- Billing Procedures

IX. General Provisions

- Duration of Emergency Assignments
- Loaned Equipment
- Mutual Sharing of Information
- Local Cooperation (levels in terms of geographical authority)
- Accident Investigations
- NonWildland Fire and Medical Aid Responses
- Previous Agreements (replacement intentions)
- Employment Policy
- Suppression and Damage Collection
- Waiver of Claims (liability responsibility to remain with employing party)
- Third Party Claims (liability to third parties)
- Officials Not to Benefit ("No member of, or delegate to Congress or Resident commissioner shall be admitted to any share or part of this Agreement or to any benefit to arise therefrom, unless it is made with a corporation for its general benefit.")
- Amendments Procedures
- Examination and Audit (specific auditable agreement provisions)
- Civil Rights
- Duration of Agreement (number of years or indefinite—describe termination progress)

SIGNATURES

2.3 HURRICANES

Hurricanes and related tropical storms cause many types of destruction including rain, flooding, tidal surges, tornadoes and in the aftermath, mold. On August 13, 2004, Hurricane Charley, a category 4 storm, slammed into the western cost of Florida with a vengeance, causing billions of dollars in damage and over twenty deaths. While the storm was predicted days before, in typical hurricane style, it veered at the last minute, striking much farther south than predicted by most of the experts. Since predicted to hit farther north and no major storm had hit this area for decades, many people did not heed the warnings nor evacuate.

CHARACTERISTICS

A hurricane is a tropical storm with winds that have reached a constant speed of 74 miles per hour or more. Hurricane winds blow in a large spiral around a relative calm center known as the eye. The eye is generally 20 to 30 miles wide, and the storm may extend outward 400 miles. As a hurricane approaches, the skies will begin to darken and winds will grow in strength. As a hurricane nears land, it can bring torrential rains, high winds, and storm surges. A single hurricane can last for more than 2 weeks over open waters and can run a path across the entire length of the eastern seaboard. August and September are peak months during the hurricane season that lasts from June 1 through November 30.

The center, or eye, of a hurricane is relatively calm. The most violent activity takes place in the area immediately around the eye, called the eye-wall. At the top of the eyewall (about 50,000 feet), most of the air is propelled outward, increasing the air's upward motion. Some of the air, however, moves inward and sinks into the eye, creating a cloud-free area.

Tropical disturbances are classified as follows:

- **Tropical Depression**—An organized system of clouds and thunderstorms with a defined circulation and maximum sustained winds of 38 mph (33 knots) or less.
- **Tropical Storm**—An organized system of strong thunderstorms with a defined circulation and maximum sustained winds of 39 to 73 mph (34–63 knots).
- **Hurricane**—An intense tropical weather system with a well-defined circulation and maximum sustained winds of 74 mph (64 knots) or higher. Hurricanes are called typhoons in the western Pacific, while similar storms in the Indian Ocean are called cyclones.

Hurricanes form in the Atlantic Ocean, Gulf of Mexico, Indian Ocean, Caribbean Sea, and Pacific Ocean. Hurricane winds in the Northern Hemisphere circulate in a counterclockwise motion around the hurricane's eye, while hurricane winds in the Southern Hemisphere circulate clockwise. Natural phenomena, which affect a storm, include temperature of the water, the Gulf Stream, and steering wind currents. Powered by heat from the sea, they are steered by the easterly trade winds and the temperate westerlies as well as by their own ferocious energy. Around their core, winds grow with great velocity, generating violent seas. Moving ashore, they sweep the ocean inward while spawning tornadoes and producing torrential rains and floods.

In the eastern Pacific, hurricanes begin forming by mid-May, while in the Atlantic, Caribbean, and Gulf of Mexico, hurricane development starts in June. For the United States, the peak hurricane threat exists from mid-August to late October although the official hurricane season extends through November. Over other parts of the world, such as the western Pacific, hurricanes can occur year-round. Areas in the United States vulnerable to hurricanes include the Atlantic and Gulf coasts from Texas to Maine, the territories in the Caribbean, and tropical areas of the western Pacific, including Hawaii, Guam, American Samoa, and Saipan.

Before hurricane season starts:

- Plan an evacuation route.
- Protect windows. Permanent shutters are the best protection.
- Have disaster supplies on hand.
- Stock emergency food and water (enough for staff and clients, in case you are caught unable to evacuate).
- Trim back dead or weak branches from trees.
- Check into flood insurance.

During a hurricane watch:

A Hurricane Watch is issued when there is a threat of hurricane conditions within 24–36 hours.

- Listen to a battery-operated radio or television for hurricane progress reports.
- Check emergency supplies.
- Secure buildings by closing and boarding up windows.
- Remove outside antennas.
- Review evacuation plan.

During a Hurricane Warning:

A Hurricane Warning is issued when hurricane conditions (winds of 74 miles per hour or greater, or dangerously high water and rough seas) are expected in 24 hours or less.

- Listen constantly to a battery-operated radio or television for official instructions.
- Avoid elevators.
- Stay inside, away from windows, skylights, and glass doors.
- Keep a supply of flashlights and extra batteries handy.
- Avoid open flames, such as candles and kerosene lamps, as a source of light.
- If power is lost, turn off equipment and other appliances to reduce power "surge" when electricity is restored.

If officials indicate evacuation is necessary:

- Leave as soon as possible.
- Avoid flooded roads and watch for washed-out bridges.
- If time permits, and your library is in an identified surge zone, elevate furniture to protect it from flooding or better yet, move it to a higher floor.

After the storm:

- Refer serious first aid emergencies to authorities.
- Stay tuned to local radio for information.
- Return to the building only after authorities advise that it is safe to do so.
- Avoid loose or dangling power lines and report them immediately to the power company, police, or fire department.
- Beware of snakes, insects, and animals driven to higher ground by floodwater.
- Open windows and doors to ventilate and dry the building.
- Take pictures of the damage, both to the building and its contents for insurance claims.
- Use telephone only for emergency calls.
- Leave inspection of utilities to professionals.

PUTTING IT ALL TOGETHER

The University of Florida's (UF) Natural Disaster and Hurricane Emergency Plan says it best:

Because hurricane warnings are posted several hours prior to anticipated landfall, each of the libraries' plans assumes that there will be plenty of time for a leisurely evacuation of the building and for completion of preparatory tasks.

The UF plan (see George A. Smathers Libraries Preservation Department Natural Disaster and Hurricane Emergency Plan) addresses the following key components:

- Responsibility/chain of command/communication.
- Distribution of plan/training of staff.
- Location of designated shelters.
- Evacuating staff and patrons.
- Closing procedures.
- Responsibilities during the hurricane itself.
- Post-hurricane/reopening procedures.
- Additional contact information.

Sample 2.6

George A. Smathers Libraries Preservation Department Natural Disaster and Hurricane Emergency Plan, University of Florida

NATURAL DISASTER and HURRICANE EMERGENCY PLAN
Smathers Library, Building 005

This plan is specific to the Smathers Library, Building 50005. Plans specific to other library buildings are also available. All of the Libraries' plans are based on a single template. Comments on and revisions to this plan are always welcome, send them to Cathy Mook at cathy@smathersnt2.uflib.ufl.edu.

This plan is specifically for the one natural disaster most likely to befall Florida, hurricane. Because hurricane warnings are posted several hours prior to anticipated landfall, this plan assumes that there will be plenty of time for a leisurely evacuation of the building and for completion of preparatory tasks.

Smathers Library Building Emergency Coordinator Information

Contact	Work Phone	Home Phone	E-mail Address
• Cathy Mook (Coordinator) Preservation Department			
• Bill Covey (Alternate) Systems Department			
• (Alternate)			

Emergency Preparations

1. The Smathers Library building emergency coordinator is responsible for planned measures both to evacuate and secure the building and to protect valuable and delicate equipment. Alternates have been named in the event of the primary coordinator's absence. The emergency coordinators are members of the electronic Emergency list service.

2. Individual Department Chairs will prepare specific, written plans, for submission to the building emergency coordinator, both to evacuate and secure their area(s) and to protect valuable assets. Written plans will include plans for egress, designating or mapping primary and secondary exits. Plans will also include the names and work locations of staff requiring assistance evacuating the building.

3. The University of Florida in accord with state regulation requires that these plans be assessed and revised annually. The building emergency coordinator is responsible for reminding department chairs of review dates and deadlines. Department chairs are responsible for reminding staff of plans specific to their department.

During a Hurricane Watch

Department Chairs should ensure that all staff are briefed and that tasked staff implement all pre-hurricane preparation measures.

Hurricane Warning Procedures

1. The University Emergency Operations Center will notify the director of libraries and the facilities planning officer that a hurricane warning has been declared. The facilities planning officer will notify the building emergency coordinator, who will notify department chairs. Department chairs will notify all their staff.

2. The university will be declared closed and all persons, except those assigned planned duties, will be instructed to secure their areas and leave the campus. Individuals who cannot leave the campus should go to a designated shelter as assigned by University Police Department (UPD).

3. The building emergency coordinator will ensure that building entrances are closed and appropriate signs posted. Assistance from the University Police Department (UPD) is available if requested at 392-1111.

4. After evacuating staff from their area(s), department chairs and tasked staff will close and lock windows, close blinds and drapes, unplug all terminals, control units, modems, and other electrical equipment. They should also move library materials and equipment, as appropriate, away from windows and other areas of potential water damage. (Some or all of these tasks may be completed prior to general evacuation.) Department chairs will have designated, in advance, an alternate(s) in the event of the chair's absence.

5. Following completion of tasks, tasked staff will be evacuated, and department chairs will lock all internal doors securing their area(s). They will report by telephone at the number above to the building emergency coordinator or the alternate when this has been accomplished. If telephone contact can not be made, department chairs will report to the coordinator or alternate in the coordinator or alternate's department. They should indicate the need for any additional requirements for protection or security of their area. Department chairs, except for those designated to assist the building emergency coordinator with final procedure, will be evacuated.

6. The building emergency coordinator and designated assistants, among the department chairs (or their alternates), will tour the entire building to ensure that evacuation is complete and that materials and equipment are secure. Department chairs who are responsible for areas off master-key are necessarily designated as assistants to the coordinator. In the Smathers Library, designated assistants include the chairs of preservation, special collections and systems or their designated alternates when the chairs are unavailable. Designated assistants will be evacuated, and the building emergency coordinator will then lock the building.

7. The building emergency coordinator will report to the facilities planning officer at 392-xxxx or, if the facilities planning officer can not be contacted, to the emergency operations director at 392-yyyy. If telephone communication with either of these persons is not available, the building emergency coordinator should summon the first available police officer to report via two-way radio. The building emergency coordinator will be evacuated after reporting.

During a Hurricane

- All persons, including the building emergency coordinator, not required for the conduct of emergency operations, will have been notified to leave the campus by the emergency operations director after completing their Hurricane Warning duties.

- Persons remaining on campus will have reported to a designated shelter where they will remain until an all-clear signal has been issued.

Post Hurricane Procedures

1. The facilities planning officer will be notified by the emergency operations director of clearance to return to particular buildings, and will notify the building emergency coordinator, who will return as soon as possible.

2. Building emergency coordinator will survey damage and report to the library facilities planning officer at 392-xxxx and to the Emergency Operations Center at 392-xxxx. If telephone service is unavailable, or if phone lines are jammed, reports should be hand delivered to the Facilities Planning at 145 Library West and to the Emergency Operations Center at the University Police Department. If possible, reports will include floor plans with problem areas clearly marked.

3. The facilities planning officer will report to the director for library support services and to the director of libraries who will decide when general staff may return.

4. The facilities planning officer will coordinate facilities damage repair and clean up efforts with work management division. The facilities planning officer will also notify the preservation and systems officers of damage requiring their attention.

5. The preservation librarian will bring together library materials recovery and salvage teams. Teams will take necessary actions, consistent with prior planning, to preserve and restore damaged library materials. Damage assessments and needs will be communicated to director for library support services.

6. The systems officer will bring together systems recovery and salvage teams. Teams will take necessary actions salvage damaged equipment and, contingent upon reliable supply of power, will return other equipment to operability. Damage assessments and needs will be communicated to director for library support services.

7. Smathers library staff should listen to local radio stations for information regarding reopening of the University of Florida and particular buildings. Staff will not be required to return to the university if personal property requires attention.

Distribution

This plan has been submitted to the library facilities planning officer who has forwarded it to Environmental Health & Safety. Copies have also been distributed to the alternate building emergency coordinator and department chairs in the Smathers Library.

Department chairs will be responsible for distribution of this plan to their staff.

The building emergency coordinator will report written changes to the facilities planning officer and department chairs.

2.4 TSUNAMIS, TIDAL WAVES, TIDAL SURGES

The December 2004 Indian Ocean tsunami drastically raised the world's consciousness with respect to these oceanographic phenomena. In addition to claiming more than 200,000 lives, the tsunamis wreaked tremendous physical destruction. Libraries in the affected countries were not exempt.

Many factors can cause an influx of large amounts of water in coastal areas, including hurricanes and earthquakes. While storm surge has been the number one cause of hurricane related deaths in the past, more people have died from inland flooding associated with tropical systems in the last 30 years. Since the 1970s, inland flooding has been responsible for more than half of all deaths associated with tropical cyclones in the United States. Flooding from hurricanes can occur hundreds of miles from the coast placing communities, which would not normally be affected by the strongest hurricane winds, in great danger.

CHARACTERISTICS

A tsunami, also known as a tidal wave, is a series of waves generated by an undersea disturbance such as an earthquake. Waves will travel outward in all directions from the area of the disturbance, much like ripples caused by throwing a rock into a pond. The time between wave crests may be from 5 to 90 minutes, and the wave speed in the open ocean will average 450 miles per hour. Tsunamis reaching heights of more than 100 feet have been recorded. As the waves approach the shallow coastal waters, they appear normal and the speed decreases. Then as the tsunami nears the coastline, it may grow to great height and smash into the shore, causing much destruction. Tsunamis can originate hundreds or even thousands of miles away from coastal areas. Local geography may intensify the effect of a tsunami. Areas at greatest risk are less than 50 feet above sea level and within one mile of the shoreline.

People who are near the seashore during a strong earthquake should listen to a radio for a tsunami warning and be ready to evacuate at once to higher ground. Rapid changes in the water level are an indication of an approaching tsunami. Tsunamis arrive as a series of successive "crests" (high water levels) and "troughs" (low water levels). These successive crests and troughs can occur anywhere from 5 to 90 minutes apart. They usually occur 10 to 45 minutes apart.

Storm surge is water that is pushed toward the shore by the force of the winds swirling around the storm. This advancing surge combines with the normal tides to create the hurricane storm tide, which can increase the mean water level 15 feet or more. In addition, wind driven waves are superimposed on the storm tide. This rise in water level can cause severe flooding in coastal areas, particularly when the storm tide coincides with the normal high tides. Because much of the United States' densely populated Atlantic and Gulf Coast coastlines lie less than 10 feet above mean sea level, the danger from storm tides is tremendous.

While caused by different metrological events, tsunamis and tidal surges have the same effect, so planning for both can be treated similarly.

Before a tsunami occurs:

- Determine if your library is in a danger area.
- Know the height of your location above sea level and your distance from the coast. Evacuation orders may be based on these numbers.
- Be familiar with the tsunami warning signs.
- Because an underwater disturbance such as an earthquake can cause tsunamis, people living along the coast should consider an earthquake or a sizable ground rumbling as a warning signal. A noticeable rapid rise or fall in coastal waters is also a sign that a tsunami is approaching.
- Make sure staff and patrons know how to respond to a tsunami.
- Make evacuation plans.
- Practice evacuation drills.
- Have disaster supplies on hand.

During *a tsunami:*

- Listen to a radio or television to get the latest emergency information, and be ready to evacuate if asked to do so.
- If you hear an official tsunami warning or detect signs of a tsunami, evacuate at once.
- Climb to higher ground. A tsunami warning is issued when authorities are certain that a tsunami threat exists.
- Stay away from the beach. If you can see the wave you are too close to escape it.

After *a tsunami:*

- Stay tuned to a battery-operated radio for the latest emergency information.
- Contact authorities to help injured or trapped people.
- Stay out of damaged buildings. Return to the library only when authorities say it is safe.
- Use a flashlight when entering damaged buildings.
- Have authorities check for electrical shorts and live wires.
- Do not use equipment or lights until an electrician has checked the electrical system.
- Open windows and doors to help dry the building.
- Shovel mud while it is still moist to give walls and floors an opportunity to dry.[6]

PUTTING IT ALL TOGETHER

As with wildfires, no library is able to deal with a tsunami on its own. The possibility of tsunami inundation must be dealt with on a community basis. The West Coast & Alaska Tsunami Warning Center (http://wcatwc. arh.noaa.gov/) recommends that communities wishing to become "TsunamiReady" address six critical issues:

- Communication and Coordination
- NWS Warning Reception

[6] http://www.fema.gov/hazards/tsunamis/tsunami.shtm

- Hydrometeorological Warning
- Warning Dissemination
- Communicative Preparedness
- Administration

Each issue is addressed more fully in the Center's TsunamiReady Community Requirements. In addition to addressing the usual concerns (responsibility, training, communication, preparations, evacuation procedures, post-disaster procedures), the library's disaster plan should be written with these guidelines in mind.

Sample 2.7

Tsunami Ready Community Requirements

Guideline 1: Communications and Coordination Center

A key to effective hazards management is effective communication. This is especially true in tsunami emergencies, since wave arrival times may be measured in just minutes. Such a "short-fused" event requires an immediate, but careful, systematic and appropriate response. To ensure such a proper response, communities must have established the following:

24–Hour Warning Point. To receive recognition under the TsunamiReady Program, an applying agency will need to have a 24–hour warning point (WP) that can receive NWS tsunami information and provide local reports and advice. Typically, this might be a law enforcement or fire department dispatching point. For cities or towns without a local dispatching point, another jurisdiction within the county could act in that capacity for them. For communities in the Alaska and Pacific Regions with less than 2,500 residents and no county agency to act as a 24–hour warning point, the community must designate responsible persons who are able to receive warnings 24 hours per day and have the authority to activate local warning systems. The warning point will need to have:

- 24–hour operations.
- Warning reception capability.
- Warning dissemination capability.
- Ability and authority to activate local warning system(s).

Emergency Operations Center. All agencies must have an emergency operations center (EOC). For communities with less than 15,000 residents, the EOC may be provided by another jurisdiction within the county. The EOC must be staffed during tsunami events to execute the warning point's tsunami warning functions. Summarized below are tsunami-related roles of an EOC:

- Activated based on predetermined guidelines related to NWS tsunami information and/or tsunami events.
- Staffed with emergency management director or designee.

- Must have warning reception/dissemination capabilities equal to or better than the warning point.
- Ability to communicate with adjacent EOCs/Warning Points.
- Ability to communicate with local NWS office or Tsunami Warning Center.

Guideline 2: NWS Warning Reception

Warning points and EOCs each need multiple ways to receive NWS tsunami warnings. TsunamiReady guidelines to receive NWS warnings in an EOC/WP require a combination of the following, based on population:

- NOAA Weather Radio (NWR) receiver with tone alert. Specific Area Message Encoding (SAME) is preferred. Required for recognition only if within range of transmitter.
- NOAA Weather Wire drop: Satellite downlink data feed from NWS.
- Emergency Managers Weather Information Network (EMWIN) receiver: Satellite feed and/or VHF radio transmission of NWS products.
- Statewide Telecommunications System: Automatic relay of NWS products on statewide emergency management or law enforcement system.
- Statewide warning fan-out system: State authorized system of passing message throughout warning area.
- NOAA Weather Wire via Internet NOAAport Lite: Provides alarmed warning messages through a dedicated Internet connection.
- Direct link to NWS office: e.g., amateur or VHF radio.
- E-mail from Tsunami Warning Center: Direct e-mail from Warning Center to emergency manager.
- Pager message from Tsunami Warning Center: Page issued from Warning Center directly to EOC/WP.
- Radio/TV via Emergency Alert System: Local Radio/TV or cable TV.
- US Coast Guard broadcasts: WP/EOC monitoring of USCG marine channels.
- National Warning System (NAWAS) drop: FEMA-controlled civil defense hotline.

Guideline 3: Hydrometeorological Monitoring

This Guideline relates solely to the StormReady requirements for the combined Storm/TsunamiReady program. While receipt of warnings is crucial to the success of any EOC or warning point, there should also be a means of monitoring weather information, especially radar data. To obtain combined Storm/TsunamiReady recognition, each EOC/WP (based on population) should have some combination of the following recommended means of gathering weather information:

- Internet.
- Television/Cable TV/Radio.
- Two-way radio.
- Emergency Management Weather Information Network (EMWIN).
- Local systems for monitoring weather.

Guideline 4: Warning Dissemination

Upon receipt of NWS warnings or other reliable information suggesting a tsunami is imminent, local emergency officials should communicate the threat with as much of the population as possible. To be recognized as

Storm/TsunamiReady, a community must have NOAA Weather Radio in the following facilities (when in range of an NWR transmitter):

Required Locations:
- 24–hour warning point.
- Emergency operations center.
- City hall.
- School superintendent office.

Recommended Locations:
- Courthouses.
- Public libraries.
- Hospitals.
- All schools.
- Fairgrounds.
- Parks and recreation areas.
- Public utilities.
- Sports arenas.
- Transportation departments.

In addition, recognition will be contingent upon having one or more of the following means (based on population) of ensuring timely warning dissemination to citizens:

- Cable television audio/video overrides.
- Local flood warning systems with no single point of failure.
- Other locally-controlled methods like a local broadcast system or sirens on emergency vehicles.
- Outdoor warning sirens.
- Phone messaging (dial-down) systems.
- Counties Only: A countywide communications network that ensures the flow of information between all cities and towns within its borders. This would include acting as a warning point for the smaller towns.

Guideline 5: Community Preparedness

Public education is vital in preparing citizens to respond properly to tsunami threats. An educated public is more likely to take steps to receive tsunami warnings, recognize potentially threatening tsunami events, and respond appropriately to those events. Communities seeking recognition in the Storm/TsunamiReady Program must:

- Conduct or sponsor tsunami and weather safety awareness programs in schools, hospitals, fairs, workshops, and community meetings (number of talks per year is based on population). These may be part of multi-hazard presentations affecting local communities/regions (e.g., flood, tsunami, wildfire).
- Define tsunami evacuation areas and evacuation routes, and install evacuation route signs.
- Designate a tsunami shelter/area outside the hazard zone.

- Provide written tsunami hazard information to the populace, including:

  Hazard zone maps

  Evacuation routes

  Basic tsunami information

  These instructions can be distributed through mailings, i.e., utility bills, within phone books, and posted at common meeting points such as libraries and public buildings throughout the community.

- Encourage local schools to meet the following guidelines:

  Inclusion of tsunami information in primary and secondary school curriculums. NWS will help identify curriculum support material.

  Practice tsunami evacuation drills when located within the defined hazard zone at least biennially.

  Provide written safety material to all staff and students.

Guideline 6: Administrative

No program can be successful without formal planning and pro-active administration. To be recognized in the Storm/Tsunami Ready Program:

  Tsunami warning and hazardous weather plans must be in place and approved by the local governing body. These plans must address the following:

- Hazard/risk assessment.
- Warning point procedures.
- EOC activation guidelines and procedures.
- Tsunami hazard zone map with evacuation routes.
- Procedures for canceling an evacuation for less-than-destructuve tsunamis.
- Procedures for reporting storm and tsunami damage to the local NWS office in near real-time.
- Storm spotter activation criteria and reporting procedures if applicable.
- Storm spotter roster and training record if applicable.
- Guidelines and procedures for activation of sirens, cable TV overide, and/or local system activation in accordance with state Emergency Alert System (EAS) plans, and warning fan-out procedures, if necessary.
- Annual exercises.

  Local community officials must conduct a bi-yearly visit/discussion with local NWS Forecast Office Warning Coordination Meteorologist or Tsunami Warning Center personnel. This can be a visit to the NWS office, phone discussion, or e-mail contacts.

From http://wcatwc.arh.noaa.gov/tsunamiready/criteria.htm

Figure 2-1. Flood Damage at the Houston Academy of Medicine—Texas Medical Center (HAM-TMC) Library, June 2001

2.5 FLOODS

Flooding is another type of disaster that knows no geographic boundaries, and can be caused by many different events. The lower tunnel area of the Central Library in the Houston Public Library system regularly takes on water from the plaza above. While the flooding caused by Tropical Storm Allison destroyed the street level of the Houston Academy Medicine—Texas Medical Center (HAM-TMC) Library, a broken pipe in 1996 destroyed a large range of bound journals on the second floor of the same library. The Michel Orradre Library at Santa Clara University in California suffered from a recurring influx of dirty groundwater into its basement, from 1997–2001. Probably any library that has experienced a fire, has also felt the effects of water damage to collections and furnishings.

CHARACTERISTICS

Floods are the most common and widespread of all natural disasters—except fire. Most communities will experience some kind of flooding after spring rains, heavy thunderstorms, or winter snow thaws. Not all floods are natural, though. Dam failures resulting in faulty maintenance or a natural event such as an earthquake or intense water upstream, are potentially the worst flood events. Floods can be slow or fast rising, but generally develop over a period of days. Communities particularly at risk are those located in low-lying areas, near water, or downstream from a dam.

Floods usually result from intense storms dropping large amounts of rain within a brief period, as is often the case with a hurricane or tropical storm. Flash floods occur with little or no warning and can reach full peak in only a few minutes. The June 2001 flooding in the HAM-TMC Library happened in a short 30–minute time span. Such rapid rise of water usually eliminates any chance of on-the-spot measures to minimize the damage.

Some characteristics of floods include:

- Floodwaters can be extremely dangerous. The force of six inches of swiftly moving water can knock people off their feet.
- Flash flood waters move at very fast speeds and can roll boulders, tear out trees, destroy buildings, and obliterate bridges.
- Walls of water can reach heights of 10 to 20 feet and generally are accompanied by a deadly cargo of debris.
- Cars can be easily swept away in just 2 feet of moving water.

For these reasons, it is important to take steps in advance to minimize damage, and to evacuate when advised by authorities.

Before a flood:

Nobody can stop a flood. But if you are faced with one, there are actions you can take to protect your staff and client, and to keep property losses to a minimum.

- If in a flood prone area, install floodwalls and floodgates that are easily operated.
- Eliminate as much solid ground around the building by installing porous concrete for parking lots and sidewalks. Porous concrete allows water to seep in rather than just run off or puddle.

- If possible, install green areas, such as lawns and flower gardens in the place of parking lots. In the case of gardens, plant foliage that is indigenous to the geographic area to increase longevity.

- Install a green roof.

- Buy flood insurance, if available in your area.

- Create a relationship with professional recovery agents in the area. Immediately after a flood, these agents will be flooded (forgive the pun) with calls from businesses and residents. If you already have already created a relationship, you could be bumped to the top of the list.

- If a flood is imminent and time permits:

    Turn off all utilities at the main power switch and close the main gas valve if evacuation appears necessary.

    Move collections, equipment, computers, furniture and other valuables to upper floors or higher elevations.

Figure 2-2. Flood Damage at the HAM-TMC Library Computer Lab, June 2001

***During** a flood:*

- Monitor weather and maintain contact with authorities.[7]
- Close floodgates when advised by authorities, or on your own judgment.
- Evacuate the area when advised.
- Do not drive through a flooded area. If you come upon a flooded road, turn around and go another way.
- Do not walk through flooded areas. As little as six inches of moving water can knock you off your feet.
- Avoid downed power fines and electrical wires. Electrocution is another major source of deaths in floods. Electric current passes easily through water.
- Look out for animals—especially snakes and in the southern United States, fire ants.

***After** a flood:*

- Call your recovery agent before you do anything else.
- Call your insurance agent next.
- Enter the building only when allowed by officials.
- Use flashlights, not candle or open flames, for light.
- Keep power off until an electrician has inspected your system for safety.
- Do not use water for consumption until local authorities proclaim it safe. It is okay to use untested water to begin clean-up efforts or to flush toilets.
- Be careful walking around. After a flood, steps and floors are often slippery with mud and covered with debris, including nails and broken glass. Wear sturdy shoes.
- Immediately begin assessment of the collection and begin recovery process. It is important to contact your recovery agent immediately, since everyone else will be doing the same.[8]

Even if your library is not in a flood-prone area, you can still suffer

---

[7] Since the area around the Texas Medical Center and Rice University in Houston is prone to flooding, a local flood alert system has been created to help local institutions monitor weather and rising waters. Go to http://fas2.rice.edu to see this system.

[8] http://www.fema.gov/hazards/floods/flood.htm

water damage from floods caused by broken pipes or a leaky roof. For this reason, all libraries should keep a stock of large plastic sheeting at hand. Since there is no way to predict when a pipe will burst, it is of utmost importance to be ready to cover shelves, work stations and archives as quickly as possible.

PUTTING IT ALL TOGETHER

Along with fire, flooding is the chief threat to libraries. It covers a tremendous range of possibilities, from minor incursions of water resulting from faulty plumbing to catastrophic inundations. Floods can occur at any time, including:

- When the building is full of patrons.
- In evenings when full-time staff are largely absent.
- After hours when no one is present in the building.

With respect to flooding, the library disaster plan needs to be flexible enough to address any of these contingencies. James Madison University's (JMU) library disaster plan is highly targeted, providing clear and concise directions for particular types of events.

Flood/Water Leakage in the Library (from http://www.jmu.edu/safetyplan/library/flood.shtml)

- Staff should determine exact location and source of the problem.
- During work day, call Emergency Coordinator who will call Facilities Management (ext. 6315).
- Evenings and weekends call Campus Police (ext. 6911) to report the problem. Then call Emergency Coordinator at home.
- Evacuate patrons and staff from wet areas to prevent patrons from walking through the water. If the electrical system has not been disconnected this could cause disastrous consequences.
- If water is coming from above, get plastic sheeting and drape the collection.

Sample 2.8

James Madison University Comprehensive Safety Plan Table of Contents

1. Comprehensive Safety Overview
2. Master Fire Safety Plan
3. Facilities Management Operational Safety
4. Emergency Response Plan
5. Laboratory Safety
6. Hazardous Materials
7. Bloodborne Pathogens
8. Radiological Safety
9. Threats, Violence & Terrorism
10. Continuity of Operations Plans (COOP)
11. Office Safety
12. Theater Safety
13. Your Right to Know (Clery Law Provisions)
14. Field Trip Contingency Plans
15. Student Handbook Safety Section
16. Vehicle Operation Safety
17. Lighting & Safety Tours
18. Weapons on Campus
19. Aviation on Campus
20. Floods
21. Bicycle & Pedestrian Safety

- If water is coming from below, move collection to higher shelves or book trucks.
- When area is safe, remove items in order of priority.

The JMU Library's flood/water leakage contingency plan is one component of the University's Comprehensive Safety Plan, which addresses hundreds of possibilities in significant detail. Just on its own the table of contents for the JMU Comprehensive Safety Plan (http://www.jmu.edu/safetyplan/contents/table.shtml) consists of twenty-nine separate headings, many of which have dozens of subpoints.

2.6 TORNADOES

Tornadoes are more prevalent in some states of the United States, occurring more frequently in the area known as *Tornado Alley*. This area, which includes Alabama, Arkansas, Florida, Iowa, Kansas, Mississippi, Missouri, Nebraska, Oklahoma, and Texas, is where the intense killer tornadoes are likely to occur. Tornadoes are not exclusive to this region, though, as the storm that hit the National Agricultural Library in Maryland in 2001 indicates. In 1974 a super tornado outbreak took place in Georgia, Illinois, Indiana, Kentucky, Michigan, Mississippi, North Carolina, Ohio, South Carolina, Tennessee, Virginia, and West Virginia. In November of 2002 a tornado outbreak occurred in Alabama, Tennessee and Ohio, killing at least thirty-six people.

The peak time for tornadoes in the southern states is between March and May, and between April and June in the northern states. Experts estimate there are approximately 770 tornadoes per year in the United States. The average tornado travels at approximately 45 kilometers per hour, follows a path 26 kilometers long, and has a diameter of between 150 and 600 meters. Most tornadoes move in a northwest direction, and often follow underground water supplies.[9]

CHARACTERISTICS

A tornado is a violent windstorm characterized by a twisting, funnel-shaped cloud. It is spawned by a thunderstorm (or sometimes as a result of a hurricane) and produced when cool air overrides a layer of warm air, forcing the warm air to rise rapidly. As with hurricanes, there are categories of tornadoes:

---

[9] www2.sunysuffolk.edu/mandias/honors/student/tornado

- *Category F0*—Gale tornado with winds between 42 and 72 miles per hour. This storm brings light damage including broken tree branches, uprooted small trees, and damage to sign boards.

- *Category F1*—Moderate tornado with winds between 73 and 112 miles per hour. This storm brings moderate damage to roofs, mobile homes or buildings, cars blown off roads or turned over.

- *Category F2*—Significant tornado with winds between 113 and 157 miles per hour. This storm brings considerable damage such as roofs torn from buildings, mobile homes and buildings demolished, boxcars pushed over, large trees snapped or uprooted, light objects becoming missiles.

- *Category F3*—Severe tornado with winds between 158 and 206 miles per hour. This storm brings sever damage such as roofs and walls torn off well-constructed buildings, trains over turned, most trees uprooted, heavy cars lifted off the ground and tossed around.

- *Category F4*—Devastating tornado with winds between 207 and 260 miles per hour. This storm causes devastating damage, including destruction of well-constructed buildings, structures with weak foundations blown some distance, heavy cars becoming missiles.

- *Category F5*—Incredible tornado with winds between 261 and 318 miles per hour. This storm brings grave damage including houses lifted off foundations and being carried long distances, cars thrown over 100 feet, and trees debarked.[10]

The National Weather Service issues a *tornado watch* when tornadoes are possible in your area. A *tornado warning* is issued when a tornado has been sighted or indicated by weather radar.

Sample 2.9

Fort Worth (TX) Public Library Interview on Disaster Planning

Does your library have a disaster plan?

Yes it was done after the March 2000 Tornado.

---

[10] www.outlook.noaa.gov/tornadoes/fujita.htm

Who overseas it?

Emergency Management with City of Fort Worth had all departments do a plan after the tornado.

Who draws up the plan?

Staff and the Library Director.

How often is it updated?

As needed.

Have you ever had to use it?

No, because was done after the March 2000 storm.

How did staff react during the tornado?

Staff used good common sense and knew to get to lower level and get away from the blowing debris. No staff or client was injured.

Were you able to salvage your library collection?

Yes. Only approximately 285 library books were unusable due to the tornado including imbedded glass, water, and debris damage and others that were destroyed while checked out.

What kind of damage was done?

Windows to the building were broken, delivery trucks were damage, skylight was broken, there was roof damage, and trees around facility damaged. There was also some water damage from rain coming in through the damaged windows and roof.

What salvaging techniques did you use?

The City of Fort Worth Transportation and Public Works Department, which maintains city facilities came the night of the storm and secured the building. The next morning they had Blackmon Mooring in the facility cleaning the debris. Every item was removed from the shelves on both levels.

How much had to be replaced?

We purchased approximately 285 library books, some furniture, story time items, posters, draperies, flags, banners. We also expended funds on staff overtime and replacement lease of trucks which were damaged.

Where did the funds come from?

City funds, some of which were reimbursed by FEMA.

Was your rare collection affected by the disaster?

No, for the most part none of this was lost.

Did the disaster affect your automation system?

The main frame of the automation system is located in the facility and during the whole time it did not ever go down. We did have to have some of the computers which the public use on the floor cleaned.

Did it cause your facility to close down?

Yes, we were closed from the 28th of March until April 15, 2000.

If it did how long was it closed and were you able to relocate to a different location?

Staff worked at other locations and also other city departments as were appropriate. We have 15 facilities in our system. So we put people at other locations.

Tessie Hutson
Assistant to the Library Director
Fort Worth Public Library
Fort Worth, TX

When a tornado threatens, individuals need to have a safe place to go and time to get there. Even with advances in meteorology, warning times may be short or sometimes not possible. Lives are saved when individuals receive and understand the warning, know what to do, and know the safest place to go. Advance planning and quick response are the keys to surviving a tornado.

Before a tornado:

- Conduct tornado drills each tornado season.
- Designate an area in the library as a shelter.
- Invest in preventive mitigation steps complying with local building codes and ordinances about wind-resistant designs.
- Strengthen un-reinforced masonry.
- Have disaster supplies on hand.
- Know the difference between a tornado watch and a tornado warning.
- Be familiar with tornado danger signs:

  An approaching cloud of debris can mark the location of a tornado even if a funnel is not visible.

  Before a tornado hits, the wind may die down and the air may become very still.

  Tornadoes generally occur near the trailing edge of a thunderstorm. It is not uncommon to see clear, sunlit skies behind a tornado.[11]

---

[11] Growing up in the Midwest, one author of this book remembers her father often going outside and sniffing the air when tornadoes were possible. His explanation was that if a tornado was near, you could smell sulfur. While not a scientific fact, we always made it to the basement before a tornado came near.

During *a tornado, if at the library:*

- Make an announcement over the public address system, or by shouting if the electricity is off.
- Instruct everyone to go to the secure area designated in your tornado plan.
- Avoid places with wide-span roofs such as auditoriums, cafeterias, or large hallways.
- Get under a piece of sturdy furniture such as a work-bench or heavy table or desk and hold on to it.
- Use arms to protect head and neck.

If outdoors:

- If possible, get inside a building.
- If shelter is not available or there is no time to get indoors, lie in a ditch or low-lying area or crouch near a strong building.
- Be aware of the potential for flooding.
- Use arms to protect head and neck.

If in a car:

- Never try to out-drive a tornado in a car or truck.
- Get out of the car immediately and take shelter in a nearby building.
- If there is no time to get indoors, get out of the car and lie in a ditch or low-lying area away from the vehicle.
- Be aware of the potential for flooding.

After *a tornado:*

- Contact your disaster recovery agency immediately.
- Contact your insurance agency.
- Enter the building only when deemed safe by authorities.
- Wear sturdy, hard-soled shoes.
- Begin disaster recovery immediately. Remember, with a tornado, you can experience damage from both wind and rain, and possibly even fire.[12]

---

[12] http://www.fema.gov/hazards/tornadoes

PUTTING IT ALL TOGETHER

With respect to tornado situations, the library disaster plan should focus on:

- Staying abreast of tornado threats during severe weather conditions.
- Identifying tornado-safe spaces within the library.
- Getting patrons and staff to shelter within the library.

The disaster plan (see Sample 2.10) of the James G. Library at Texas A&M University Commerce addresses these key points.

Sample 2.10

James G. Gee Library Disaster Plan, Texas A&M University

TORNADO WATCH OR WARNING

In the event of a tornado watch or tornado warning, university police will call the director's office between 8:00 A.M. and 5:00 P.M., the circulation department or reference after 5:00 P.M. and weekends. University police will inform the library of the appropriate warning as issued to them by the National Weather Service. The person receiving the alert should notify all departments in the library.

Tornado Warning: A tornado has been sighted, all library occupants should stay in the building away from windows, and move to the center of the building (staff lounge or pre-shelve area).

Tornado Watch: Conditions are favorable for a possible tornado.

The circulation department will place the proper warning sign close to the entrance way, to inform patrons upon entering the library of the impending weather situation. The sign is located in the closet next to the automatic doors. Next, reference and/or circulation personnel should go to the upper floors to inform all patrons of the warning and strongly suggest to them that it would be safer to remain on the first floor. Encourage patrons to stay in the building and away from windows.

During a tornado warning a campus wide emergency alarm will be sounded by university police. It is possible that during a tornado warning, Security may only have time to sound the alarm rather than call each building. The library will never close during a tornado watch/warning, unless told to do so by university police or the president of university.

From http://www7.tamu-commerce.edu/library/displan25.htm

2.7 EARTHQUAKES

An earthquake is a sudden, rapid shaking of the earth caused by breaking and shifting beneath the surface. This shaking can cause buildings and bridges to collapse; disrupt gas, electric, and phone service; and sometimes trigger avalanches, landslides, flash floods, fires, and tsunamis (huge, destructive ocean waves). Earthquakes can happen anywhere, but are most prevalent in areas where the earth's tectonic plates meet and shift. In the United States there are 45 states that have a moderate to high risk of experiencing an earthquake, with California and Alaska being the most frequent. Other areas, including Alabama, Arkansas, Indiana, Kentucky, Missouri, Mississippi, Ohio, and Tennessee have experience ground shaking.

CHARACTERISTICS

Earthquakes strike suddenly, without warning and can occur at any time of the year and at any time of the day or night. On a yearly basis, 70 to 75 damaging earthquakes occur throughout the world. Estimates of losses from a future earthquake in the United States approach $200 billion.

There are forty-five states and territories in the United States at moderate to very high risk from earthquakes, and they are located in every region of the country. California experiences the most frequent damaging earthquakes; however, Alaska experiences the greatest number of large earthquakes—most located in uninhabited areas. The largest earthquakes felt in the United States were along the New Madrid Fault in Missouri, where a three-month long series of quakes from 1811 to 1812 included three quakes larger than a magnitude of 8 on the Richter Scale. These earthquakes were felt over the entire Eastern U.S., with Missouri, Tennessee, Kentucky, Indiana, Illinois, Ohio, Alabama, Arkansas, and Mississippi experiencing the strongest ground shaking.[13]

Sample 2.11

Northridge (CA) Earthquake, Oviatt Library at California State University, Northridge

On January 17, 1994 at 4:31 A.M., a 6.7 magnitude earthquake hit Northridge, CA. The epicenter was within one mile of the California State University (CSU) campus, which is located 32 miles northwest of Los Angeles, in the San Fernando Valley. Because it's earthquake country and there had been a ferocious earthquake in the 1970s in Sylmar, which is within a few miles of the CSU Northridge campus, there was good disaster planning, and a written plan in place at the time of the 1994 earthquake. The book stacks were anchored to the floor and braced across the top. Many, but not all, filing cabinets were anchored to walls. A staff communication and location plan, complete with phone trees, existed.

The earthquake occurred early in the morning of Martin Luther King Jr., Day, a university holiday. Due to the early hour and the holiday, only a handful of people were on campus. Almost everyone was at home. Additionally, since it was our intersession period, many people were away on vacation or at conferences. Even the president of the university was in a remote location on vacation. An interesting thing about disaster plans is how often they are oriented solely to taking action if you are present in your facility.

---

[13] http://www.fema.gov/hazards/earthquakes/

Thank goodness that no one was here, because there would have been widespread injury or worse. But the Northridge earthquake caused a different kind of nightmare because most people were at home.

The damage from the earthquake was so severe within a 20–mile radius that people had to tend to their own homes and families first. Even those who wanted to get to the campus had difficulty. There was no power so street lights and stoplights did not work. Some of the fatalities were victims of car accidents, including doctors speeding to hospitals and people racing to check on their extended families who collided at dark, unregulated intersections.

The dean of the library lived (still does) nearby. After assuring her family and home were safe, she drove with her family (who wants to be separated at this time?) to the campus and the library. She saw the damage to the building. The 235,000 square foot library was built in two stages. The central core, built in 1971–1972, was a big concrete box and contained most stack areas. The east and west wings, built just a few years before the earthquake, were boxes made of steel reinforced concrete. They suffered grievous structural damage. Huge four-story tall concrete pillars surround the library. Some of these pillars were snapped from their supports. Glass was broken, windows gaping open, all the books on the floor, unsupported stacks twisted, computers on the floor, offices upside down.

It was a few days before anyone was permitted into the library building. At that time, the dean and a few selected others used the short window they were permitted to go directly to special collections to retrieve the most valuable rare books and archives. There was a collection prioritization plan, which was very important for our library's recovery, and they followed it whenever they were permitted into the building. Staff members were permitted into the building on one day for 20 minutes to retrieve their own personal things. Colleagues tell me of officials lining up groups of people, handing out hard hats and flashlights, and accompanying them into different office spaces. (I was not employed by the library when the earthquake hit, but was hired later to lead the recovery team.)

The most immediate problem on campus was science labs, some of which were on fire. Because no one was present to tell firefighters what chemicals were in which labs, they could not respond to the fires. By the time faculty reached the campus, some were only able to watch their life's research burning.

In 1994, cell phones did not have the ubiquity of today. The disaster plan provided for managers and others to have the phone numbers of those whom they work with. The dean of the library and other administrators were attempting to locate and verify the safety of all members of the staff. None of the campus phones, even those in buildings, which were safe to enter, could work without electricity! This was not in the disaster plan then (it is now). So people lined up at two pay phones, which were still working, putting in quarters to call and locate staff members. This went on for days. A local business was kind enough to open its doors, and supply quarters and bottled water among other things.

The campus President was notified, but she could not reach the campus. Interstate 5, the route to the San Fernando Valley from most of northern California, had suffered major damage. This was shown extensively on television, the freeway bridges elevated quite high which cracked and lost entire sections. Eventually the president was brought in by helicopter. This made a very big difference, and it was critically important since she was able to make a number of key decisions quickly.

Many people have reported to me that when they arrived as daylight was beginning, they saw the damage all over the campus and concluded that campus might not come back from this disaster. The Northridge earthquake remains the single most expensive natural disaster to affect a university campus in this country, costing more than $60 million of FEMA recovery dollars. Some people lost their homes and wept because they felt they would lose the university as well.

Even though vicious aftershocks were occurring with frequency for days and still weeks after the event, a decision needed to be made about the upcoming spring semester. Registration, which was conducted then via telephone modem, would continue thanks to CSU's Bakersfield and Fresno campuses, which donated computer banks. The data files containing registrations, which had already been completed were on the top floor of a building, which was unsafe to enter. The dean of the library, who was also the vice provost for information technology at that time, rode a cherry picker to enter the area and retrieve the computer tapes, which were also transferred to Fresno and Bakersfield.

Most importantly, the president decided that classes would resume. The semester was supposed to begin at the end of January. She identified that resources could be secured so that classes could begin February 14. Trailers and computers from all over the region were brought in and set up to establish classrooms. Tents were erected in the middle of the campus, phone lines brought to them, and staff members were put to work answering phones, giving out information, and trying to contact faculty and students.

The library set up an operation on the lawn in front of the library building. There was a little tent with a telephone and a computer. Students could look at our catalog (running on a server, which was brought up from a duplicate kept offsite, again part of the disaster plan), connect to other libraries' catalogs, and staff could answer reference questions and request interlibrary loans. The library staff and faculty pulled together as a team to reorganize services and find substitute services and access for our students.

Arrangements were made for students to become users of the UCLA libraries. Buses went hourly to the UCLA campus, about an hour's drive from Northridge. Reference librarians from Northridge went to the UCLA libraries to help serve the demand.

After several months, the central part of the library building was made available for use again. The damage was repaired, exposed asbestos had to be removed, and then the library's services and stacks were reorganized into a smaller space. Service areas that did not fit, including microforms, fine arts, and the young readers' collection were housed in temporary structures nearby. A temporary building was erected to permit for extra study space. A building, which had last been used as a goat barn, was converted into work pace for the entire Technical Services Department, with additional study space for students.

The recovery was long and slow, from 1994 to the completion of the rebuilt library in 2000. Staff members, especially those who were located in temporary buildings or trailers in remote locations, had difficulty maintaining routine, but they did it with amazing persistence. Many individuals had lost their homes, or suffered great damage to them. There were financial issues, along with issues of fear and separation. When I arrived in 1997, I was one of the few in the library who did not have earthquake experience of any kind. I was responsible for overseeing the rebuilding projects, the reorganization of services and operations, and the return of all services, staff, and operations into the rebuilt library building. It was a great help to me, and to the library, to have someone who had not been through the earthquake, who had no history with the building. I could make and facilitate decisions and move people forward when they themselves occasionally were stuck. Obviously, strong bonds were forged.

The tenth anniversary of the earthquake was a week and a half ago (as of this writing). The campus is now almost completely rebuilt, and about two thirds of the faculty and staff members are people who were here at the time of the earthquake remain. We have a revised disaster plan which accounts for many of the things learned during the Northridge earthquake and which were not covered in the previous disaster plan. We practice at least once a year and add to the plan when we discover something new. The library is also part of the campus emergency response plan, which establishes satellite operations centers to form during a disaster. We will be responsible for oversight of the library building in this case, and we are coordinated with the entire campus through the campus plan.

Because the earthquake affected the entire campus, there is wonderful support for the library and its recovery needs, in addition to those elsewhere on campus. The earthquake recovery was a campus-wide issue, and the library did not need to face advocacy on its own for recovery money. Because there was a disaster plan in place and because campus and library leadership could also improvise when there was a scenario outside of the plan, the library recovery was a team effort.

Susan E. Parker
Associate Dean, Oviatt Library
California State University, Northridge

Before an earthquake:

- Designate "safe places" in each area of the building. A safe place could be under a sturdy table or desk or against an interior wall away from windows, bookcases, or tall furniture.
- Conduct drills that include dropping under a sturdy desk and hold on to one leg of it and protecting eyes by keeping head down.
- Bolt bookcases and other tall furniture to wall studs.
- Brace or anchor high or top-heavy objects.
- Secure items that might fall (books, computers, video equipment, etc.).
- Install strong latches or bolts on cabinets to ensure they remain shut.
- Move large or heavy objects and fragile items to lower shelves.
- Hang heavy items, such as pictures and mirrors, away from seating areas.
- Brace overhead light fixtures.
- Install flexible pipe fittings to avoid gas or water leaks.
- Get expert advice on repairing cracked walls and foundations.
- Follow local seismic building standards and safe land use codes that regulate land use along fault lines.
- Keep staff and patrons informed about the earthquake plan.
- Everyone in your library should know what to do if an earthquake occurs.

During an earthquake:

- Wait in your safe place until the shaking stops.
- Be on the lookout for fires. Fire is the most common earthquake-related hazard, due to broken gas lines, damaged electrical lines or appliances, and previously contained fires or sparks being released.
- If you must leave a building after the shaking stops, use the stairs, not the elevator.
- Stay away from windows.
- In a high-rise building, expect the fire alarms and

sprinklers to go off during a quake. Earthquakes frequently cause these systems to go off even if there is no fire.

- Once the shaking has stopped, check for and extinguish small fires.
- If you are in a coastal area, move to higher ground. Earthquakes often cause tsunamis or tidal waves. (See Section 2.4 for more information.)
- If you are in a mountainous area or near unstable slopes or cliffs, be alert for rock and other debris that could be loosed by the earthquake.

After an earthquake:

- Contact your disaster recovery agency immediately.
- Contact your insurance agent.
- Consult authorities before reentering the building or beginning recovery efforts.
- Look for and extinguish small fires.
- Leave the gas on at the main valve, unless you smell gas or think it's leaking. It may be weeks or months before professionals can turn gas back on using the correct procedures.
- Open cabinet doors cautiously. Contents may have shifted during the shaking of an earthquake and could fall, creating further damage or injury.
- Be aware that aftershocks following earthquakes can cause further damage to unstable buildings. Vacate any building that is seriously damaged.
- Watch out for fallen power lines or broken gas lines, and stay out of damaged areas. Hazards caused by earthquakes are often difficult to see, and you could be easily injured.
- Use battery-powered lanterns or flashlights to inspect the building. Kerosene lanterns, torches, candles, and matches may tip over or ignite flammables inside.
- Use the telephone only to report life-threatening emergencies.[14]

[14] http://www.fema.gov/hazards/earthquakes/

PUTTING IT ALL TOGETHER

Despite recent advances scientists do not yet have the ability to predict earthquakes. With that in mind, the library disaster plan should pay particular attention to:

- Risk assessment.
- Mitigation efforts.
- What to do during an earthquake event.
- Stabilization and recovery efforts.

There are some areas (the northern coast of the Gulf of Mexico) at virtually no risk for earthquake activity. Other areas experience earthquakes (California) routinely and have a long history of earthquake mitigation efforts. Still other areas (Upper Mississippi Valley) experienced severe earthquakes in the distant past but none in living memory. These latter areas are perhaps most at risk of experiencing a catastrophic earthquake, both because they are heavily developed and because most construction has occurred without earthquakes in mind. The library of Washington & Lee University, located in Lexington, Virginia, addresses the possibility of earthquakes in its disaster plan (see Sample 2.12).

Sample 2.12

Washington & Lee University Disaster Plan

Other Natural Disasters: Earthquakes

Earthquakes may occur in Virginia. The danger from earthquakes is caused by what they do to man-made structures—debris falling from damaged buildings, flying glass from broken windows, fires caused by broken gas lines, and flooding due to broken water mains. There is no warning before an earthquake occurs. When one does strike, there is a loud rumbling noise which sounds like a train.

Evacuation

When an earthquake happens, the building should not be evacuated. Persons in the building should stay in the inner core of the building away from windows. Shelter should be taken in a doorway, in a narrow corridor, or under a heavy table, desk, or bench. Exits which lead into stairways should not be used because they may have collapsed or be jammed with people. Also, be aware that after-shocks may follow for several hours or days after the earthquake. A battery-powered radio should be available so that instructions concerning the earthquake can be monitored.

For further information on evacuation, see the *Evacuation Team* section.

Recovery and Recovery Resources

Damage from an earthquake may include structural damage to the building, collapsed shelving, damage to equipment and furniture, water damage from broken pipes, and fire and/or smoke damage caused by broken gas lines. All damage will need to be assessed by someone in charge of building maintenance before re-entering to begin recovery operations.

From http://library.wlu.edu/howto/DisasterPlan.asp

2.8 LANDSLIDES AND DEBRIS FLOWS

CHARACTERISTICS

Landslides are a serious geologic hazard common to almost every state in the United States. It is estimated that nationally they cause up to $2 billion in damages and from 25 to 50 deaths annually. Globally, landslides cause billions of dollars in damage and thousands of deaths and injuries each year. Individuals can take steps to reduce their personal risk.

Some landslides move slowly and cause damage gradually, whereas others move so rapidly that they can destroy property and take lives suddenly and unexpectedly. Gravity is the force driving landslide movement. Factors that allow the force of gravity to overcome the resistance of earth material to landslide movement include: saturation by water, steepening of slopes by erosion or construction, alternate freezing or thawing, earthquake shaking, and volcanic eruptions.

Landslides are typically associated with periods of heavy rainfall or rapid snow melt and tend to worsen the effects of flooding that often accompanies these events. In areas burned by forest and brushfires, even low amounts of precipitation may initiate landslides.

Mudflows (or debris flows) are rivers of rock, earth, and other debris saturated with water. They develop when water rapidly accumulates in the ground, such as during heavy rainfall or rapid snowmelt, changing the earth into a flowing river of mud or slurry. A slurry can flow rapidly down slopes or through channels, and can strike with little or no warning at avalanche speeds. A slurry can travel several miles from its source, growing in size as it picks up trees, cars, and other materials along the way.

Before a landslide or debris flow:

- Learn about landslide risk in your area.
- Contact local officials, state geological surveys or departments of natural resources, and university departments of

geology. Landslides occur where they have before, and in identifiable hazard locations.

- Ask for information on landslides in your area, specific information on areas vulnerable to landslides, and request a professional referral for a very detailed site analysis of your property, and corrective measures you can take, if necessary.
- Talk to your insurance agent. Debris flow may be covered by flood insurance policies from the National Flood Insurance Program (NFIP).
- Develop an evacuation plan.
- Conduct evacuation drills.

Before *an intense storm:*

- Watch the patterns of nearby storm-water drainage on slopes near the library, and especially the places where runoff water converges, increasing flow over soil-covered slopes.
- Watch nearby hillsides for any signs of land movement, such as small landslides or debris flows, or progressively tilting trees.

During *a landslide:*

- Be aware that intense, short bursts of rain may be particularly dangerous, especially after longer periods of heavy rainfall and damp weather.
- Listen to battery-operated radios for updates on local conditions.
- If you are in areas susceptible to landslides and debris flows, evacuate when instructed by local officials. Remember that driving during an intense storm can be hazardous.
- If you remain in the library, move to a second story if possible. Staying out of the path of a landslide or debris flow saves lives.
- Listen for any unusual sounds that might indicate moving debris, such as trees cracking or boulders knocking together. A trickle of flowing or falling mud or debris may precede larger landslides. Moving debris can flow quickly and sometimes without warning.

- If you are near a stream or channel, be alert for any sudden increase or decrease in water flow and for a change from clear to muddy water. Such changes may indicate landslide activity upstream, so be prepared to move quickly.

After the landslide:

- Stay away from the slide area. There may be danger of additional slides.
- Check for injured and trapped persons near the slide, without entering the direct slide area. Direct rescuers to their locations.
- Listen to local radio or television stations for the latest emergency information.
- Watch for flooding, which may occur after a landslide or debris flow. Floods sometimes follow landslides and debris flows because they may both be started by the same event.
- Look for and report broken utility lines to appropriate authorities. Reporting potential hazards will get the utilities turned off as quickly as possible, preventing further hazard and injury.
- Check the building foundation and surrounding land for damage.
- Replant damaged ground as soon as possible since erosion caused by loss of ground cover can lead to flash flooding.
- Seek the advice of a geotechnical expert for evaluating landslide hazards or designing corrective techniques to reduce landslide risk. A professional will be able to advise you of the best ways to prevent or reduce landslide risk, without creating further hazard.[15]

PUTTING IT ALL TOGETHER

With respect to landslides, libraries must rely on local officials to:

- Control development on naturally dangerous slopes.
- Take actions to mitigate the development-related effects (e.g., water runoff) that may precipitate a landslide.

[15] http://www.fema.org/hazards/landslides

- Monitor the safety of slopes during times of intense or prolonged adverse weather conditions.
- Inform the public when landslide risk is high.

The Oregon Department of Land Conservation and Development Web site (see Sample 2.13) offers advice to local governments regarding planning for planning with respect to natural hazards such as landslides.

Sample 2.13

Oregon Department of Land Conservation and Development

Landslides—Local Government

This section provides guidance to local governments in planning and mitigating landslide hazards and regulating development activities in such a way as to decrease the risk to people and property.

Goal 7 Guidelines

Statewide Planning Goal 7 provides general guidelines for both natural hazards planning and implementing natural hazards-related regulations. The Goal 7 guidelines below are relevant for landslide hazards planning and the implementation of landslide hazards-related regulations. The Land Conservation and Development Commission adopted *amendments to Goal 7* PDF) in September 2002. The amendments took effect on June 1, 2002. For more information on Goal 7, see the *Statutory Background* of this Web site.

Guidelines for Natural Hazards Planning

- Areas subject to natural hazards should be evaluated as to the degree of hazard present. Proposed developments, which could be affected by a natural hazard, should be designed to avoid damage even if it means that limitations on use are imposed for developments located in the planning area.
- Plans taking into account known areas of natural disasters and hazards should consider as a major determinant, the carrying capacity of the air, land and water resources of the planning area. The land conservation and development actions contemplated by such plans should not exceed the carrying capacity of such resources.
- Planning for known areas of natural disasters and hazards should include an evaluation of the beneficial impact on natural resources and the environment from letting such events naturally reoccur.

Guidelines for Implementation of Natural Hazards-Related Regulations

- When locating developments in areas of known natural hazards, the density or intensity of the development should be limited by the degree of the natural hazard.
- When regulatory programs and engineering projects are being considered, the impacts of each should be considered.
- Natural hazard damage that can occur as a result of new developments, such as an increase in water runoff from paving projects or soil slippage due to weak foundation soils, should be considered, evaluated and accommodated in order to avoid damage to neighboring properties.

Existing Ordinances

This section is intended to provide a summary of existing hazards-related ordinances in Oregon that exemplify the principles contained in Goal 7 and that can serve as models for local governments in the development of hazard ordinances.

Douglas County Grant Project—SB 12 Rapidly Moving Landslides (Debris Flows)

Marion County Geologically Hazardous Areas Overlay Zone Ordinance

City of Salem Landslide Hazard Ordinance

Transfer of Development Rights Programs

State Agencies

Oregon Office of Emergency Management

Oregon Department of Geology and Mineral Industries

Oregon Department of Forestry

Oregon Coastal Management Program

From http://159.121.112.22/hazards/landslide_guidance.html

2.9 WINTER STORMS

The Olympia College Learning Resources Center in Bremerton, Washington felt the effects of intense snow and rainstorms in December 1997, when the roof collapsed under the weight of two feet of melting snow and 18 inches of rain. Fortunately, the disaster happened on a Sunday during semester break, so no one was injured, but this incident illustrates how winter storms can be devastating.

CHARACTERISTICS

A major winter storm can be lethal. Preparing for cold weather conditions and responding to them effectively can reduce the dangers caused by winter storms. The National Weather Service issues a winter storm watch to indicate that severe winter weather may affect your area. A winter storm warning indicates that severe weather conditions are definitely on the way. A blizzard warning indicates that large amounts of falling or blowing snow and sustained winds of at least 35 miles per hour are expected for several hours. "Wind chill" refers to the calculation of how cold it feels outside when the effects of temperature and wind speed are combined.

Before *a winter storm:*

- Be familiar with winter storm warning messages.
- Service snow removal equipment and have rock salt on hand to melt ice on walkways and kitty litter to generate temporary traction.
- Winterize the library building.
- Caulk and weather-strip doors and windows.
- Install storm windows or cover windows with plastic from the inside.
- Have safe emergency heating equipment available.
- Keep pipes from freezing by:

    Wrap pipes in insulation or layers of old newspapers.

    Cover the newspapers with plastic to keep out moisture.

    Let faucets drip a little to avoid freezing.

    Know how to shut off water valves.

During *a severe winter storm, if you are indoors:*

- Stay indoors and dress warmly.
- Conserve fuel.
- Lower the thermostat to 65° during the day and 55° at night.
- Close off unused rooms.
- If the pipes freeze, remove any insulation or layers of newspapers and wrap pipes in rags.
- Completely open all faucets and pour hot water over the pipes, starting where they were most exposed to the cold (or where the cold was most likely to penetrate).
- Listen to the radio or television to get the latest information.

If you are outdoors:

- Dress warmly.
- Wear loose-fitting, layered, lightweight clothing. Layers can be removed to prevent perspiration and chill. Outer garments should be tightly woven and water repellant.
- Wear mittens rather than gloves because fingers generate warmth when they touch each other.

- If you go out to remove snow, do a few stretching exercises to warm up your body. Also take frequent breaks.
- Cover your mouth.
- Protect your lungs from extremely cold air by covering your mouth when outdoors. Try not to speak unless absolutely necessary.
- Avoid overexertion. Cold weather puts an added strain on the heart.
- Be aware of symptoms of dehydration.
- Watch for signs of frostbite and hypothermia.
- Keep dry. Change wet clothing frequently to prevent a loss of body heat. Wet clothing loses all of its insulating value and transmits heat rapidly.

After a severe winter storm:

- Report downed power lines and broken gas lines immediately.
- After blizzards, heavy snows or extreme cold, check to see that no physical damage has occurred and that water pipes are functioning.
- Check the roof for heavy accumulations of snow.

PUTTING IT ALL TOGETHER

How a library plans for winter storm emergencies is governed by two factors:

- Whether the library is part of a larger organization
- Local climate conditions

If the library is part of a larger organization, whether the library closes for a winter storm is apt to be determined from above, rather than within the library itself. If the university remains open, the library is likely to remain open, unless the storm is occurring at a particularly slow time of the year. Whether the university closes will be influenced by such factors as the number of students who live on campus versus the number of students who commute to campus. Likewise, the biggest factor in a school library closing is likely to be road conditions affecting school buses; having major highways clear is less important than the conditions of residential streets.

Local climate conditions are the other big factor. Places that routinely experience snow and ice and that have a local infrastructure for responding to such conditions are less likely to shut down than places where snow and ice are relatively rare events. Conditions that would not cause a hiccup in Buffalo can create major disruptions in cities like Atlanta and Washington, D.C.

The approach of the library at Minnesota State University Moorhead (see Sample 2.14) is fairly standard.

Sample 2.14

Winter Storms General Notes, Minnesota State University, Moorhead

About 90% of the students and employees of Moorhead State University live in the immediate Moorhead/Fargo area. Consequently, if travel is possible in the two cities, the university will usually try to avoid calling off classes and/or closing the campus. All individuals must take into account their own circumstances for travel to/from MSU and decide accordingly whether or not it is safe for them to travel.

The vice president for student affairs has the responsibility for decisions about the cancellation of classes, and the vice president for administrative affairs has the responsibility for decisions about the closure of the university/personnel matters. Notification is sent to the MSU information telephone operator, campus security, the Tri-College University office, the early education center, continuing studies, and the local television and radio stations.

If evening classes are canceled, the library will remain open until 8:00 P.M. on Monday–Thursday and until 4:45 P.M. on Friday.

If all classes are canceled by the university but the university remains open, the library will be open from 7:30 A.M. to 8:00 P.M. on Monday–Thursday and from 7:30 A.M. to 4:45 P.M. on Friday.

If the university has been declared closed, the library will be open (with only student assistants on duty) from 10:00 A.M. to 8:00 P.M. on Monday–Thursday and from 10:00 A.M. to 4:45 P.M. on Friday.

The student assistant supervisor maintains a list of student assistants willing to work during storm emergencies and is responsible for contacting and scheduling student assistants during university closings.

If inclement weather occurs on Saturdays, Sundays, holidays, or evenings when the library is scheduled to be open, closing decisions will be made by the librarian on duty and the dean of academic services.

From http://www.mnstate.edu/instructres/manual/winter.cfm

2.10 AVALANCHES

While not as common as other types of disasters, any library located in a mountainous area needs to be aware of the possibility of an avalanche. Destruction by an avalanche can be very similar to that of a landslide.

CHARACTERISTICS

An avalanche or snowslide is a mass of snow sliding down a mountainside. Avalanches can occur in any situation where snow, slope, and weather conditions combine to create proper conditions. Four conditions must be present for an avalanche to occur: a steep slope; a snow cover; a weak layer in the snow cover; and a trigger.

Avalanche danger increases with major snowstorms and periods of thaw. About 2,000 avalanches are reported to the U.S. Forest Service Avalanche Center in an average winter and more than 80% occur during or just after large snowstorms.

Although most avalanches occur in the back country, outside of developed areas, avalanches can take place anywhere the four conditions are present, including heavily populated areas. They can occur on small slopes well below the timberline, such as gullies, road cuts, and small openings in trees.

Before an avalanche:

The best way to avoid an avalanche is by recognizing and avoiding avalanche terrain. If your library happens to be in an avalanche-prone area, learn how to recognize unstable snow. When the snow cover is very unstable, nature often broadcasts clear danger signals. Snow that cracks, collapses, or makes hollow sounds is also unstable. Weak layers that are found by digging snow pits are also signs of unstable snow. Snow that has become wet from thaw or rain can also be dangerous.

If your library is located in an avalanche-prone area, it is advisable to have on hand an avalanche transceiver (or beacon), shovel, and a collapsible or ski pole probe. Always keep enough food and water and other equipment on hand to spend the night. If an avalanche occurs, you, as well as your staff and patrons, could either be trapped inside the library building or outside when trying to evacuate. If situated in an avalanche-prone area, always have an evacuation plan on hand.

During an avalanche:

The best way to survive an avalanche is to avoid it altogether. If that is not possible, keep in mind that only one in three victims caught in an avalanche without a transceiver or beacon survives. If you are caught, try to escape to the side. If you are knocked down, swim with the avalanche to try to stay on top. When the avalanche slows down, reach the surface or make an air pocket.

After *an avalanche:*

- Stay away from the slide area. There may be danger of additional slides.
- Check for injured and trapped persons near the slide, without entering the direct slide area. Direct rescuers to their locations.
- Listen to local radio or television stations for the latest emergency information. This might require a battery-operated radio.
- Look for and report broken utility lines to appropriate authorities. Reporting potential hazards will get the utilities turned off as quickly as possible, preventing further hazard and injury.

PUTTING IT ALL TOGETHER

As is the case with landslides and mudslides, the key to library preparedness with respect to avalanches includes:

- Hazard assessment.
- Staying alert when conditions are threatening.

Since most avalanches occur in back country areas, hazard assessment is a fairly straightforward activity. Very few libraries are likely to be located in avalanche-prone areas. Libraries located in mountainous areas that experience severe winter weather may be at risk. Consult with local emergency management officials to help assess your risk.

If your library is located in an at risk area, keeping abreast of threatening conditions is the centerpiece of any preparedness plan. There are multiple avalanche forecasting centers throughout the western United States and other alpine regions of the world. Avalanche.org (http://www.avalanche .org), a Web site maintained by the American Avalanche Association, provides a comprehensive listing of avalanche centers in the United States and Canada, with links to European sites.

Although most of their information is oriented to individuals engaging in back country recreational activities (e.g., skiing, snowboarding, snowmobiling, climbing, hiking), some give specific information to local residents. The City and Borough of Juneau, Alaska (the municipal area in the

United States most at risk from damaging avalanches) has developed a detailed Urban Avalanche Response Plan, which can be found at: http://www.juneau.org/emergency/documents/AvplanAdopted.pdf. Highlights of this plan can be found on the following pages.

Sample 2.15

The City and Borough of Juneau, Alaska Urban Avalanche Response Plan

I. Purpose

II. Situation

   a. Background

   b. Path Details

      i. Path descriptions.

      ii. Avalanche path maps.

   c. Resources

      i. Primary avalanche responders.

      ii. Avalanche equipment.

III. Assumptions

IV. Concept of Operations

   a. Scene Safety

      i. Secondary avalanches.

      ii. Avalanche specialist.

      iii. Additional scene safety considerations.

      iv. Explosive avalanche reduction work.

   b. Response Organization

      i. Response organizational chart.

      ii. Urban avalanche sequence of events chart.

   c. Incident Command

   d. Communications

V. Roles and Responsibilities

   a. Checklists

      i. Incident command summary sheet.

      ii. Field operations chief summary sheet.

      iii. First responders summary sheet.

      iv. First responding team summary sheet.

      v. Team leader summary sheet.

      vi. Team member summary sheet.

      vii. Scribe summary sheet.

      viii. Gear checklist.

b. Roles of Responding Agencies and Groups
   i. Capital City Fire and Rescue
   ii. Alaska State Troopers
   iii. Juneau Police Department
   iv. CBJ Emergency Management Coordinator
   v. Juneau Mountain Rescue
   vi. SEADOGS
   vii. Ski Patrol
VI. Search Procedures
   a. Goals
   b. Scene Rules
   c. Initial Search Procedures
      i. Urban avalanche SAR
      ii. Highway avalanche SAR
   d. Interviews
VII. Notification Tree

Purpose

The CBJ Urban Avalanche Response Plan outlines the City's procedures for managing an avalanche event that impacts residential areas and infrastructures of the City of Junea. The plan identifies departments, agencies and individuals that are directly responsible for emergency response and critical support services. It provides a management structure for coordinating and deploying essential resources following that of the nationally recognized Incident Command System.

Background

Avalanches are of special concern to Juneau because parts of the city are located directly beneath avalanche paths. National experts consider Juneau one of the largest municipal avalanche hazard areas in the country because of the combined threat from the Behrends and White paths as well as the many paths that empty onto Thane Road. Avalanches have hit, damaged or destroyed at least 72 buildings within a 10–mile radius of downtown Juneau in the past century.

There are 62 houses, 1 hotel, 2 sections of the Egan Expressway, a number of streets and roads, parts of the Flume, and much of Aurora Basin boat harbor in mapped avalanche zones. There are 40 houses in the severe hazard zone and 22 plus the hotel in the moderate hazard zone.

Avalanches from these paths have very high destructive potential. No historical avalanches has reach the destructive potential of its path. It is likely that 100 to 300 year events have not yet occurred in the relatively short time since the town of Juneau was established.

A 100 to 300 year avalanche event could easily destroy most buildings in the avalanche zone, sweep cars off the highways, and damage or destroy boats in Aurora Basin. Such large slides could also block the Glacier Highway and the Egan Expressway at the White and Behrends Avenue paths, hindering emergency response and possibly blocking road access to the hospital. Large slides can also occur on Thane Road and in heavily used areas near Basin Road.

From http://www.juneau.org/emergency/documents/AvplanAdopted.pdf

2.11 VOLCANOES

The most memorable volcanic eruption in the United States in the last few decades was that of Mount St. Helen's in the Pacific Northwest in May of 1980. While some libraries, such as the Spokane Public Library, had to close for a few days, other library workers in the affected area wore surgical masks, swept ash, collected clothing for victims, asked patrons to leave their shoes at the door, and provide reference on volcanoes. For example, the Washington State Library circulated information on how to remove ash from engines, electrical equipment, and computers.

CHARACTERISTICS

A volcano is a mountain that opens downward to a reservoir of molten rock below the surface of the earth. Unlike most mountains, which are pushed up from below, volcanoes are built up by an accumulation of their own eruptive products lava, ashflows, and airborne ash and dust. When pressure from gases and the molten rock becomes strong enough to cause an explosion, eruptions occur. Gases and rock shoot up through the opening and spill over, or fill the air with lava fragments. Volcanic products are used as building or road-building materials, as abrasive and cleaning agents, and as raw materials for many chemical and industrial uses. Lava ash makes soil rich in mineral nutrients. Dangers associated with volcanoes include:

- Volcanic ash can affect people hundreds of miles away from the cone of a volcano. Several of the deaths from the Mount St. Helens volcano in 1980 were attributed to inhalation of ash. Volcanic ash can contaminate water supplies, cause electrical storms, and collapse roofs.
- An erupting volcano can also trigger tsunamis, flash floods, earthquakes, rockfalls, and mudflows.
- Sideways directed volcanic explosions, known as "lateral blasts," can shoot large pieces of rock at very high speeds for several miles. These explosions can kill by impact, burial, or heat. They have been known to knock down entire forests. The majority of deaths attributed to the Mount St. Helens volcano were a result of lateral blast and tree blow-down.

In the United States, volcanic eruptions are most likely in the Pacific Rim states of Hawaii, Alaska, Washington, Oregon, and California. The chance of eruptions that could damage populated areas is the greatest for the active volcanoes of Hawaii and Alaska. Active volcanoes of the Cascade Mountain Range in California, Oregon, and Washington have created problems recently. The danger area around a volcano covers approximately a 20-mile radius. Some danger may exist 100 miles or more from a volcano, leaving Montana and Wyoming at risk.

Before *a volcanic eruption:*

- Learn about your community warning systems.
- Be prepared for other disasters that can be spawned by volcanoes, including earthquakes, flash floods, landslides and mudflows, thunderstorms, and tsunamis.
- Make evacuation plans. You want to get to high ground away from the eruption. Plan a route out and have a backup route in mind.
- Have a pair of goggles and a disposable breathing mask for each staff member.
- Comply with evacuation instructions. Although it may seem safe to stay in the library to wait out an eruption, doing so could be very dangerous. The rock debris from a volcano can break windows and set buildings on fire.

During *a volcanic eruption:*

- Follow the evacuation order issued by authorities.
- Avoid areas downwind of the volcano.
- If trapped outdoors, seek shelter indoors.
- If caught in a rockfall, roll into a ball to protect head.
- Avoid low-lying area where poisonous gases can collect and flash floods can be most dangerous.
- If caught near a stream, beware of mudflows.
- Protect yourself by wearing long sleeved shirts and pants; using goggles to protect eyes; using a dust-mask or a damp cloth over face to help breathing.
- Watch out for mudflows, powerful "rivers" of mud that can move faster than people can walk or run.

After *a volcanic eruption:*

- Listen to a battery-powered radio or television for the latest emergency information.

- Stay away from volcanic ashfall.
- When outside, cover your mouth and nose.
- Wear goggles to protect your eyes.
- Keep skin covered to avoid irritation or burns.
- If you have a respiratory ailment, avoid contact with any amount of ash. Stay indoors until local health officials advise it is safe to go outside.
- Avoid driving in heavy ashfall. Driving will stir up more ash that can clog engines and stall vehicles.
- Clear roofs of ashfall. Ashfall is very heavy and can cause buildings to collapse.[16]

PUTTING IT ALL TOGETHER

As is the case with hurricanes and other widespread phenomena, volcanic activity is something that must be confronted by the community or region at large, not just the library alone. Since the Nevada del Ruiz disaster in Colombia twenty years ago, volcanologists and emergency preparedness officials have made tremendous strides in predicting volcano eruptions and the consequences thereof.

Developed by the Office of the United Nations Disaster Relief Coordinator and UNESCO, "Developing a Volcano Emergency Plan" identifies more than a dozen key issues that need to be addressed by local and regional officials, including:

- Key assumptions.
- Basic elements of the plan.
- Time scales.
- Identification of hazard zones.
- Population census and inventory of property.
- Identification of safe transit points and refuge zones.
- Identification of evacuation routes.
- Means of transport, traffic control.
- Accommodation in refuge zones.
- Rescue, first aid and hospital services.
- Security in evacuated zones.

[16] http://www.fema.gov/hazards/volcanoes/volcano.shtm

- Alert procedures within government.
- Formulation and communication of public warnings.
- Review and revision of plans.

The Lincoln County, Montana disaster plan includes a section on volcanic active, reproduced from volcanic emergency management (office of the U.S. Nations Disaster Relief Coordinator [UNDRO] and the United Nations Educational Scientific and Cultural organization, U.N., NY, 1985).

Sample 2.16

United Nations Disaster Relief Coordinator (UNDRC) Development of Volcanic Emergency Plans

Developing a Volcano Emergency Plan

Chapter Five

The Development of Volcanic Emergency Plans

Reproduced from: *Volcanic Emergency Management,* Office of the United Nations Disaster Relief Coordinator (UNDRO) and United Nations Educational Scientific and Cultural Organization, United Nations, New York, 1985.

Basic Assumptions

It will be assumed in this chapter:

a.   That in any community exposed to volcanic hazards there is general awareness of the hazard and of the attendant risks to life and property, and a general desire to take collective action to reduce these risks.

b.   That a legislative framework exists within which it is possible to plan, organize, and put into effect, at the national and at the local level, appropriate protective measures, including if necessary the evacuation of threatened areas and assistance to evacuees.

c.   That scientific knowledge of the potentially dangerous volcanoes is sufficiently advanced to permit the elaboration of "scenarios" of possible eruptions, their destructive effects and their social and economic consequences.

d.   That it will be possible to have some warning of impending eruptions, either from visible signs of volcanic activity or from scientific monitoring of the volcanoes, and that this warning will be given in time for appropriate action to be taken.

e.   That, if the above conditions are fulfilled, an emergency plan of action in case of eruption will be prepared for each potentially dangerous volcano.

Time Scales

One important question, which must be examined at the outset, is the relation between the time-scale of volcanic events and the time needed to put various protective measures (i.e., on-site protection and/or evacuation) into effect.

Experience has shown that the interval between the onset of an eruption, or of significant precursory phenomena, and a violent climax, eruption, may range from a few hours to several days, weeks or months.

On the other hand, the time required to put emergency protective measures into effect depends on the size of the area at hazard, the density of population and settlement, the degree of mobility of the population, the transport and communication facilities available, and the general technological level of development. It will generally be measured in hours or days.

In practice, it will usually be appropriate to plan for two types of action:

1. Phased response to a gradually developing volcanic crisis, during which one may expect to have warning of potentially dangerous volcanic events at least 24 hours before they occur.

2. Immediate response to a situation calling for the fastest possible evacuation of people by whatever means are immediately available.

The more that is known about the history of a volcano, and the greater the effort that have been devoted to scientific studies and monitoring of its behavior, the easier it will be to foresee how much time may be available to take protective action when an eruption does occur.

Identification of Hazard Zones

The first element of a volcanic emergency plan is a map showing the hazard zones around the volcano which are liable to be affected by one or more destructive phenomena (pyroclastic flows, mudflows, lava flows, heavy ash falls, etc.) during an eruption. Such maps normally include the subdivision of the area exposed to each type of hazard into two or three subzones corresponding to eruptions of different magnitudes.

Indentification of Safe Transit Points and Refuge Zones

If the evacuation of a hazard zone is to proceed in an orderly manner, it is essential that each person in the zone knows where to go when evacuation starts. For each hazard zone (or part of each zone), the nearest easily accessible point outside the zone may be identified, to which the people should go or should be taken, as quickly as possible, and where they may assemble in safety while arrangements are made for their reception in a refuge zone.

At each such safe transit point, arrangements will be made for evacuees to be identified so that, if necessary, a search can be made for any persons who may be missing. If several such transit points are set up, there should be good facilities for telephone or radio communication between them. All evacuees, including those proceeding to their own alternative accommodation in a safe area, should register their departure from the danger zone at one or other of the transit points.

The safe transit points will probably have only minimal facilities for the shelter and feeding of the evacuees. They should nevertheless be selected on the basis of a survey of buildings outside the hazard zones but easily accessible from them, to provide the best possible shelter for the anticipated maximum number of evacuees. In volcanic eruptions, tents are not suitable as temporary shelter, especially if sited close to a high-hazard zones, because they can be easily damaged by falling ash or lava lumps. Schools, community centers, warehouses, or other large buildings will be preferred.

The plan will also specify the arrangements for the transfer of evacuees as quickly as possible from transit points to temporary accommodation in refuge zones elsewhere.

Identification of Evacuation Routes

The next element in emergency planning will be to carry out a survey of the number of people to be moved to safety, the number of vehicles (and, if appropriate, boats and aircrafts) available, and the serviceability and traffic capacity of each of the roads leading out of the hazard zones to the location, type and magnitude of the eruption, and according to the direction of the wind at the time. The main objective will obviously be to distribute the expected traffic flow as evenly as possible along all the escape routes which are likely to remain open. In this context, it will be advisable to consider the vulnerability of each route not only to ash falls, pyroclastic flows, mudflows or lava flows emanating from the volcano, but also to landslides and bridge or tunnel damage which may be caused by strong local earthquakes. Fine ash fall, even if only a few centimeters thick, may make asphalt road surfaces slippery, causing traffic congestion on steep slopes or accidents at corners and road junctions. Each of the escape routes will need to be examined, and measures taken as far as possible to control and maintain the traffic flow at expected danger points.

It is hardly necessary to point out that although the first consideration in selecting escape routes will be to move people as quickly as possible out of the immediate danger zone, it will also be desirable to bring them with the minimum delay to those safe areas where facilities exist for the reception and accommodation.

Means of Transport, Traffic Control

As has already been indicated, the plan for transporting people and their property out of the danger zones should be designed for two levels of emergency: namely, phased response and immediate evacuation. In a phased evacuation, when there is sufficient time between the official evacuation order and the onset of destructive eruption, one may assume that each family possessing its own vehicle or boat will look after itself and any neighbors for whom it has space and has made a specific commitment. All other evacuees will be collected by public transport from pre-arrange pick-up points. Each public transport driver, including especially hired or requisitioned truck drivers, will be instructed to collect people from one of these pick-up points (and not elsewhere). All private and public vehicle drivers will be briefed on which escape roads to use and when to leave. The public transport will continue to make return trips as long as roads remain open or until all evacuees and as much property as possible have been removed. In the event of an unexpectedly rapid escalation of destructive activity, transport will become increasingly difficult to control (due to attempts of people to scramble on to the nearest available truck or bus), and traffic movement along the escape routes out of urban areas may become impossible because of the large number of people leaving on foot. In this case, the plan will have to be abandoned in favor of a "crash" plan allowing any vehicles returning to the hazard zone to collect fleeing pedestrians at ad hoc pick up and turning points (preferably under police or civil defense control) along the escape route.

In order to plan evacuation transport in detail, it will be necessary:

a. To establish how many people have private vehicles and/or boats, and to designate the routes these will follow.

b. To make an inventory of the numbers and locations of people needing public transport.

c. To designate pick-up points for public transport.

d. To make an inventory of available public transport and drivers and to assign pick-up points to each of them.

e. To make arrangements for requisitioning and fueling private trucks and buses (and boats if appropriate) and to provide any other necessary incentives to those normally based outside the hazard zones whose services may be required. It may be judged necessary or appropriate, for example, for the government to undertake to make good any loss or damage suffered by private vehicles or boats brought into the danger zone to assist with the evacuation.

Alert Procedures Within Government

As distinct from other natural hazards, volcanic hazards are strongly localized, the most destructive effects of eruptions being limited to areas within a few tens of kilometers of each volcano. The main responsibility for action of the kind described above may often devolve on local or provincial rather than national government agencies, except when the magnitude of the disaster is such that the local government is unable to cope with the situation.

The emergency plan will define the responsibilities of the various departments of government in dealing with the situation and the procedures by which the various elements of the plan will be put into effect when required.

Overall responsibility will generally be vested in an inter-departmental committee composed of representatives of the government departments concerned and presided over by the head of the national, provincial or local government. Each government department represented on the committee will prepare its own plans for action in response to alerts, in accordance with the directives given by the committee.

In general, it will be possible to define several stages of alert, each corresponding to a different level of hazard as assessed by the scientific team monitoring the volcanic activity. The responsibility for declaring the various stages of alert will lie with a designated official, who will act on the advice of the scientific team monitoring the volcano. There will usually be an element of personal scientific judgment in deciding what interpretation to place on the observed volcanic phenomena and much will depend on knowledge of the past history of the particular volcano. In practice, the decision as to which stage of alert has been reached may often be based not so much on an objective assessment of the probability of a violent eruption as on the number of false alarms which can be tolerated without loss of confidence by the civil authorities and by the public.

Formulation and Communication of Public Warnings

Since the measures that can be taken to protect life and property during a volcanic eruption will affect to some degree the whole population, it is of vital importance to keep the public fully and accurately informed of the nature of the hazard and of what is being done (and what they should do) for their protection. This inevitably entails some degree of control of the information transmitted to the public by the news media. This control will usually be exercised by a responsible official on behalf of the government. In order to avoid panic or other adverse reactions to the situation, the form and content of public announcements will, as far as possible, be decided in advance of any emergency, and the public will be familiarized with the arrangements made for their information, so that they know what to expect. The details of these arrangements will vary from place to place and from country to country, according to the political and social structure of the community and the technical means available. It is therefore difficult to lay down any detailed guidelines for public information and warning. However, as an example, we give here model texts that could be used to announce by radio the two highest levels of alert.

VOLCANIC ASH FALLOUT
SECTION 3.12

(X) = EOC File

A. PURPOSE:

This section identifies response procedures and provides information necessary to protect public health, safety, and welfare.

B. TACTICAL OPERATIONS:

   1. **General Considerations:**

     a. Incident Command

      A volcanic ash fallout event will necessitate a unified command structure involving the Lincoln County Commissioners and the Lincoln County Sheriff.

b. Operating Concept:

An incident is caused by an influx of airborne erupting volcanic ash material, likely originating from the West Coast area. Immediate public health effects involve eye and respiratory damage. Public safety is most impacted by vehicle travel impairment, and volcanic ash's clogging effects on water and sewer plants, and other machinery.

2. **Response Operations**

   a. Agency responsibilities

      i. Dispatch

         (a) Notify the EMA Director

         (b) Assist the EMA Director when the operation center has been activated.

      ii. Law Enforcement

         (a) Be prepared to initiate commissioner's resolutions and ordinances pertaining to closures, curfews, and traffic control.

      iii. Fire

         (a) Be prepared to initiate Commissioner's resolutions and ordinances pertaining to closures, curfews, and traffic-control.

      iv. Health Department

         (a) Assist Commissioners and EMA Director in matters related to health and welfare of the public.

      v. Emergency Operating Center and EMA Director

         (a) Notify staff and Commissioners

         (b) Be prepared to inform the public and Commissioners in other County jurisdictions.

3. **Effects of volcanic ash and individual responses to it.**

   a. Hazard:

   The volcanic ash fallout in Montana from the May 18, 1980, eruption of Mount St. Helens and the threat of more eruptions, has demonstrated a need for contingency planning with respect to volcanic ash fallout. The May 18 eruption has proven Montana can receive considerable amounts of volcanic ash from the West Coast. This constitutes a definite threat to the public health and safety of every citizen in Lincoln County.

   b. What is volcanic ash?

   Volcanic ash is pulverized rock. It often contains small pieces of light, expanded lava called pumice or cinders. Although gases are usually too diluted to constitute danger to the average person, the combination of acidic gas and ash which may be present within a few miles of the eruption could cause lung damage to small infants, the very old and infirm, or those already suffering from severe respiratory illness.

   c. Effect of ash fallout:

      i. A heavy ash fall blots out light. Sudden heavy demand for electric light may cause power supplies to brown out or fail.

      ii. Ash clogs water courses, reservoirs, sewers, and machinery of all kinds.

   Alternate Water Sources, see Section 4.19

      iii. Ash drifts onto roadways, railways, and runways like snow but resembles soft, wet sand.

iv. Fire ash may be slippery.

v. The weight of ash may cause roofs to collapse.

Building Collapse Plan. *See Section 4.09 Manual #42*

d. Citizen instruction if volcanic ash is falling:

    i. Don't panic. Stay calm.

    ii. Stay indoors.

    iii. If outside, seek shelter (e.g., car, building), use mask or dampened cloth.

    iv. If at work, go home if possible, before the ash begins to fall. If the ash is falling stay indoors until the heavy ash has settled.

    v. Go directly home, do not run errands.

    vi. Unless an emergency, do not use telephone.

    vii. Use your radio for information.

e. If in your auto

    i. Get vehicle inside, ash is abrasive.

    ii. Don't speed, and don't follow closely behind other vehicles.

    iii. Change oil and filter right away, don't drive without an air filter.

f. If in your home:

    i. Close doors and windows.

    ii. Close dampers.

    iii. Place damp towels at door thresholds and other draft sources.

    iv. Do not run fan or cloths dryer.

    v. Remove ash from flat roofs and gutters.

    vi. Clothes—brush, shake, and presoak because they may gum up.

From http://www.montana-grassroots.com/emergopsplan.htm

2.12 MOLD

It seems that in the last decade, stories of mold outbreaks in libraries, offices, homes, etc., have become more prevalent. Insurance rates in Texas alone have skyrocketed due to the payouts caused by mold claims. While the University of Texas School of Public Health Library in Houston suffered no damage from the 2001 floods, the next month they fell victim to a mold outbreak that shut down the library for weeks. The cause of the outbreak was inconsistent HVAC handling, not the suspected cause, Tropical Storm Allison.

Sample 2.17

Mold Outbreak, University of Texas School of Public Health at Houston Library

The first week of July 2001, staff of the University of Texas School of Public Health (UTSPH) Library began a project weeding the collection. I initiated this project as the newly appointed Interim Director. On Monday morning of the second week of weeding, a staff member casually asked, "What's that?" while pointing to a book. We were in full mold bloom!

We took a quick look through the stacks to determine how affected we were, then called the University of Texas Health Science Center Houston (UTHSCH) environmental people. A crew was sent that very day to begin taking readings. An investigation also began to determine how this occurred as the bloom took place well after Tropical Storm Allison flooded the Texas Medical Center. The UTSPH had taken in no water during the flooding and there were no plumbing leaks, so attention was turned to the HVAC. I learned that the air chillers were left running over the weekend but the air handlers had been turned off to save energy. The handlers are what removed humidity from the air. As a result, the library had weekend readings of 76% to 78% humidity with a temperature of 71° to 72°, perfect for mold.

We stayed in the library a few weeks while a plan was developed. This is something that I would change if I could do it all over. I would have had the staff out immediately, but hindsight is 20/20. Staff counted approximately 2,150 affected books by the first week of August, including all of our *Index Medicus* from 1983 forward. We also found mold behind the vinyl wall covering which covered much of the first and part of the second floor of the library.

I began doing research, both on the Web and for journal articles. Conservation OnLine (http://palimpsest.stanford.edu/) was indispensable for providing an authoritative, quick source for mold information, mold remediation, and mold prevention. I also found an article describing a mold infiltration at the University of Oklahoma Library in Norman, OK. The author described placing packets of chlorine dioxide around the library to reduce continuing humidity problems and, hence, reduce the mold. I contacted the author, Pat Weavers-Meyer about it and she was absolutely convinced that it had been a miracle worker. Chlorine dioxide is odorless and there are no OSHA warnings so I got ordering information and ordered multiple packets. Once they arrived, I placed the packets around the library. We also had a Phoenix dehumidifier put into the library; a second was added a few weeks later.

A full evaluation of the library was eventually done, both inside and out. I had pointed out some rotten wood on a low window ledge facing the east side of the library. The wood, when pulled away, revealed a full termite infestation. Ultimately, a leaking irrigation line was found outside the window, which provided an ideal environment for the termites.

A plan was developed which included the following:

- Temporary containment areas should be erected around the areas to be remediated that would prevent the further contamination of the rest of the facility.

- Prior to cleaning, items identified by library staff for immediate disposal were to be packaged in a manner, which minimized the spread of particles. The shelves holding these items were cleaned in a manner that minimized the spread of particles.

- Relative humidity in the containment area affected by the mold growth was reduced to no higher than 7% moisture content in the books in the collection including those with visible mold growth. Remediation could not begin until the mold was dry and inactive.

- The relative humidity of the containment area during remediation was maintained at no more than 35% while the temperature was maintained below 68°.

- Recording instruments were installed with dehumidifiers to monitor the temperature and relative humidity.

- Once the mold was inactivated, the bookstacks of the first floor, including books and shelving, but excluding walls, ceilings, ducts, and floors, were manually cleaned in a manner, which minimized the spread of particles.

Figure 2-3. University of Texas School of Public Health at Houston Library, Fall 2001

The guidelines specifying moisture content and humidity were taken from Conservation OnLine and other web sites. Specifications also indicated that no biocides were to be used in the cleaning process, only HEPA vacuums and dry sponges. The ceiling tiles, furniture, shelves, and carpets were also cleaned. Treated air was pumped into the library to maintain the required temperature and humidity; the air tube for the supplemental air stayed through March 2002 when an additional air handler could be installed.

The books were cleaned and we moved back into the library. However, staff members cleaning the books were not well trained so, while the books were cleaned, they were horribly mis-shelved. Whole shelves of books would be placed upside down; those that weren't were out of call number order. Again, in hindsight, I wish I had spot-checked the workers. However, to be a Pollyanna about it, we did need to shelf read anyway and we certainly needed to do some weeding and shifting so this provided the extra motivation to get started.

The whole process, from the day the mold was found to the day we moved back into a clean library, took approximately three months. Because we are a state institution, I assisted with some of the technical language for an RFP for remediation, but we were essentially bound to go with the low bid contractor. On the positive side, the mold provided an impetus for a library renovation. I was very clear in my reports in describing the conditions that allowed the mold to flourish in the library: the poor air flow throughout the space, the lack of lighting in some of the aisles, the use a vinyl wall covering on outside walls, the dirty ceiling tiles, and the musty smelling air that was continually recycled through the library. The UTHSCH decided to do a renovation which included complete removal of the wall covering, new lights and new ceiling tiles throughout the library, and new duct work including additional air ductwork in areas that had previously had none.

We moved out of the library in early December 2001 and back in 8 weeks later. What had originally been a rather dark place is now clean and well lighted. The indoor air is kept at 50% RH; the temperature hovers between 71° to 72°. Students, staff, and faculty enjoy using the library and we still get compliments on what a nice place it is to be in.

Helena M. Von Ville
Library Director
University of Texas School of Public Health
at Houston

CHARACTERISTICS

Molds produce tiny spores to reproduce, spores which waft through the indoor and outdoor air continually. When mold spores land on a damp spot indoors, they may begin growing and digesting whatever they are growing on in order to survive. There are molds that can grow on wood, paper, carpet, and foods. When excessive moisture or water accumulates indoors, mold growth will often occur, particularly if the moisture problem remains undiscovered or un-addressed. There is no practical way to eliminate all mold and mold spores in the indoor environment; the way to control indoor mold growth is to control moisture. Potential health effects and symptoms associated with mold exposures include allergic reactions, asthma, and other respiratory complaints.

Before a mold outbreak:

- Remember, there is no practical way to eliminate all mold and mold spores in the indoor environment; the way to control indoor mold growth is to control moisture.

- Reduce indoor humidity (to 30–60%) to decrease mold growth by: venting moisture-generating sources to the outside; using air conditioners and de-humidifiers; increasing ventilation; and using exhaust fans whenever cooking, dishwashing, and cleaning.

- Identify any potential moisture hazards such as old pipes, uncalked windows, leaky roofs.

- Leave the HVAC on 24×7.

- Prevent condensation by reducing the potential on cold surfaces (i.e., windows, piping, exterior walls, roof, or floors) by adding insulation.

- In areas where there is a perpetual moisture problem, do not install carpeting (i.e., by drinking fountains, sinks, or on concrete floors with leaks or frequent condensation).

- Engage the services of a firm licensed to check for possible mold outbreak.
- If the environment is found to be susceptible to mold, follow the advice of the experts as quickly as possible.

During *a mold outbreak:*

- Eliminate the source of the moisture.
- Fix the source of the water problem or leak to prevent mold growth.
- Reduce indoor humidity (to 30–60%) to decrease mold growth by: venting moisture-generating sources to the outside; using air conditioners and de-humidifiers; increasing ventilation; and using exhaust fans whenever cooking, dishwashing, and cleaning.
- If the outbreak is extensive, contact a professional mold removal contractor.
- Clean and dry any damp or wet building materials and furnishings within 24–48 hours to prevent mold growth.
- Clean mold off hard surfaces with water and detergent, and dry completely. Absorbent materials such as ceiling tiles, that are moldy, may need to be replaced.[17]

After *a mold outbreak:*

Follow the steps listed above in ***Before*** a mold outbreak.

PUTTING IT ALL TOGETHER

Mold is in some ways a post-disaster disaster. For whatever reason (power failure, flood, human error) temperature and humidity in the library are uncontrolled long enough for a mold outbreak. The effective library disaster plan is oriented toward identifying the presence of an outbreak, isolating mold-affected materials (whether books, furniture, or other products in the library), and, most importantly, remediation. The Northeast Document Conservation Center's Technical Leaflet (Section 3, Leaflet 9) provides a detailed, step-by-step approach to for dealing with mold salvage operations (see Sample 2.18).

[17] http://www.epa.gov/iaq/molds/moldresources.html#Introduction%20to%20Molds

Sample 2.18

Emergency Salvage of Moldy Books and Paper by Beth Lindblom Patkus, Preservation Consultant, Walpole, MA

EMERGENCY SALVAGE OF MOLDY BOOKS AND PAPER

Introduction

Most librarians and archivists have seen the effects of mold on paper materials, but many have never experienced an active mold outbreak. Dealing with such an outbreak (large or small) can be overwhelming. This leaflet provides some basic information about mold and outlines the steps that need to be taken to stop mold growth and begin to salvage collections.

Please note that the actions recommended here are basic stabilization techniques to be undertaken in-house for small to moderate outbreaks. The complexities of dealing with a large number of wet and moldy materials will usually require outside assistance, and some suggestions for dealing with a major mold outbreak, appear at the end of this leaflet. In all cases, a conservator or preservation professional should be consulted if any questions arise or if further treatment is necessary.

What is Mold?

Mold and *mildew* are generic terms that refer to various types of fungi, microorganisms that depend on other organisms for sustenance. There are over 100,000 known species of fungi. The great variety of species means that patterns of mold growth and the activity of mold in a particular situation can be unpredictable, but it is possible to make some broad generalizations about the behavior of mold.

Mold propagates by disseminating large numbers of spores, which become airborne, travel to new locations, and (under the right conditions) germinate. When spores germinate, they sprout hair-like webs known as mycelium (visible mold); these in turn produce more spore sacs, which ripen and burst, starting the cycle again. Molds excrete enzymes that allow them to digest organic materials such as paper and book bindings, altering and weakening those materials. In addition, many molds contain colored substances that can stain paper, cloth, or leather. It is also important to realize that mold can be dangerous to people and in some cases can pose a major health hazard. Mold outbreaks should never be ignored or left to "go away on their own."

Why Does Mold Grow?

To germinate (become *active*), spores require a favorable environment. If favorable conditions are not present, the spores remain inactive (*dormant*); in this state they can do little damage.

The most important factor in mold growth is the presence of moisture, most commonly in the air, but also in the object on which the mold is growing. Moisture in the air is measured as relative humidity (RH). In general, the higher the RH the more readily mold will grow. If the RH is over 70% for an extended period of time, mold growth is almost inevitable. It is important to remember, however, that it is possible for some species of mold to grow at lower RH as well. If collections have become wet as the result of a water disaster, this increases their susceptibility to mold growth. Other factors that will contribute to mold growth in the presence of moisture are high temperature, stagnant air, and darkness.

Mold spores, active or dormant, are everywhere. It is not possible to create an atmosphere free of spores. They exist in every room, on every object in the collection, and on every person entering the collection area. The only wholly dependable control strategy is to keep the humidity and temperature moderate so the spores remain dormant, keep collections as clean as possible, and prevent the introduction of new active mold colonies.

Basic Principles of Salvage

Reduce the Humidity: As noted above, moisture initiates mold growth. Reducing the humidity is essential to stopping the mold growth.

Do not Turn up the Heat: This will not help to dry out collections and storage areas. Additional heat in the presence of moisture will cause the mold to grow faster.

If Collections are Wet, Dry or Freeze Them: Mold will normally grow on wet materials in about 48 hours (sometimes sooner). If you know you cannot get the affected material dry within 48 hours, it is best to freeze it. This will not kill the mold, but it will stop further growth until you have a chance to dry and clean the material.

Consider the Health Risks: A few mold species are toxic to people, and many molds are powerful sensitizers. Exposure to mold can lead to debilitating allergy even among people not prone to allergies. Everyone who works with moldy objects must be properly protected.

Avoid "Quick and Easy" Cures: "Quick cures" that you may have heard about (such as spraying Lysol on objects or cleaning them with bleach) may cause additional damage to items or be toxic to people; they are also often ineffective. In the past, mold-infested collections were often treated with fumigants. Ethylene oxide (ETO) will kill active mold and mold spores; other chemicals that have been used are less effective. All of these chemicals can have adverse effects on both collections and people, and none of them will keep the mold from recurring.

Beth Lindblom Patkus
Preservation Consultant
Walpole, MA

From: http://www.nedcc.org/plam3/tleaf39.htm

STEP-BY-STEP SALVAGE

This section provides specific steps for responding to a small or moderate mold outbreak. While the steps are numbered for convenience, they may not be carried out in exactly this order, and some of these activities will occur simultaneously.

1. **Find out what is causing the mold growth.** You need to know what is causing the problem so that additional mold on collections not yet affected can be avoided.

   • Look first for an obvious source of moisture, such as a water leak.

   • If there is no obvious source of moisture, use a monitoring instrument to measure the relative humidity in the affected area. If the humidity is elevated, there might be a problem with the HVAC (heating, ventilating, and air conditioning) system, or the area might be subject to higher humidity for another reason, such as having shelves placed against an outside wall. Mold might also develop in areas with poor air circulation or in areas where there is a lot of dust and dirt that might provide a food source for mold.

- Initiate repairs or resolve the problem as soon as possible. If the problem cannot be resolved quickly, salvage the collections as directed below and develop a strategy for frequent monitoring of the area for additional mold growth.

2. **Take steps to modify the environment so that it is no longer conducive to mold growth.**

- Mop up and/or use a wet-dry vacuum to remove any standing water. Bring in dehumidifiers, but be sure that a mechanism is in place to drain them periodically so they do not overflow. Bring in fans to circulate the air, and open the windows (unless the humidity is higher outside).

- Your goal should be to reduce the relative humidity to 55% or lower. Temperature should be moderate, below 70°F. Get a monitoring instrument that can measure the relative humidity and temperature accurately, and record the measurements in a log several times a day. Do not rely on your own impression of climate conditions.

3. **Implement safety precautions for staff and others working with moldy items.**

- A mycologist should be consulted to insure that no toxic mold species are present (a local hospital or university should be able to provide a reference). If toxic molds are present, DO NOT attempt to salvage materials yourself.

- If there are no toxic molds present, collections can be salvaged in-house, but everyone working with the affected materials must wear disposable plastic gloves and clothing, and use a protective mask when working with moldy objects.

- Use a respirator with a HEPA (high efficiency particulate) filter; pollen dust masks available in drug and hardware stores are not adequate. If you cannot use disposable clothing, be sure to leave dirty clothes in a designated area and wash them in hot water and bleach. Respirators should be wiped periodically with rubbing or denatured alcohol.

- Be aware that some people cannot wear respirators. The respirator must fit well with good contact around the nose and mouth area. In addition, they make breathing somewhat difficult and can be problematic for people with asthma or heart conditions, or people who are pregnant. It is a good idea to consult your doctor before wearing a respirator to work with moldy materials.[18]

4. **Isolate the affected items.**

   - Quarantine items by removing them to a clean area with relative humidity below 45%, separate from the rest of the collection. Items should be transferred in sealed plastic bags to avoid transfer of mold to other items during the move, but they should not remain in the bags once in the clean area, since this will create a micro-environment that can foster further mold growth.

   - In the case of a large mold outbreak it may be impractical to move the items; in that case the area in which they are housed should be quarantined and sealed off from the rest of the building to the extent possible (remember that this includes shutting off air circulation from the affected area).

5. **Begin to dry the materials.** Your goal is to make the mold go dormant, so that it will appear dry and powdery rather than soft and fuzzy. This will allow you to remove the mold residue more easily.

   - Wet material should be dried in a cool, dry space with good air circulation. An air-conditioned space is the best for this purpose, but if that is impossible, use fans to circulate air (do not aim fans directly at objects, however, as this can damage materials and further scatter mold spores). Place paper toweling or unprinted newsprint (regular newspapers may transfer print to the wet objects) under the drying items to absorb moisture, and change this blotting material often. Air drying takes time and attention, since you must check drying materials often, and you must maintain cool, dry conditions and air circulation in the space.

---

[18]Hilary Kaplan. "Mold: A Follow-up." Available on-line at http://palimpsest.stanford.edu/bytopic/mold.

- Collections may also be dried outside in the sun (sunlight or ultraviolet light can cause some molds to become dormant). The outside humidity must be low. Be aware that the sun causes fading and other damage to paper-based collections, however. Materials should be monitored closely and left outside no more than an hour or so.

- Special attention should be paid to framed objects (such as prints and drawings) and to the interior of the spines of books. A frame provides an ideal environment for mold; the back is dark, air does not circulate, and humidity can be trapped inside. Similarly, the interior of the spine of a book is particularly vulnerable to mold growth. Spines should be checked regularly during the drying process. Framed materials should be unframed immediately, and dried as above. If the item appears to be stuck to the glass in the frame, remove the backing materials from the frame and leave the item in the frame and attached to the glass. Place the framed item in a cool, dry space as described above, and consult a professional conservator.

6. **If immediate drying is not possible, freeze the affected items.**

   - If the item is small enough, it can be placed in the freezer compartment of a home refrigerator, with freezer paper loosely wrapped around it to prevent it from sticking to other items.

   - For items that are too big for a freezer compartment or for larger numbers of items, a commercial freezer may be necessary (grocery store, university food service, or commercial cold storage facility). It is a good idea to make arrangements for commercial freezer storage before an emergency arises, since there may be restrictions on storing moldy items in a freezer that normally holds foodstuffs.

   - Once time and resources are available, frozen materials can be thawed and dried in small batches, or they can be freeze-dried or vacuum freeze-dried (with the exception of photographs, which should not be freeze-dried or vacuum freeze-dried).

7. **Clean the affected items.** DO NOT try to clean active mold (soft and fuzzy) yourself. This should be done only by a conservator, who will use a vacuum aspirator

to avoid further embedding the mold into the paper. The following instructions apply only to inactive (dry and powdery) mold and materials that do NOT have artifactual value:[19]

- Remove mold residue outdoors rather than in an enclosed space whenever possible. Be sure to wear protective gear (see above). If you must work indoors, use a fume hood with a filter that traps mold or in front of a fan, with the fan blowing contaminated air out a window. Close off the room from other areas of the building (including blocking the air circulation vents).

- Vacuum the mold. Use a vacuum with a HEPA filter; this will contain the mold spores. A normal vacuum will simply exhaust the spores out into the air. You can also use a wet-dry commercial-strength vacuum if the tank is filled with a solution of a fungicide such as Lysol diluted according to the label instructions. A tube from the hose inlet should extend into the solution so that incoming spores are directed there.

- Do not vacuum fragile items directly, since the suction can easily cause damage. Papers can be vacuumed through a plastic screen held down with weights. A brush attachment covered with cheese-cloth or screening should be used for books to guard against loss of detached pieces. Boxes can be vacuumed directly. When disposing of vacuum bags or filters, seal them in plastic trash bags and remove them from the building.

- It is also acceptable to clean off mold with a soft brush, but this must be done carefully. Once moldy material is dry and the residue appears powdery, take a soft, wide brush (such as a watercolor wash brush) and lightly brush the powdery mold off the surface of the item. This should be done outside or the mold should be brushed into a vacuum nozzle. Be careful not to rub the mold into the surface, since that will attach it permanently to paper fibers or the cover of a book.

---

[19]For these and other cleaning suggestions, see Lois Olcott Price's *Managing a Mold Invasion: Guidelines for Disaster Response*. Philadelphia, PA: Conservation Center for Art and Historic Artifacts, 1996, CCAHA Technical Series No. 1.

8. **Dry and thoroughly clean the room(s) where the mold outbreak occurred.** You may do this yourself or hire a company to provide dehumidification and/or cleaning.

   - Vacuum shelves and floors with a wet-dry vacuum filled with a fungicide solution such as Lysol, then wipe them down with Lysol or a similar solution. Allow them to dry fully before returning any materials. If a musty odor lingers in the room, open containers of baking soda may help.

   - It is also a good idea to have the HVAC system components (heat-exchange coils, ductwork, etc.) cleaned and disinfected, particularly if you suspect they have caused the problem.

9. **Return materials to the affected area.** Do this ONLY after the area has been thoroughly cleaned AND the cause of the mold outbreak has been identified and dealt with.

10. **Continue to monitor conditions and take steps to avoid additional mold growth.**

    - Take daily readings of temperature and relative humidity, and be sure that the climate is moderate. It is particularly important to keep humidity below 55% to insure that mold will not reappear. Temperature should not exceed 70°F.

    - Check problem areas frequently to insure that there is no new mold growth. Be sure to examine the gutters of books near the endbands and inside the spines.

    - Keep areas where collections are stored and used as clean as possible, since dust and dirt are a source of spores, both active and dormant. Clean floors with a HEPA filter vacuum rather than sweeping, since sweeping scatters dust. House collections in protective enclosures whenever possible to keep them free of dust. Vacuum shelves and the tops of unboxed, shelved books, or clean them with a magnetic wiping cloth.

    - If funds permit, install a multi-stage particulate filtration system in the building or storage area.

    - Keep windows closed to prevent active spores from entering, and prohibit live plants in collection storage or use areas, since these are also a source of spores.

- Quarantine new acquisitions for a few days, and check them carefully for signs of mold.
- Avoid storing collections in potentially damp areas or in locations where water accidents are possible. Insure that regular maintenance is carried out on the building to reduce the chance of water emergencies.
- Regularly inspect the HVAC system, which is a good breeding ground for mold. Regularly clean the heat exchange coils, drip pan, and ductwork. Change air filters frequently.
- Prepare a disaster plan. This will prevent some accidents and provide strategies for dealing quickly and effectively with problems. Be sure that all employees are familiar with the plan.

DEALING WITH A MAJOR MOLD OUTBREAK

If a large portion of the collection is affected by the mold outbreak, if dangerous species of mold are present, or if the HVAC system and the building itself are also infected with mold, outside assistance will be needed. Particularly in the latter cases, it is essential to make sure that the building is safe for occupancy by staff. There are a variety of companies experienced in working with cultural collections that can assist institutions with recovery.

Most of the disaster recovery companies that provide drying services will also clean surface mold off collections. Conservators or regional conservation centers provide treatment services for individual items with artifactual value.

There are also several disaster recovery companies that specialize in dehumidifying and cleaning of buildings. In the case of a severe infestation of mold and/or an infestation that poses serious health risks to staff, companies specializing in indoor air quality can help to insure that the building is safe for occupancy. In severe cases, fumigation of the affected area may be necessary. Due to the potential for damage, fumigants should not be used directly on or in the presence of collections unless there is no other choice. Fumigation should always be done by a licensed professional.

A list of service providers is given at the end of this section. Be sure that the company you choose is familiar with the requirements of cultural collections. If you are not sure how to choose a service provider, always contact a conservator or preservation professional for advice.

SUMMARY

Spores, active or dormant, are ubiquitous. Although it is impossible to get rid of all the spores, mold growth can be controlled. Most important for mold control is maintaining RH conditions below 55%, or, better, below 45%. Use of protective enclosures, meticulous housekeeping, monitoring of RH and temperature, and a watchful eye are also important. If resources allow, high-level filtration of storage areas, if not of the whole building, is recommended. Protecting library and archival collections from water accidents should be among the highest priorities for any institution. Wet collections must be immediately dried or stabilized by freezing. Moldy materials must be isolated, dried if wet, then cleaned using the strictest precautions.

FURTHER READING

Chamberlain, William R. "A New Approach to Treating Fungus in Small
　　Libraries." *Abbey Newsletter* 15, no. 7 (November 1991): 109.
　　A practical article describing the response to a mold outbreak and
　　the preventive measures that were subsequently undertaken at the
　　Virginia State Library. Available online at http://palimpsest
　　.stanford.edu/byorg/abbey/.
"Mold As a Threat to Human Health." *Abbey Newsletter* 18, no. 6
　　(October 1994).
　　A short article on mold as a workplace hazard for library and
　　archival workers. Summarizes articles relevant to the subject and
　　anecdotes from the field. Available online at http://palimpsest
　　.stanford.edu/byorg/abbey/.
Nyberg, Sandra. *Invasion of the Giant Spore*. SOLINET Preservation
　　Program Leaflet Number 5. Atlanta, GA: Southeastern Library
　　Network, 1987, 19 pp.
　　An updated version of this leaflet (emphasizing preventive activi-
　　ties and non-chemical treatments) is available from SOLINET
　　on its web page at http://www.solinet.net/preservation/leaflets/
　　leaflets-fs.cfm?leafletpgname=leaflets_templ.cfm?doc_id=122 or
　　from Alicia Riley-Walden, Preservation Administrative Assistant,
　　SOLINET Preservation Services, 1438 West Peachtree Street,
　　NW, Suite 200, Atlanta, GA 30309-2955 (email: alicia_riley-
　　walden@solinet.net or ariley@solinet.net). The older version
　　of the leaflet gives a good summary of mold prevention and

treatment, and also presents detailed information on various chemical treatment methods that in most cases would no longer be recommended.

Price, Lois Olcott. *Managing a Mold Invasion: Guidelines for Disaster Response*. Philadelphia, PA: Conservation Center for Art and Historic Artifacts, 1996, CCAHA Technical Series No. 1.
    An excellent summary of response and recovery techniques. Includes a good bibliography that cites articles on the effects of fumigation on collections. Available from CCAHA, 264 South 23rd Street, Philadelphia, PA, 19103; (215) 545-0613, Fax (215) 735-9313, or email CCAHA@shrsys.hslc.org.

SOURCES OF SUPPLIES AND SERVICES

This list is not exhaustive, nor does it constitute an endorsement of the suppliers and services listed. We suggest that you obtain information from a number of vendors so that you can make comparisons of cost and asses the full range of available products and services.

A more complete list of suppliers is available from NEDCC. Consult the Technical Leaflets section of NEDCC's Web site at www.nedcc.org or contact NEDCC for the most up-to-date version in print.

American Freeze-Dry, Inc.
P.O. Box 264
39 Lindsey Avenue
Runnemede, NJ 08078
(800) 817-1007; (856) 546-0777
Fax (856) 939-1220
john@americanfreezedry.com
http://www.americanfreezedry.com
Vacuum freeze drying, cleaning of collections.

Blackmon-Mooring Steamatic Catastrophe, Inc.
International Headquarters
303 Arthur Street
Fort Worth, TX 76107
(800) 433-2940 24 hr. hotline; (817) 332-2770
Fax (817) 332-6728
info@bmscat.com
www.bmscat.com
Vacuum freeze drying, cleaning of collections, cleaning of interiors.

Disaster Recovery Services, Inc.
2425 Blue Smoke Court South
Fort Worth, TX 76105
(800) 856-3333; (817) 535-6793
Fax (817) 536-1167
Vacuum freeze drying, cleaning of collections, dehumidification.

Document Reprocessors
5611 Water Street
Middlesex, NY 14507
(888) 437-9464 24 hours; (585) 554-4500
Fax (585) 554-4114
http://www.documentreprocessors.com
Vacuum freeze drying, cleaning of collections.

EnviroCenter
http://envirocenter.com
A Web resource specializing in the indoor environment and indoor air quality. Provides a list of companies that specialize in indoor air quality products and services.

Ethylene Oxide Sterilization Association
1815 H Street NW, Suite 500
Washington, DC 20006-6604
(202) 296-6300
Fax (202) 775-5929
info@eosa.org
http://www.eosa.org
An industry trade group established by parties with an interest in ethylene oxide sterilization. A place to start if a company specializing in ETO fumigation is needed.

Lab Safety Supply
P.O. Box 1368
Janesville, WI 53547-1368
(800) 356-0783
Fax (800) 543-9910
http://www.labsafety.com
Respirators, HEPA filter vacuums.

Munters Corporation
Headquarter Region Americas
79 Monroe Street
P.O. Box 640
Amesbury, MA 01913
Toll-Free: (800) 686-8377 24 hours; (978) 241-1100

Fax (978) 241-1219
muntersinfo@muntersamerica.com
http://www.munters.us
Dehumidification, cleaning of interiors.

Nilfisk-Advance of America
300 Technology Drive
Malvern, PA 19355
(800) NILFISK; (800) 645-3475
http://www.pa.nilfisk-advance.com
HEPA filter vacuums.

Sigma-Aldrich Corporation
P.O. Box 355
3050 Spruce Street
St. Louis, MO 63103
(800) 325-3010; (314) 771-5765
Fax (314) 771-5757
custserv@sial.com
http://www.sigmaaldrich.com
Respirators.

MANMADE DISASTERS

2.13 TERRORISM, BIOTERRORISM, AND CYBERTERRORISM

Recent events worldwide show that terrorism can occur at any time, and at the hand of citizens or foreigners. Many things can be used to cause terroristic acts including vehicles, airplanes, biologic agents, computers, or even shoes. While many libraries have been affected by terrorism, especially the bombing of the Murrah Building in Oklahoma City in 1995 and the tragic events of September 11, 2001 in New York and Washington, it is a sad sign of the times that we are all affected in our daily lives. Terrorism is not restricted to the United States, as multiple tragic events in Russian in the summer of 2004 illustrated. It is sad, but in the current state of the world, many communities have begun conducting disaster drills to test the preparedness of emergency workers for a possible terrorist attack. Such a drill was held in Houston, TX in September 2004, response to the 2001

September attack. Major newsworthy events such as the Olympics, Super Bowl, and political conventions are conducted with extremely heightened security.

CHARACTERISTICS

In the United States, terrorism is legally defined as the use of force or violence against persons or property in violation of the criminal laws for purposes of intimidation, coercion or ransom. Terrorists often use threats to create fear among the public, to try to convince citizens that their government is powerless to prevent terrorism, and to get immediate publicity for their causes.

The U.S. Federal Bureau of Investigation categorizes terrorism in as one of two types—domestic terrorism or international terrorism. Domestic terrorism involves groups or individuals whose terrorist activities are directed at elements of our government or population without foreign direction. The 1995 bombing of the Murrah Building in Oklahoma City is an illustration of domestic terrorism. International terrorism involves groups or individuals whose terrorist activities are foreign-based and/or directed by countries or groups outside the United States or whose activities transcend national boundaries. September 11, 2001 is an example of international terrorism.

Bioterrorism refers to the use of biological or chemical agents to inflict terror. Biological agents are infectious microbes or toxins, which produce illness or death in people, animals or plants. Biological agents can be dispersed as aerosols or airborne particles. Terrorists may use biological agents to contaminate food or water because they are extremely difficult to detect. Chemical agents kill or incapacitate people, destroy livestock or ravage crops. Some chemical agents are odorless and tasteless and are difficult to detect. They can have an immediate effect of a few seconds to a few minutes or a delayed effect of several hours to several days.[20]

Biological and chemical weapons have been used primarily to terrorize an unprotected civilian population and not as a weapon of war. This is because of fear of retaliation and the likelihood that the agent would contaminate the battlefield for a long period of time. The Persian Gulf War in 1991 and other confrontations in the Middle East were causes for concern regarding the possibility of chemical or biological warfare. While no incidents occurred, there remains a concern that such weapons could be involved in an accident or be used by terrorists.

Chemical Agents—Chemical agents are poisonous gases, liquids, or solids that have toxic effects on people, animals, or plants. Common traits of chemical agents used in terroristic events include:

- Most agents cause serious injuries or death.
- Severity of injuries depends on the type and amount of the chemical agent used, and the duration of exposure.

[20]http://www.fema.gov/hazards/terrorism/terror.shtm

- In the event of a chemical agent attack, authorities would instruct citizens to either seek shelter where they are and seal the premises or evacuate immediately.
- Leaving the shelter for any reason can be a deadly decision.

Biological Agents—Biological agents are organisms or toxins that have illness-producing effects on people, livestock and crops. Common traits of biological agents used in terroristic events include:

- Because biological agents cannot necessarily be detected and may take time to grow and cause a disease, it is almost impossible to know that a biological attack has occurred.
- If government officials become aware of a biological attack through an informant or warning by terrorists, they would most likely instruct citizens to either seek shelter where they are and seal the premises or evacuate immediately.
- A person affected by a biological agent requires the immediate attention of professional medical personnel.

Some agents are contagious, and victims may need to be quarantined. Also, some medical facilities may not receive victims for fear of contaminating the hospital population.

Cyberterrorism refers to unlawful attacks and threats of attack against computers, networks, and the information stored therein when done to intimidate or coerce a government or its people in furtherance of political or social objectives. It is distinct from computer crime, economic espionage, and "hactivism," although terrorists may employ any of these forms of computer abuse to further their agendas.

The weapons of cyberterrorism—computers—differ from weapons of mass destruction such as biological agents, chemical agents, and radiological agents in that they don't *directly* cause death and injury. However, acting indirectly, they can cause serious consequences to individuals, businesses, industry, government, and the public at large. Depending on how they are used, they can lead to injury and death.[21]

Before a terrorist attack:

- Learn about the nature of terrorism and the types of terrorism that might affect your library.
- Be aware of near-by visible targets such as international airports, large cities, major international events, resorts,

---

[21]http://www.fema.gov/doc/reg-viii/tkapp-d.doc

and high-profile landmarks. Since the Texas Medical Center is only about one mile from the site of the 2004 Super Bowl, the entire Center was on alert for a possible attack. Not only might the campus be in the path of an attack, we would have also been the institutions depended upon for first-response. All of this had an impact on the HAM-TMC Library for many days surrounding the even.

• Prepare to deal with a terrorist incident by adapting many of the same techniques used to prepare for other crises, such as conducting emergency evacuation drills. A bomb threat to a nearby building in 2002 provided the HAM-TMC Library with a wonderful opportunity for an impromptu drill.

Bomb Threats. If you receive a bomb threat:

• Get as much information from the caller as possible.
• Keep the caller on the line and record everything that is said.
• Notify the police immediately.
• After you've been notified of a bomb threat, do not touch any suspicious packages.
• Clear the area around the suspicious package and note the location.
• Evacuate the building using your regular evacuation plan.
• Follow instructions from emergency officials.

During a terrorist attack:

• In a building explosion, evacuate the building as quickly and calmly as possible.
• If unable to evacuate, get under a sturdy table or desk to avoid items are falling off of bookshelves or from the ceiling.

After a terrorist attack, if you are trapped in debris:

• Use a flashlight.
• Stay in your area so that you don't kick up dust. Cover your mouth with a handkerchief or clothing.

The bombing of the Murrah Building in Oklahoma City in 1995 profoundly affected all of us. The OUHSC Library is just a few blocks from downtown, so we felt the affects of the blast. It was as though someone had pushed over scores of fully packed filing cabinets all at the same time. When we rushed outside the billow of smoke in the skyline told another story. Members of the Oklahoma Health Center community rushed to the site: health care workers, staff, and students. Although the library wasn't impacted immediately in terms of services, library staff was affected emotionally and psychologically. The Medical Examiner's office is just south of the library, and we would see semi trucks arrive to deliver the remains of victims. The library served it's usual role in providing information. It didn't take long for us to realize that we needed to collect information on terrorism or war and post-traumatic stress disorder, to make readily available to those who inquired. It's an instance such as this that instantaneously draws people together, and makes you vividly aware of how fragile and vulnerable we are.

Joy Summers-Ables
Head, Library Computing and Information Systems
Robert M. Bird Health Sciences Library
University of Oklahoma Health Sciences Center
Oklahoma City, Oklahoma

Figure 2-4. Bombing of the Murrah Building, Oklahoma City, OK

- Tap on a pipe or wall so that rescuers can hear where you are. Use a whistle if one is available. Shout only as a last resort—shouting can cause a person to inhale dangerous amounts of dust.

PUTTING IT ALL TOGETHER

In addressing the threat of terrorism the library's disaster plan must take into account a wide array of possible assaults, including actions such as bomb threats, civil disorder, vandalism, mail terrorism, and so forth. The disaster plan (see Sample 2.19) of the D. Hiden Ramsey Library at the University of North Carolina, Asheville establishes response guidelines and recovery guidelines for a number of possible terrorist situations.

Sample 2.19

Terrorism, Civil Disorder, Bomb Threat, Vandalism from the D. Hiden Ramsey Library, University of North Carolina

In the Event of Terrorism, Civil Disorder, Bomb Threat, Vandalism or Theft

I. *RESPONSE GUIDELINES*

A. Initial response for BOMB THREATS

1. Remain calm, be polite and show interest in caller.
2. If a phone call is received reporting a bomb, attempt to get answers from the caller to the following: TAKE BOMB THREATS SERIOUSLY!

   Bomb Threat Checklist:

   When is the bomb going to explode?

   Where is it right now?

   What does it look like?

   What kind of bomb is it?

   What will cause it to explode?

   Did you place the bomb?

   Why?
3. Complete the *Bomb Threat Checklist* immediately with the caller, if possible. Write down as much detail as you can remember.
4. If possible, while you are on the phone, signal another staff member to call Public Safety, at extension 6710.
5. Try to keep the caller talking to learn more information.
6. Alert the Library Director of the threat. Do not discuss the threat with other staff.
7. Follow the instructions in the Public Safety Manual regarding Bomb Threats.
8. Evacuate when directed by ANY Disaster Team Coordinators or Library Director.
9. Do not spread rumors.

B. Initial response if a **BOMB EXPLODES** in area:

1. Remain calm.
2. Take cover under a table or desk.
3. Be prepared for possible further explosions.
4. Stay away from windows, mirrors, overhead fixtures, filing cabinets, bookcases, etc.
5. Follow the instructions of the Public Safety personnel and Disaster Team Coordinators.
6. Evacuate calmly, when directed, to the Assembly Area. Assist disabled persons.
7. Do not move seriously injured persons, unless they are in immediate danger (fire, building collapse, etc.)
8. Open doors carefully. Watch for falling objects.
9. Do not use elevators.
10. Avoid using the telephone, except in a life threatening situation.
11. Do not use matches or lighters.

12. Do not re-enter the affected area until directed by emergency preparedness personnel.

13. Do not spread rumors.

C. Initial response for SUSPICIOUS PACKAGE OR OBJECT

1. If an unaccompanied suspicious package or object is noticed in the library, do not attempt to move the item. Call Public Safety, extension 6710.

2. Decisions to evacuate the building should be made after consultation with one of the disaster plan coordinators or with the library director, or based on the imminent danger of the suspected terrorist activity.

D. Initial response to VANDALISM

1. If the vandalism appears to be a random and minor act such as writing in a book or dog-earing pages, ask the individual to STOP.

2. If the activity is more serious and involves destruction of property such as chairs, equipment, or tables, go to the nearest phone and **call Public Safety at extension 6710.**

E. Initial response to TERRORISM

1. Call Public Safety at extension 6710.

2. Follow the instruction of the security and emergency preparedness personnel.

3. If an explosion occurs, take cover immediately and anticipate there may be other explosions.

4. Notify campus authorities of any known hazards (e.g., fire, bomb threat, chemical or biological threat).

4. Stay indoors and away from windows unless directed to evacuate.

5. Evacuate when directed and follow procedures for evacuation (above) and any instructions of the evacuation coordinators.

6. If released from work early, follow the instructions of the emergency preparedness personnel. Do not remain in the vicinity to sightsee.

7. Do not spread rumors.

F. **MAIL TERRORISM**

1. Do not try to open the mailpiece if it looks suspicious.

2. Isolate the mail.

3. Evacuate the immediate area.

4. Request assistance from campus Public Safety office, **extension 6710.**

5. If biological or chemical agents are suspected, request medical assistance.

6. List all persons who have come in contact with the material and include personal contact information.

Center for Disease Control

Emergency Response: (770) 488-7100

URL: http://www.bt.cdc.gov

G. Initial response to **CIVIL DISORDER AND DEMONSTRATIONS**

1. Call Public Safety at extension 6710.

2. Notify authorities immediately of any information received, factual or rumored, of a demonstration or other form of civil disorder which is planned or in progress in the vicinity of the facility.

3. Follow the instructions of public safety personnel and disaster team coordinators.

4. Assist with protecting objects (art, sculptures, and expensive books).

5. If an explosion occurs, take cover immediately and anticipate there may be others.

6. Notify Authorities of any potential/actual hazards (e.g., fire, bomb threat) incurred during a threatening situation.

7. Stay indoors and away from windows unless directed to evacuate by the emergency preparedness personnel.

8. Evacuate when directed and follow the evacuation procedures included at the beginning of this handbook.

8. If released from work early, follow instructions of the emergency preparedness personnel and the local authorities. Do not remain in the vicinity of the disturbance to sight-see.

9. Do not spread rumors.

II. *RECOVERY GUIDELINES*

1. Do not re-enter area or building until area or building is clear of all threats to personal safety.

2. Recovery of materials will depend on the nature of the terrorism and the nature of the destruction of property.

From http://bullpup.lib.unca.edu/displan/section_6d.html

2.14 HAZARDOUS MATERIALS

Characteristics: We tend to think of chemical and industrial accidents as happening "somewhere else" but the fact is a hazardous materials accident can occur anywhere. Communities located near chemical manufacturing plants are particularly at risk but given that hazardous materials are transported on our roadways, railways and waterways daily, any area is considered vulnerable to an accident.

Before *a hazardous materials accident:*

- Learn to search the *Toxnet* family of databases made available through the National Library of Medicine. The librarians role in the event of a hazardous materials accident might be to find information on the contaminant for the emergency officials.

- Contact your local emergency management office for information about hazardous materials and community response plans. Offer your library as a resource in the case of an accident.

Conduct drills as specified earlier in this section of the books. Be ready to evacuate.

During *a hazardous materials accident:*

- If you learn of an accident, turn on a radio or television for further emergency information.

If asked to stay indoors (sheltering-in place):

- Seal building so contaminants cannot enter by locking windows and doors.
- Seal gaps under doorways and windows with wet towels and duct tape.
- Seal gaps around window and air conditioning units, with duct tape and plastic sheeting, wax paper or aluminum wrap.
- Close off nonessential rooms such as storage areas.
- Turn off ventilation systems.

Immediately after the "in-place sheltering" announcement is issued:

- Fill large containers for an additional water supply.
- Turn off all HVAC units.
- If gas or vapors could have entered the building, take shallow breaths through a cloth or a towel.
- Monitor the Emergency Broadcast System station for further updates and remain in shelter until authorities indicate it is safe to come out.

If Asked to Evacuate:

Authorities will decide if evacuation is necessary based primarily on the type and amount of chemical released and how long it is expected to affect an area. Other considerations are the length of time it should take to evacuate the area, weather conditions, and the time of day.

- Stay tuned to a radio or television for information on evacuation routes, temporary shelters, and procedures.
- Follow the routes recommended by the authorities—shortcuts may not be safe. Leave at once.

After *a hazardous materials accident:*

- Return to the building only when authorities say it is safe.

- Follow local instructions concerning the safety of food and water.
- Contact emergency officials concerning clean-up methods if the library itself has been contaminated.

PUTTING IT ALL TOGETHER

A key factor in determining how to respond to a disaster involving hazardous materials is whether to evacuate or to shelter in place. Inasmuch as the library itself is unlikely to be the source of the hazardous materials incident, communication with local emergency responders is critical. James Madison University's Emergency Response Plan for Hazardous Materials addresses the myriad factors a responder organization must consider when confronted by a hazardous materials disaster.

Sample 2.20

James Madison University's Emergency Response Plan for Hazardous Materials

I. Initial Responder (usually a campus police officer)

1. Attempt to identify the hazard and immediately notify the fire department in the event of a chemical spill, chemical fire, or suspected chemical contamination.

2. When responding to a chemical emergency, avoid contamination.
   a. Do not walk into or touch any spilled material.
   b. Avoid inhalation of all gases, fumes, and smoke. Stay up wind.
   c. Don't assume that gases/vapors are harmless because they lack odor.

3. Isolate the area. Move and keep people away from the incident scene (Safe distances from the scene will vary. Consult with the orange "Guidebook" for the safe distance chart. Copies of the book are placed in each patrol vehicle and at the communications dispatch desk).

4. Establish a COMMAND POST outside the perimeter, again up wind.

5. If it can be done safely, make an immediate attempt to identify the chemical/hazardous materials.
   a. Laboratory chemicals should be labeled (USDOT HazMat Warning Labels).
   b. Tanks or vehicles should have a black four digit identification number on a placard or orange panel (UNITED NATIONS or NORTH AMERICAN ID).
   c. Shipping papers or packages should contain a name or four digit number preceded by the letters "UN" or "NA."
   d. Only if no ID number or shipping name can be found, search for a diamond shaped placard (USDOT HazMat Warning Placard System).

     e. Many laboratories and other permanent facilities use the system recommended by the National Fire Protection Association (NFPA 49 and 704M) for identification of the Fire Hazards of Materials (the red, blue, yellow, and white diamond).

     f. If none of the above means can be used to identify the substances, call CHEMTREC (800) 424-9300 for assistance.

  6. Refer to the orange "Guidebook" when the substance is identified and follow all instructions for that substance. Simultaneously call CHEMTREC for any updated information pertaining to safety action for the chemicals involved.

II. Resources and Assistance

1. CHEMTREC 1(800) 424-9300.
2. Harrisonburg Fire Department and its HazMat team at 911.
3. VA Dept. of Emergency Services, HazMat Officer 1(540) 491-7044.
4. VA State Police, Motor Carrier Safety & Hazardous Materials Team by calling the State Police dispatcher at 1(800) 572-2260.
5. VA Dept. of Environmental Quality, Valley Regional Office 828-2595.
6. Identified chemical shippers and/or manufacturers (local or involved).
7. Military and other federal agencies (EPA, USDOT, etc.).
8. Utilities (HEC 434-5361/5363, Hbg. Water/Sewer 434-9959/2545, Commonwealth Gas Co. 434-7620 or 1[800]531-7648/544-5606).
9. Rockingham Memorial Hospital 433-4100.
10. Professional clean-up and abatement firms.

III. Background on the University's and Local Community's Preparedness Hazardous Materials Incidents, Response, & Evacuations

1. Demonstrating the multi-disciplinary approach to environmental safety and health issues on campus is the cooperative effort between JMU's Chemistry Department, the university's Safety Engineer, and the Harrisonburg Fire Department's Hazardous Materials Response Team. A chemistry faculty member acts as an advisor to the HAZMAT team and is "on call" as an unpaid consulting supervisor. The HAZMAT team is stationed at a facility in close proximity to the campus. The HAZMAT team responds to all Hazardous Materials incidents occurring on campus. The Safety Engineer routinely provides familiarization tours of the campus to Harrisonburg Fire Department personnel. Indirectly related, the Public Safety Director facilitates training and familiarization of the campus in liaison with the Harrisonburg Police Department's Tactical Response unit.

2. Initiated during the early 1980's, the Chief of the Harrisonburg Fire Department, the Hazardous Materials officer of the Virginia State Police, and the university's Safety Engineer presented a workshop on management of hazardous materials incidents, followed by periodic update programs. This was prompted by heightened concerns related to hazardous materials emergencies and federal mandates calling for local governmental bodies' involvement in such responses. Clearly stated were responsibilities for making the public aware of the ramifications of such incidents. Police officers, fire fighters, and municipal officials joined with personnel from this department in the formulation of a campus HAZMAT program.

3. Subsequently, the department developed a general response policy in outline format. Supplied to each officer through placement in each patrol vehicle and at the communications desk are copies of the U.S. Department of Transportation's *Emergency Response Guidebook for Hazardous Materials Incidents*. This serves as a quick and handy reference for the initially responding officer.

4. In the event of a spill or disaster, consideration of limited or mass evacuations depends on the nature and extent of the emergency. Measured response would be the approach taken (see reference # 1 at the end of Hazardous Materials Incidents, Response, & Evacuations).

5. The Harrisonburg Fire Department, with fully paid, trained, and certified personnel, is up to the task with its continuously trained and comprehensively equipped Hazardous Materials Response Team previously cited in this report. The fire department provides, in addition the fire fighting, first medical response pending the arrival of a Rescue Squad unit.

6. The Virginia State Police maintains a similar unit regionally located ready to respond at a moment's notice.

7. The Harrisonburg Police Department maintains a ready tactical response team which can assist in deliberate acts involving hazardous materials. The team periodically conducts practical exercises in representative campus facilities (see related city/county/campus law enforcement MUTUAL AID AGREEMENT).

8. Maintained at the Campus Police Headquarters is a constantly updated floor plan directory available to all appropriate response teams.

9. The Harrisonburg Volunteer Rescue Squad headquartered in close proximity to campus is well staffed, trained, certified, and comprehensively equipped. A significant number of its Emergency Medical Technicians are students of this institution (see reference # 2 at the end of Hazardous Materials Incidents, Response, & Evacuations); all with a vested interest in the welfare of the campus and its community.

10. One Campus Police officer is a fully certified EMT and is an instructor in CPR and First Responder Basic First Aid at the regional police academy. This officer provides training in those areas "in house" as well.

11. Rockingham Memorial Hospital is located directly contiguous to the campus.

12. The University maintains an alternative landing zone to Rockingham Memorial Hospital's primary rotary wing medical evacuation site. These sites principally serve the "Pegasus" medivac helicopters, stationed at the University of Virginia's Medical Center, fifteen minutes air time away from Harrisonburg (see reference # 3 at the end of Hazardous Materials Incidents, Response, & Evacuations).

13. UVA's Medical Center is one of the nation's most advanced facilities for emergency trauma, critical, and burn care. The campus is also thirty to forty-five minutes flying time from equivalent emergency medical units in Richmond and Roanoke. These units are served by similar medivac ships.

14. With a major pharmaceutical manufacturer, Merck, and a chemical producer, Dupont located within thirty to forty minutes, other highly trained hazardous materials response teams are available to provide highly technical expert assistance in the event of toxic or hazardous spills. Both are involved with ongoing community interfacing with public safety agencies. Merck provides community based awareness programs for local industries, businesses, and governmental bodies in cooperation with the local Chamber of Commerce, in which this department has participated.

IV. Commonly utilized reference materials and resources:

1. U.S. Dept. of Transportation's Emergency Response Guidebook for Hazardous Materials Incidents DOT P 5800.3*.

2. Hazardous Waste Management at Educational Institutions published by the National Association of College & University Business Officers.

3. Chemical Transportation Emergency Center (Chemtrec) of the Chemical Manufacturer's Association (800) 424-9300.

4. Superfund Hotline (800) 424-9346.

5. Notification of Hazardous Waste Activity (US-EPA) Form 8700-12.

6. Hazardous Waste Regulations, Virginia Bureau of Hazardous Waste Management, Virginia Department of Health.

7. National Fire Codes, promulgated by the National Fire Protection Association (NFPA) including Life Safety Code 101.

8. Emergency Handling of Hazardous Materials in Surface Transportation, Norfolk Southern Railway.

9. Virginia OSHA Standards for General Industry, Dept of Labor and Industry.

10. Work Area Protection Manual, VA Department of Transportation.

11. Fire Resistance Directory, Underwriters Laboratories.

12. Building Materials Directory, Underwriters Laboratories.

13. The BOCA National Building Code, Building Officials & Code Administrators.

14. The BOCA National Fire Prevention Code.

15. The BOCA National Plumbing Code.

16. The BOCA National Mechanical Code.

17. The BOCA National Existing Structures Code.

18. The BOCA National Energy Conservation Code.

19. The Virginia Hazard Communication Standard, VOSH/OSHA.

20. The Federal Hazard Communication Standard: An Introduction to the New Legislation and How It Will Effect James Madison University.

21. Dept. of Waste Management, Hazardous Waste Management Regulations, 672–10–1, Commonwealth of Virginia.

22. Guide to Preventative Maintenance of State Facilities, Virginia Division of Engineering & Buildings.

23. Virginia Confined Space Standard for General Industry and the Construction Industry.

24. Underground Storage Tank Regulations, Virginia Dept. of Community Development and the State Water Control Board.

25. JMU's Dept. of Biology Laboratory Information, Safety and Policy Manual.

26. JMU's Dept. of Chemistry Laboratory Information, Safety and Policy Manual.

27. JMU's Theater Safety Handbook.

28. JMU's Master Fire Safety Plan and Emergency Procedure Manual.

29. JMU Campus Police's Standard Operating Procedure and Field Training Manual.

30. American National Standards (ANSI) Code 117.1 pertaining the Handicapped Accessibility.

31. Uniform Federal Accessibility Standards, FED-STD-795 Federal Register, Friday July 26, 1991, Part III, Department of Justice, 28 CFR, Part 36.

32. Nondiscrimination on the Basis of Disability by Public Accommodations and Commercial Facilities; Final Rule.

33. Americans with Disabilities Act Accessibility Guidelines for Buildings and Facilities (Commonly known as "ADAAG") Uniform Standards for Accessible Design.

34. Occupational Exposure to Bloodborne Pathogens; Final Rule, Federal Register, Friday December 6, 1991, Part II, Department of Labor, Occupational Safety and Health Administration.

NOTE: All cited publications and documents are available for review at the Department of Public Safety, Shenandoah Hall, 921 South Main Street.

V. Reference Item # I:

1. With the affected zone limited to a relatively confined area, residents in close proximity are to be relocated to residential units outside the zone of danger.

2. In evacuations of a larger scope, the University, as a contractual participant in the Harrisonburg Transit System, would utilize city buses in addition to coaches from the institution's motor pool. All city bus routes originate and terminate at the "hub" bus stand, centrally located on campus contiguous to the Campus Police headquarters. All city buses are radio equipped and dispatched from the municipal transit office.

3. Harrisonburg and Rockingham county provide numerous sites for emergency assembly such as two other colleges, all with auditoriums and gymnasiums. All could, and have, serve as remote evacuation sites, witness the tragic flood of November 1985 that left so many homeless in outlying areas of the county. Harrisonburg/Rockingham mobilized to meet the emergency needs of the affected populations and is prepared to do so again in the event of a man-made or natural disaster.

4. With a hazardous materials disaster wide in scope and long in duration (protracted and complicated cleanup) with direct impact on campus, normal operations and classes could be suspended. Students then would be sent home; or alternative arrangements made for their welfare. They would be summoned back to classes upon safe resolution of the incident. Such an incident would involve not only the campus, but contiguous residential communities, and would call for involvement by state, federal, and local emergency preparedness and coordination officials. The university's Safety Engineer maintains ongoing liaison and excellent working relationships with all counterpart agencies and peer personnel.

VI. Reference Item # III.I.:

1. Some of these student volunteers with the Harrisonburg Rescue Squad are also employed as Campus Police Patrol Cadets.

VII. Reference Item # III.L & III.M.:

1. "Pegasus" is equipped with dedicated, purpose built Bell and MBB/Kawasaki medivac helicopters, both twin engined craft featuring sufficient redundancy in the event of failure of one of the turbines. This provides sufficient power in marginal conditions for enhanced safety.

VIII. Reference the companion policy "Crisis Communications Plan for JMU" prepared by the Director of Media Relations for primary use by the Media Relations Staff. Important telephone numbers are included in this Media Relations policy that would be a useful resource in this Public Safety/Facilities Management Emergency Response Plan.

From http://www.jmu.edu/safetyplan/hazmaterial/plan.shtml

SUMMARY

The information provided in this section should serve as an adjunct to the Library's disaster planning process. While all libraries may be at risk for some disasters, most libraries are not at risk for ALL disasters.

This information addresses another aspect of disaster planning, namely, the impact on the librarian as an individual. Our responses to disasters necessarily occur on at least two levels, not just the institutional but also the personal. During Tropical Storm Allison one of the three authors of this book had to contend not only with a damaged building and a waterlogged collection but also a flooded home.

How we respond individually depends a great deal on where we are at the time the disaster occurs (on site or off site) and to what extent we have any warning that the library or the community is at risk. Our responses also informed by how much we *know* about individual types of disasters. Reading about a hurricane is not the same thing as experiencing one first hand but knowing the dangers posed is a help.

III RESOURCES ON THE WEB

In Part I we discussed disaster planning and in Part II we presented information, gleaned from freely available sources on the World Wide Web, about specific types of disasters. In Part III we provide thumbnail sketches of more than fifty additional websites for disaster-related information. These have been categorized according to the information services they provide, including:

3.1 Library Specific Sites

3.2 Sites for Communication and Collaboration

3.3 Disaster Planning

3.4 Financial Information Sources

3.5 Specific Hazards

Each listing contains evaluative details for the site that provide information on the languages spoken on the site and the degree of commercialism of the site. The **Special Features** section lists just that, special features of each site. Notes on the authorship of the site found in the **About** section. The **Description** contains notes on the site's offerings. A **Content** section is included if the site offers specialized information on separate pages. When available, **Contact** information for the site's publishers has been supplied.

3.1 LIBRARY SPECIFIC SITES

These sites provide disaster planning specific for libraries. Included are a few examples of library disaster plans that are posted on the Web.

DISASTER PREPAREDNESS AND TRAINING PLAN FOR THE VOLPE LIBRARY (http://www2.tntech.edu/library/disaster/disaster_plan.html)

Languages: English
Privacy Policy: No
Advertisements: No
Availability: Free
Direct Sales: No

Special Features: Direct link to the library's disaster plan.
Authority: The Volpe Library is part of the Tennessee Technological University.

Contact:
Angelo & Jennette Volpe Library and Media Center
Tennessee Technological University
Campus Box 5066
1100 N. Peachtree Ave.
Cookeville, TN 38505
(931) 372-3326
Fax (931) 372-6112

JAMES MADISON UNIVERSITY LIBRARY DISASTER PLAN (http://www.jmu.edu/safetyplan/library/index.shtml)

Languages: English
Privacy Policy: No
Advertisements: No
Availability: Free
Direct Sales: No

Special Features: Direct link to the library's disaster plan.
Description: Included in the disaster plan are power failure, fire, tornado or hurricane, flood, bomb, explosion, biopredation (mold, mildew, rodent, insect infestation), earthquake and salvage procedures for the James Madison University Library. Links on the left side of the page take the user to more general disaster information from the University.
Authority: James Madison University in Harrisonburg, Virginia, developed and posted to its Web site a disaster plan that addresses the issues specific to its library.

Contact:
James Madison University
Office of Public Safety

Shenandoah Hall, RM 103, MSC 6302
Harrisonburg, VA 22807
(540) 568-6764

LIBRARYHQ.COM (http://www.libraryhq.com)

Languages: English
Privacy Policy: No
Advertisements: Yes
Availability: Free
Direct Sales: Yes

Special Features: Library disaster planning and recovery page.

About: LibraryHQ.com, a web-based portal site for the library profession, is developed and managed by Katharine Garstka. She holds a BA from UCLA and an MLS from the University of Arizona, and has worked in public, university, health care, and zoology libraries. She has developed websites for Intergraph Corporation, a computer hardware and software developer, and Sirsi Corporation.

Description: The library disaster and planning page provides valuable links to numerous sites that offer advice and help for physical and digital library disasters.

Content: *Library Disaster Planning and Recovery.* http://www.libraryhq .com/disaster.html. There is no obvious link from the main Libraryhq.com Web page to the disaster page. The easiest way to find it is to go to it directly or use the site map.

Contact:
LibraryHQ.com
One Seaport Plaza
199 Water Street, 20th Floor
New York, NY 10038
(877) 401-9535 toll free
webmaster@libraryhq.com

MUNTERS CORPORATION MOISTURE CONTROL SERVICES (http://www.muntersamerica.com)

Languages: English.
Privacy Policy: No
Advertisements: Yes
Availability: Free
Direct Sales: Yes

Special Features: Commercial site for a world-wide restoration company.

About: Munters is a world leader in humidity control. The company designs, supplies and services dehumidification systems; provides domestic and commercial water and fire damage restoration, leak detection and temporary solutions for dehumidification, heating and cooling. After the 2001 flood in the HAM-TMC Library, Munters was on the scene immediately.

Description: Munters is a world-wide company. The site has a clickable map which makes it easy to find the nearest location. The local office in Houston contacts libraries on a regular basis, just to remind administrators that they are available if needed.

Contact:
Munters Corporation Moisture Control Services
79 Monroe Street,
P.O. Box 640
Amesbury, MA 01913
(800) 422-6379
mcsinfo@untnersamerica.com

OCLC ONLINE COMPUTER LIBRARY CENTER, INC. (http://www.oclc.org/home)

Languages: English
Privacy Policy: No
Advertisements: No
Availability: Free
Direct Sales: No

Special Features: Digitization and preservation information.

About: OCLC is a nonprofit membership organization serving 43,559 libraries in eighty-six countries and territories around the world. OCLC's mission is to further access to the world's information and reduces library costs by offering services for libraries and their users.

Description: OCLC Digital & Preservation Resources services provide the technology, infrastructure, resources and services you need for complete digital collection life cycle management. These new services allow you to create, access and preserve collections; to collaborate to build new collections and a clearinghouse of information about projects, funding and best practices; and to learn about digitization and preservation issues.

Content: Digitization and Preservation. http://www.oclc.org/digitalpreservation/. There are many reasons libraries, museums and historical societies digitize some, or all, of their treasures including access, security, longevity and simplification of management. This section provides more information about digitization solutions, special centers that process materials and the cooperative education programs available to help learn about building and developing digital collections.

Contact:
OCLC Online Computer Library Center, Inc.
6565 Frantz Road
Dublin, OH 43017
(614) 764-6000; (800) 848-5878; (614) 764-6096
oclc@odc.org

ROBINSON LIBRARY DISASTER CONTROL PLAN (http://www.ncl.ac.uk/bindery/disaster.html)

Languages: English
Privacy Policy: No
Advertisements: No
Availability: Free
Direct Sales: No

Special Features: Full-text of the library's disaster plan.

About: The Robinson Library is part of the University of Newcastle upon Tyne, providing a British version of a library disaster plan. The purpose of this document is to outline plans at a practical level for responding to disasters or unexpected events which might have potentially destructive consequences for the library and its holdings and services.

Contact:
Robinson Library
University of Newcastle
Newcastle upon Tyne, NE2 4HQ
0191 222 7587

SECURITY LIBRARY (http://www.windowsecurity.com/whitepapers/disaster_recovery/)

Languages: English
Privacy Policy: No
Advertisements: Yes
Availability: Free
Direct Sales: Yes

Special Features: Links to White papers on various types of preparedness, including anti-virus, firewalls and disaster recovery; monthly newsletter.

About: WindowSecurity is a company, not affiliated with Microsoft, that provides information in protecting computers, servers, etc., from piracy. There is a lot of good information in the white papers listed.

3.2 SITES FOR COMMUNICATION AND COLLABORATION

Links to sites for communication and collaboration are those resources that aid in information sharing. Communication networks that provide information and seminars on public safety are listed.

AMATEUR RADIO EMERGENCY COMMUNICATION
(http://www.arrl.org/FandES/field/pscm/sec1-ch1.html)

Languages: English
Privacy Policy: No
Advertisements: No
Availability: Free
Direct Sales: Yes

Special Features: Information on amateur radio usage during disasters.

About: Amateur radio operators set up and operate organized communication networks locally for governmental and emergency officials, as well as non-commercial communication for private citizens affected by a disaster. Amateur radio operators are most likely to be active after disasters that damage regular lines of communications due to power outages, lack of electricity and destruction of telephone lines.

Description: This site describes the function of amateur radio users in times of emergency. Many times in a disaster event, these are the only lines of communication. If your organization is interested in exploring this option as a part of your disaster plan, this is a good site to review. Information is provided on purchasing amateur radios as well as how to operate them.

Content: Emergency Communications. http://www2.arrl.org/FandES/field/emergency/. This site provides links for amateur radio operaters interested others turn on the web for news and information for news and information when disasters strike.

Federal Communications Commission (FCC) Rules for Operating HAM Radios http://www2.arrl.org/FandES/field/regulations/news/part97/

This site provides links to FCC rules in .pdf and ASCII formats, as well as summaries and updates.

HAM Radio—Getting Started http://www2.arrl.org/hamradio.html. This site provides information on getting started as an amateur radio operator, including frequently asked questions.

Contact:
Jennifer Hagy
Media Relations Manager
(860) 594-0328
jhagy@arrl.org

DISASTER NEWS NETWORK (DNN)
(http://www.disasternews.net)

Languages: English
Privacy Policy: No
Advertisements: No
Availability: Free
Direct Sales: Yes

Special Features: Email updates of current information about disasters and response efforts (fee based), a list of Disaster Response Organizations, means for donating money, relief supplies or support for areas hit by disasters.

About: Produced by the Village Life Company, a not-for-profit organization founded in early 1996, DNN is a news service that tells the story of disaster response and suggests appropriate ways the public can help survivors. It also facilitates information sharing among disaster responders.

Description: DNN covers the topics of preparedness and mitigation, public violence, environmental hazards and terrorist disasters. This is a good site to consult to stay on top of current issues and events in disaster events. DNN also provides an opportunity to contribute time and money as well as share your experiences with disasters.

Content: Domestic Organizations. http://www.disasternews.net/howtohelp/orgs.php?domint=Domestic. This site provides information on disaster response organizations and Web sites in the United States.

How to Help. http://www.disasternews.net/howtohelp/. This site provides information on how to help following disasters.

Contact:
Disaster News Network Inc.
P.O. Box 8403
Elkridge, MD 21075
info@disasternews.net

THE EMERGENCY INFORMATION INFRASTRUCTURE PROJECT (EIIP) (http://www.emforum.org)

Languages: English
Privacy Policy: Yes
Advertisements: No
Availability: Free
Direct Sales: No

Special Features: Live chat and interactive question and answer sessions on specific topics and transcripts of previous programs.

About: The EIIP is a non-profit educational organization, dedicated to enhancing the practice of emergency management, and thereby public safety, through offering professional development opportunities to practitioners and other interested people.

Description: This site presents in the *Virtual Forum* timely, disaster-related topics by experts in their fields through Internet-based *Live Chat* technology. There is no charge to participants.

WEATHERRADIOS.COM (http://www.weatherradios.com)

Languages: English
Privacy Policy: No
Adverstisements: No
Availability: Free
Direct Sales: No

Special Features: Local severe weather information.

About: Weather Radio (NWR) is a nationwide network of radio stations broadcasting continuous weather information direct from a nearby National Weather Service office. NWR broadcasts National Weather Service warnings, watches, forecasts, and other hazard information 24 hours a day.

Description: This site provides product reviews for the various types of weather radios, availability of weather radio signals in specific area and accessories for the deaf. There are also instructions for programming the weather radio on this site.

3.3 DISASTER PLANNING SITES

Disaster planning sites include those information resources on the Web that provide fact sheets, tips for preparation, and those resources that can aid in recovery should a disaster occur. Look for information regarding checklists and supply list for emergency planning as well as national resources. These resources can provide crucial information regarding travel, including traffic information which is vital in the case of evacuation, and preparation techniques that will mitigate the cost of a disaster event.

AMERICAN RED CROSS DISASTER SERVICES GUIDE
(http://www.redcross.org)

Languages: English
Privacy Policy: Yes
Advertisements: No
Availability: Free
Direct Sales: No

Special Features: Local Red Cross Locator; detailed instructions for preparing a disaster kit; foreign language materials in Arabic, Cambodian, Chinese, Farsi, French, Hmong, Japanese, Korean, Laotian, Russian, Spanish, Tagalog, and Vietnamese.

About: The American Red Cross was created in 1881 to serve America in times of disaster and national distress. It is a humanitarian organization chartered by the U.S. Congress to aid the public prepare for and respond to emergency events.

Description: The American Red Cross Web site provides information that supports its mission of preparing Americans for disasterous events and providing aid in times of emergencies. Among its services are disaster services, biomedical services, services for the military, health and safety services, international services, and much more.

Content: Disaster Safety. http://www.redcross.org/disaster/safety/guide.html. This portion of the site is a collaborative work of the National Disaster Education Coalition which is comprised of the American Red Cross, the Federal Emergency Management Agency, National Oceanagraphic and Atmospheric Association/National Weather Agency, National Fire Protection Association and the U.S. Geological Survey.

The information provided in this guide is organized to assist emergency managers in communities that have been affected by disasters caused by severe weather and other naturally occurring phenomena as well as chemical and biological events. The site is designed for use by the general public rather than for those interested in research or other scientific information.

Business & Industry Guide. http://www.redcross.org/services/disaster/ 0,1082,0_606_,00.html

The Business and Industry Guide provides important information about planning for disasters and protecting employees, customers and businesses.

Financial Recovery. http://www.redcross.org/services/disaster/afterdis/ recover.html

This section describes steps to take once a disaster strikes including conducting an inventory, reconstructing lost records, notifying creditors, filing an insurance claim, obtaining loans and grants, avoiding contractor rip-offs and reducing the tax bite.

Contact:
American Red Cross National Headquarters
431 18th Street, NW
Washington, DC 20006
(202) 639-3520

ASSOCIATION OF STATE FLOODPLAIN MANAGERS (http://www.floods.org)

Languages: English
Privacy Policy: No
Advertisements: No
Availability: Free
Direct Sales: Yes

Special Features: Interactive map with state contacts, publications, annual conference information.

About: The Association of State Floodplain Managers is an organization of professionals involved in floodplain management, flood hazard mitigation, the National Flood Insurance Program, as well as flood preparedness, warning, and recovery.

Description: The publications section of this site could be beneficial to lay persons concerned with issues relating to disasters involving flooding. Also included in the site is information about current legislation that affects floodplain management.

CENTERS FOR DISEASE CONTROL (CDC) (http://www.cdc.gov)

Languages: English, Spanish
Privacy Policy: Yes

Advertisements: No
Availability: Free
Direct Sales: No

Special Features: Factsheets and brochures on specific health issues, statistical data, software and databases, 24-hour emergency telephone number.

About: The CDC is recognized as the lead federal agency for protecting the health and safety of people—at home and abroad, providing credible information to enhance health decisions and promoting health through strong partnerships.

Description: Through this site the CDC provides information for developing and applying disease prevention and control, environmental health and health promotion and education activities designed to improve the health of the people of the United States.

Content: Emergency Preparedness and Response Branch. http://www.cdc.gov/nceh/emergency/weather/default.htm. The National Center for Environmental Health's Emergency Preparedness and Response Branch (EPRB) coordinates the CDC emergency preparedness and response activities.

Disaster Epidemiology. http://www.cdc.gov/nceh/hsb/disaster/default.htm. This site provides information resources for epidemiologial consequences of disaster events.

Emergency and Environmental Health Services. http://www.cdc.gov//nceh/eehs/. This site provides Information resources for health services in response to emergency events.

Environmental Hazards and Health Effects. http://www.cdc.gov/nceh/divisions/ehhe.htm. This site provides information that addresses preventing and controlling diseases and death that result from Environmental hazards.

Agency for Toxic Substances and Disease Registry (ATSDR). http://www.atsdr.cdc.gov/. This site provides links to toxiological profiles where substances are ranked on the basis of frequency of occurrence, toxicity, and potential for human exposure. Other links go to: the ATSDR Ombudsman who serves as a mediator for disputes that involve exposure to toxic subastances, emergency response instructions, a list of sites by state, that contain hazardous substances, education and training and other information sources.

Contact:
Centers for Disease Control
1600 Clifton Rd.
Atlanta, GA 30333
(404) 639-3311; (800) 311-3435; (404) 639-3312 TTY

CENTER FOR EXCELLENCE IN DISASTER MANAGEMENT AND HUMANITARIAN ASSISTANCE
(http://coe-dmha.org/index.htm)

Languages: English
Privacy Policy: No
Advertisements: No
Availability: Free
Direct Sales: No

Special Features: The journal *Liason*; multi-media gallery.

About: The Center for Excellence in Disaster Management and Humanitarian Assistance is a federally funded project given a mandate by the U.S. Congress to improve the coordination and integration of the world's response to natural disasters, humanitarian crises and peace operations. The Center promotes civil-military management in international humanitarian assistance, disaster response and peacekeeping through education, training, research and information programs.

Description: The Center for Excellence in Disaster Management and Humanitarian Assistance provides information about training program across the United States and is helpful resource for those looking for training and keeping up with current issues in disaster management. Of particular interest is *Liason*, a newsletter that addresses current issues in disaster management.

Contact:
The Center of Excellence in Disaster Management & Humanitarian Assistance
Tripler Army Medical Center
1 Jarrett White Road (MCPA-DM)
Tripler AMC, HI 96859-5000

CITIZENCORPS.GOV (http://www.citizencorps.gov)

Languages: English, Spanish
Privacy Policy: Yes
Advertisements: No
Availability: Free
Direct Sales: 2/20/2003

Special Features: Handouts and brochures; current threat level.

About: In response to the events of September 11, 2001, the Citizen Corps was established as a component of the Freedom Corps in an effort to coordinate volunteer activities and ensure that the public is prepared in the event of a disaster of any kind.

Description: This site offers the public the opportunity to become involved by providing an online application. By joining, members are able to receive immediate information as threats become apparent. Also included on this site, are tips on preparation for disasters. Of particular interest and use are Citizens Preparedness Publications where a library has been compiled on how to prepare oneself for a disaster.

DISASTERRELIEF.ORG (http://www.disasterrelief.org)

Languages: English
Privacy Policy: No
Advertisements: No
Availability: Free
Direct Sales: No

Special Features: Photo gallery; disaster dictionary; preparedness materials.

About: A collaboration effort between the American Red Cross, Cable News Network, and IBM, DisasterRelief.org was developed to help disaster victims world-wide through the dissemination of information via the Internet.

Description: Found on this site is information on preparing for disasters, contacting family members and loved whose area was affected by a disaster, and links to a number of relief agencies.

Content: Red Cross Help World-wide. http://www.disasterrelief.org/GetHelp/world.html. This site lists the locations around the world in which Red Cross provides aid.

Disaster-Relevant Organizations. http://www.disasterrelief.org/Links/. This site includes the contact information for volunteer religious, relief, and welfare organizations, university programs and disaster/hazard research and other sources of disaster information.

DISASTER RESPONSE: PRINCIPLES OF PREPARATION AND COORDINATION
(http://orgmail2.coe-dmha.org/dr/flash.htm)

Languages: English
Privacy Policy: No
Advertisements: No
Availability: Free
Direct Sales: No

Special Features: Full-text online reference *Disaster Response*; directories of disaster-relevant organizations.

About: This is a widely used resource in the disaster management and medical communities. It is an online version of an out-of-print reference source written by disaster expert and physician, Dr. auf der Heide. Through this site the online reference source is available free of charge. Macromedia Flash Player is required to view the book.

Description: In this book, Dr. auf der Heide focuses on the systemic problems of disaster management, recognizing the fact that while the public sector is mandated by law to provide disaster management strategies and relief, it is the private sector that provides most of the resources. The lack of communication between these entities adds to the problem of ineffective disaster management. His book details solutions to inherent problems in disaster management and provides a well researched analysis of disaster management and is helpful in understanding the theory and practice of this arena as a whole. *Disaster Response* is used in undergraduate and graduate courses in the United States.

EQUIPPED TO SURVIVE™ (http://www.equipped.org)

Languages: English
Privacy Policy: No
Advertisements: Yes
Availability: Free
Direct Sales: No

Special Features: Independent reviews of survival equipment, survival and search and rescue information.

About: The Equipped To Survive™ Web site is supported by the non-profit 501(c)(3) Equipped To Survive Foundation and edited by noted survival authority, Douglas S. Ritter.

Description: This site provides reviews of survival equipment and search and rescue information. While some of this site is outside of the scope of disaster management, much of it is relevant to the topic. Several links provide helpful information about building survival kits in disaster emergencies.

Content: Disaster Preparedness. http://www.equipped.org/disastertoc .htm. This site provides vital information for creating a disaster kit.

Survival Kit. http://www.equipped.org/srvkitstoc.htm. This site provides general information on survival kits.

Urban Survival. http://www.equipped.org/urbantoc.htm. This site provides specialized information for those in urban areas.

EXTENSION DISASTER EDUCATION NETWORK (EDEN)
(http://www.agctr.lsu.edu/eden/default.aspx)

Languages: English
Privacy Policy: Yes
Advertisements: No
Availability: Free
Direct Sales: No

Special Features: Information Extension Services by state, resource database.

About: EDEN is a collaboration by multiple states to extend services across the United States to improve the delivery of services to citizens affected by disasters, EDEN receives support from the Cooperative State Research, Education and Extension Service, and the U.S. Department of Agriculture.

Description: This site provides a resource database where users can find assistance, help for psychological problems brought on by disaster, EDEN-related Web sites and directories of agencies that provide disaster relief.

FEDERAL EMERGENCY MANAGEMENT AGENCY (FEMA)
(http://www.fema.gov)

Languages: English, Spanish
Privacy Policy: Yes
Advertisements: No
Availability: Free
Direct Sales: No

Special Features: Disaster preparedness; response and recovery; tribal information; photo library; maps.

About: FEMA, a former independent agency that became part of the new Department of Homeland Security in March 2003, is tasked with responding to, planning for, recovering from and mitigating against disasters. FEMA can trace its beginnings to the Congressional Act of 1803. This act, generally considered the first piece of disaster legislation, provided assistance to a New Hampshire town following an extensive fire. In the century that followed, ad hoc legislation was passed more than 100 times in response to hurricanes, earthquakes, floods and other natural disasters.

Description: Included in this site are a library of documents that addresses the various aspects of different hazards and related threats, a library of images and maps and links to related sites. The FEMA site features links to a FEMA-created site for children, the U.S. Fire

Administration, flood Insurance and mitigation, tribal information, DisasterHelp.gov, and much more. This is a must have information resource for disaster management.

Content: Emergency Management Guide for Business. http://www .fema.gov/library/bizindex.shtm. In this document FEMA provides information for companies of all sizes in planning response and recovery with regards to disaster management. The guide analyzes the steps in the planning process, emergency management considerations, information specific to hazards and other informational sources. FEMA designed this document as a guide to emegency management rather than a outline of requirements for compliance to federal, state or local regulations.

Disasters and Emergencies. http://www.fema.gov/library/dizandemer .shtm. Information found in this library can be viewed in .pdf, html, and Microsoft Word formats. Categories of information include: Animals and Emergencies; Comprehensive HAZMAT Emergency Response—Capability Assessment Program; Disaster Information; Education; Major Disaster Summary Maps and Supplies and Warnings.

Response and Recovery. http://www.fema.gov/library/respandrecov .shtm. This site is a library of publications for response and recovery activities. Of particular interest is the *Standard Checklist Criteria for Business Recovery*.

Preparation and Prevention. http://www.fema.gov/library/prepandprev .shtm. This site provides a library of publications that focus on individual hazards and threats.

Hazards. http://www.fema.gov/hazards/. This site provides information on specific hazards and how to deal with them.

Contact:
FEMA
Federal Center Plaza
500 C Street, SW
Washington, DC 20472
(202) 566-1600

INTERNATIONAL FEDERATION OF RED CROSS AND CRESCENT SOCIETIES (IFRC) (http://www.ifrc.org)

Languages: English, French
Privacy Policy: No
Advertisements: No
Availability: Free
Direct Sales: No

Special Features: Current news on world-wide relief efforts; appeals and situation reports; meetings and events; photo gallery.

About: The IFRC was founded in 1919 in response to the aftermath of World War I and the need for cooperation between Red Cross societies to help prisoners of war and combattants. Today it focuses on disaster preparedness and response, as well community healthcare.

Description: This site contains detailed contact information for worldwide Red Cross relief efforts, including contact information for people and organizations involved. Their efforts and activities focus on health, disaster response, and disaster preparedness.

Content: Disaster Response. http://www.ifrc.org/what/disasters/response/index.asp. This site provides information on particular types of disasters including hurricanes, cyclones and typhoons, drought, earthquakes, epidemics, famine, floods, man-made disasters, population movement, volcanic erruptions, and technological disasters.

Contact:
International Federation
800 Second Avenue
Suite 355, 3rd Floor
New York, NY 10017
(212) 338-0161
Fax (212) 338-9832
secretariat@ifrc.org

NATIONAL TRAFFIC CLOSURE
(http://www.fhwa.dot.gov/trafficinfo/index.htm)

Languages: English
Privacy Policy: Yes
Advertisements: No
Availability: Free
Direct Sales: No

Special Features: Regional and local traffic information which can be invaluable when evacuations become necessary and when weather conditions make highways impassable.

About: A service of the U.S. Department of Transportation, Federal Highway Administration (FHWA), this site was created to improve the U.S. highway system, by using technology and research to maintain quality transportation information nationwide.

Description: Of great use on this site is the National Traffic and Road Closure Information which provides construction related information, traffic conditions, transit related information, regional links, as well as weather and road conditions. A clickable map provided to find out traffic information for a particular part of the United States.

Contact:
FHWA
Nassif Building
400 7th Street SW
Washington, DC 20590
(202) 366-0537
ntis.feedback@fhwa.dot.gov

PUBLIC ENTITY RISK INSTITUTE (PERI)
(http://www.riskinstitute.org)

> *Languages: English*
> *Privacy Policy: Yes*
> *Advertisements: No*
> *Availability: Free*
> *Direct Sales: Yes*

Special Features: Virtual Symposium Programs, risk management information.

About: PERI's mission is to serve public, private and nonprofit organizations as a dynamic, forward thinking resource for the practical enhancement of risk management.

Description: The PERI Web site is a source for funding information, tools and resources for risk management, as well as a clearinghouse for related publications. This site provides publications focusing on risk management, disaster management, and reference materials. PERI also offers Virtual Symposium Programs which offer valuable educational opportunities in an array of risk management subjects.

Contact:
PERI
11350 Random Hills Road, 210
Fairfax, VA 22030
(703) 352-1846
Fax (703) 352-633

READY.GOV (http://www.ready.gov)

> *Languages: English*
> *Privacy Policy: Yes*
> *Advertisements: No*
> *Availability: Free*
> *Direct Sales: No*

Special Features: Make a safety kit information; make a safety plan information; be prepared information; glossary.

About: A site sponsored by the U.S. Department of Homeland Security, Ready.gov was set up primarily for educating the public about preparing for threats to national security.

Description: The U.S. Department of Homeland Security was established in the face of terrorism. It in turn, this information resource was created to educate citizens about the different aspects of terrorist activity. Ready.gov provides information about preparation in the event of a biological, chemical or nuclear threat. Preparation activities addressed by this site include making a safety kit, making a plans and understanding the effects various types of terrorist activities.

Content: Biological Threat. http://www.ready.gov/biological.html. This site provides information on how to respond to biological attacks, or the deliberate release of germs or other biological substances that can make people sick.

Chemical Threat. http://www.ready.gov/chemical.html. This site provides information on how to respond to a chemical attack, or the deliberate release of a toxic gas, liquid, or solid that can poison people and the environment.

Explosions. http://www.ready.gov/explosions.html. This site provides information on how to respond to explosions.

Nuclear Blasts. http://www.ready.gov/nuclear.html. This site provides information on nuclear blasts, or an explosion with intense light and heat, a damaging pressure wave and widespread radioactive material that can contaminate the air, water and ground surfaces for miles around.

Radiation Threat. http://www.ready.gov/radiation.html. This site provides information on radiation threats/dirty bombs, or the use of common explosives to spread radioactive materials over a targeted area. It is not a nuclear blast.

THE DISASTER PREPAREDNESS AND EMERGENCY RESPONSE ASSOCIATION (DERA) (http://www.disasters.org/deralink.html)

Languages: English, French, German, Italian, Portuguese, Spanish

Privacy Policy: No

Advertisements: No

Availability: Free

Direct Sales: No

Special Features: Online Conference; library; newsletter.

About: DERA was founded in 1962 to assist communities worldwide in disaster preparedness, response and recovery, and to serve as a professional association linking professionals, volunteers, and organizations active in all phases of emergency management.

Description: This site serves as a collaborative resource and offers local agencies to emergency management information while learning from others.

Content: Online Conference. http://www.disasters.org/workshop/nov2002/default.htm. The continuous online conference has two purposes: bring together emergency managers, planners and academics from around the world to share insights and processes for effective strategic planning and provide a forum for DERA members to discuss their visions for the future of the organization.

Contact:
DERA
P.O. Box 797
Longmont, CO 80502
(303) 809-4412
dera@disasters.org

PAN AMERICAN HEALTH ORGANIZATION DISASTERS AND HUMANITARIAN ASSISTANCE
(http://www.paho.org/disasters)

Languages: English, Spanish
Privacy Policy: No
Advertisements: No
Availability: Free
Direct Sales: No

Special Features: Bilingual (English and Spanish) disaster information; multimedia educational materials.

About: The Pan American Health Organization Disasters and Humanitarian Assistance, a regional office of the World Health Organization, was established to aid in disaster planning, mitigation, and response for Latin American countries.

Description: This site focuses on providing information on dealing with disasters and their adverse affects on public health. These pages provide universally relevant information, education material and fact sheets though developed to aid residents of Latin America. This is also a good resource for material in Spanish.

Content: Publications. http://www.paho.org/english/ped/Publication_eng.htm. This site provides publications and training materials on all aspects of disaster preparedness and mitigation, an essential part of the work of Pan American Health Organization's Emergency Preparedness Program.

Health Library for Disasters. http://www.helid.disasters.net/. This site provides The Global Virtual Library of Essential Information Resources on Public Health for Disasters and Complex Emergencies.

Contact:
Pan American Health Organization
Pan American Sanitary Bureau
Regional Office of the World Health Organization
525 Twenty-third Street NW
Washington, DC 20037
(202) 974-3000
Fax (202) 974-3663
disaster@paho.org

3.4 FINANCIAL INFORMATION SOURCES

Financial resources listed include information from insurance organizations, federal programs, and non-profit organizations that provide relief should a disaster occur. Eligibility standards of these programs are usually listed on each site.

BUSINESS AND HOME SAFETY (http://www.ibhs.org)

Languages: English
Privacy Policy: No
Advertisements: No
Availability: Free
Direct Sales: No

Special Features: Video gallery; some publications can be downloaded from the site other are available upon request free of charge; subscriber area where users can obtain information tailored to their needs.

About: This site was created by the Institute for Business & Home Safety (IBHS), a non-profit association that provides information about protecting your assets before and after emergencies. This organization performs research, provides training and tracks relevant legislation.

Description: The IBHS site has legal and financial information to help planners prepare for and respond to emergency events brought on by severe weather and other disasters. Find information on building codes, the fortified program, land use planning, business protection, and other programs. The IBHS pages also provides resources such as current events regarding this subject matter, a library of material, and a video gallery. This site also links to the Congress Conference, an annual meeting sponsored by the IBHS that brings together emergency management professionals, the insurance industry and researchers to discuss recent developments in mitigating natural hazards.

Content: Building Codes. http://www.ibhs.org/building_codes/. This site provides building code regulations by state.

Land Use Planning. http://www.ibhs.org/land_use_planning/. This site provides resources that helps the user make informed decisions with regards to choosing a location for a business or home.

Business Protection. http://www.ibhs.org/business_protection/. This site providies brochures that include a disaster planning toolkit for businesses and guidelines for financial recovery after a disaster.

Protect Yourself. http://www.ibhs.org. This site provides links that provide information about preparing for and recovering from specific hazards.

Contact:
Institute for Business & Home Safety
4775 East Fowler Avenue
Tampa, FL 33617
(813) 286-3400
Fax (813) 286-9960
info@ibhs.org

INSURANCE INFORMATION INSTITUTE (http://www.iii.org)

Languages: English, Spanish
Availability: Free
Privacy Policy: No
Advertisements: No
Direct Sales: No

Special Features: Disaster insurance information; terrorism and insurance; information on specific types of disasters (earthquakes, fires, floods, hurricanes and tornadoes).

About: The Insurance Information Institute was designed to improve public knowledge of insurance issues.

Description: This site provides resources and informtation about insuring oneself in the case of a disaster. The disaster portion of this site discusses what to do before and after specific disasters including hurricanes, floods, earthquakes, fires, and tornadoes. Also included is a video (requires real player or windows media player) entitled *Expect a Catastophe*.

Content: Disasters. http://www.iii.org/individuals/disasters/. This site provides information on how to prepare for and recover from a disaster.

Contact:
Insurance Information Institute
110 William Street
New York, NY 10038
(212) 346-5500

NATIONAL FLOOD INSURANCE PROGRAM
(http://www.fema.gov/fima/nfip.shtm)

Special Features: A Word document that describes, in detail, the National Flood Insurance Program.

About: The Federal Insurance and Mitigation Administration (FIMA), a component of the Federal Emergency Management Agency (FEMA), manages the National Flood Insurance Program.

Description: This site provides information on the three components of the National Flood Insurance Program including flood insurance, flood-plain management and flood hazard mapping.

Content: Library. http://www.fema.gov/library/prepandprev.shtm. This site provides a library of documents provided in .pdf, html, and Word formats, with subjects including FIMA resources, maps, planning and preparing, reports and archives.

Education and Training. http://www.fema.gov/fima/education.shtm. This site provides online tutorials, software application training and training at FEMA's Emergency Management Institute.

Software: HAZUS. http://www.fema.gov/hazus/index.shtm. HAZUS is a software application that provides a natural hazard loss estimation program. Models include earthquake, wind, and flood. Training is available for this application.

Hazards. http://www.fema.gov/hazards/. This site links to the FEMA hazards site.

Contact:
FEMA
500 C Street SW
Washington, DC 20472
(202) 566-1600
opa@fema.gov

SMALL BUSINESS ADMINISTRATION (SBA)
(http://www.sba.gov)

Languages: English
Privacy Policy: Yes

Advertisements: No
Availability: Free
Direct Sales: No

Special Features: Disaster Assistance page provides detail explanations of the types of loans available and how to obtain them.

About: The U.S. SBA, established in 1953, provides financial, technical and management assistance to help Americans start, run and grow their businesses.

Description: Of particular interest on this site are the Disaster Assistance pages. When seeking relief from damages incurred by a disaster this link is the one to follow. Other features of the SBA site include business counselling services, loan programs, business management help and help marketing products and services.

Content: Small Business Administration: Disaster Assistance. http://www.sba.gov/disaster/general.html. This is a helpful assistance resource which includes information about the types of loans available for relief and how to apply to them. Additional information includes disaster preparedness and disaster updates by state.

Contact:
SBA Answer Desk
6302 Fairview Road, Suite 300
Charlotte, NC 28210
(800) UASK-SBA; (800) 827-5722; (704) 344-6640 TTY
answerdesk@sba.gov

U.S. DEPARTMENT OF HOUSING AND URBAN DEVELOPMENT (HUD) (http://www.hud.gov)

Languages: English, Spanish
Privacy Policy: Yes
Advertisements: No
Availability: Free
Direct Sales: No

Special Features: Specific details about assistance programs.

About: HUD was born in 1965, but its history extends back to the National Housing Act of 1934, with a mission to provide a decent, safe sanitary home and suitable living environment for every American.

Description: Aside from providing information about buying and selling homes, grants and programs, the HUD site also has a *Disaster Recovery Assistance* page where information about the various HUD programs can be found. Some of these programs are available to businesses located in depressed area.

Content: Disaster Recovery Assistance. http://www.hud.gov/offices/cpd/communitydevelopment/programs/dri/index.cfm. This site provides information about the various HUD programs. Some of these programs are available to businesses located in depressed area. This is another good place to look for financial assistance.

Contact:
U.S. Department of Housing and Urban Development
451 7th Street SW
Washington, DC 20410
(202) 708-1112; (202) 708-1455 TTY

3.5 SITES ABOUT SPECIFIC HAZARDS

These are sites that provide information about how to prepare for specific hazards, special concerns and warning systems.

NATIONAL GEOPHYSICAL DATA CENTER (NGDC) (http://www.ngdc.noaa.gov/ngdc.html)

> *Languages: English*
> *Privacy Policy: Yes*
> *Advertisements: No*
> *Availability: Free*
> *Direct Sales: Yes*

Special Features: Searchable natural hazard handbook.

About: The NGDC, located in Boulder, Colorado, is a part of the U.S. Department of Commerce (USDOC), National Oceanic & Atmospheric Administration (NOAA), National Environmental Satellite Data and Information Service (NESDIS).

Description: Of particular interest on this site is the *Hazards* page where one can find information about and images of the various types of geological hazards. Also provided are *Outreach and Education* links. A couple of publications offered by the site that are of interest are the *National Environmental Satellite, Data, and Information Service, Hazards Support Activities* and *Natural Hazards Data Resources Directory*.

Content: Natural Hazards Data Resource Directory. http://www.ngdc .noaa.gov/seg/hazard/resource/. The Natural Hazards Data Resource Directory is an online handbook that focuses on geological and meteorological hazards and the social response to them.

Hazards. http://www.ngdc.noaa.gov/seg/hazard/hazards.shtml. The focus is on geological hazards here.

Hazard Support Activities. http://www.ngdc.noaa.gov/noaa_pubs/ hazards.shtml. This site describes NOAA/NESDIS programs relating to the observance and assessment of natural hazards such as severe weather, geophysical activity and extreme biological events.

Contact:
NOAA
14th Street & Constitution Avenue NW
Room 6217
Washington, DC 20230
(202) 482-6090
Fax (202) 482-3154
nqdc@noaa.gov

NATURAL HAZARDS.ORG (http://www.naturalhazards.org)

Languages: English
Privacy Policy: No
Advertisements: No
Availability: Free
Direct Sales: No

Special Features: Current advisories for natural hazards in specific areas; education on the dangers of natural hazards.

About: Natural Hazards.org is a scientific, non-profit organization that aids in the understanding of natural hazards. The site was created and is maintained by a volunteer staff of geographic educators and students.

Description: This site delivers a brief introduction of natural hazards, with links to detailed information about specific hazards. Hazards addressed include climate change, El Nino, fog, hurricanes, snow and ice, tornadoes, wildland fire, drought, earthquakes, floods, slope failures, tsunamis, and volcanoes. There is an online form for anyone requiring more information. In addition, the Natural Hazard advisory page provides information on current warnings in specific areas.

Content: Current Natural Hazard Advisories. http://www.naturalhazards .org/check/index.html. This site provides current hazard advisories and information about products that can immediately alert users to future advisories.

Contact:
Since this is an organization staffed by geographically diverse volunteers, the means of contact is a form found at http://www.naturalhazards.org/ask/question.htm.

EARTHQUAKE ENGINEERING RESEARCH INSTITUTE (EERI)
(http://www.eeri.org)

Languages: English
Privacy Policy: No
Advertisements: No
Availability: Free
Direct Sales: No

Special Features: Current information on recent earthquakes worldwide; link to *World Housing Encyclopedia.*

About: EERI is a national, non-profit, technical society of engineers, geoscientists, architects, planners, public officials, and social scientists. EERI members include researchers, practicing professionals, educators, government officials and building code regulators.

Description: This site provides an information clearinghouse on earthquake information, as well as a way of tracking legislation related to building codes and other aspects touched by this phenomena.

Content: *World Housing Encyclopedia.* http://www.world-housing.net/index.asp. The purpose of the encyclopedia is to develop a comprehensive global categorization of characteristic housing construction types presented in a report using a standardized format. All relevant aspects of housing construction are included, such as socio-economic issues, architectural features, the structural system, seismic deficiencies and earthquake-resistant features, performance in past earthquakes, available strengthening technologies, building materials used, the construction process, and insurance. In addition to the text and numerical information, several illustrations (photos, drawings, sketches) are also included in the report.

EARTHQUAKE IMAGE INFORMATION SYSTEM (EQIIS)
(http://nisee.berkeley.edu/eqiis.html)

Languages: English
Privacy Policy: No
Advertisements: No
Availability: Free
Direct Sales: No

Special Features: Photographic images of earthquakes worldwide.

About: This database was developed by the Regents of the University of California and the National Information Service for Earthquake Engineering to house earthquake images.

Description: The EqIIS database includes 10,000 photographs, featuring earthquake damage.

EARTHQUAKE INFORMATION NETWORK (EQNET) (http://www.eqnet.org)

Languages: English

Privacy Policy: No

Advertisements: No

Availability: Free

Direct Sales: No

Special Features: Searchable directory.

About: The EQNET Web site is sponsored by a consortium of state and national organizations in that disseminate earthquake-related information. The purpose of EQNET is to provide links to authoritative Internet resources about earthquakes and the issues surrounding them.

Description: EQNET is a searchable directory of earthquake related information. This is a comprehensive site and a good place to start when seeking information on this phenomena.

U.S. GEOLOGICAL SURVEY EARTHQUAKE HAZARDS PROGRAM (http://earthquake.usgs.gov)

Languages: English

Privacy Policy: Yes

Advertisements: No

Availability: Free

Direct Sales: Yes

Special Features: Earthquake glossary, separate site for children, FAQs about earthquakes.

About: This Web site is provided by the U.S. Geological Survey's Earthquake Hazard Program as part of an effort to reduce earthquake hazard in the United States. Funding for the program comes from the U.S. Geological Survey Earthquake Hazards Program, which is funded, in turn, by the National Earthquake Hazards Reduction Program (NEHRP).

Description: This site provides current earthquake information as well as general earthquake information. Found on this site are maps charts, information for preparedness, and links to regional Web sites.

Contact:
U.S. Geological Survey National Center
12201 Sunrise Valley Drive
Reston, VA 20192
(703) 648-4000

FIRE SAFETY INSTITUTE (http://www.middlebury.net/firesafe)

Languages: English
Privacy Policy: No
Advertisements: No
Availability: Free
Direct Sales: No

Special Features: Fire safety information.
About: The Fire Safety Institute was founded in 1981, to encourage an integrated approach to the reduction of life and property loss from fire through rational fire safety decision making. The Institute pursues this goal by application of information science to collect and organize current and developing fire safety concepts, research methods of decision analysis to develop better ways to utilize fire safety technology and education of professionals to disseminate fire safety knowledge.
Description: This site offers links to information resources that feature fire safety concerns as well as information focusing on fire risk analysis and historic preservation issues. A bibliography is provided for further reading.

Contact:
Fire Safety Institute
P.O. Box 674
Middlebury, VT 05753
(802) 462-2663
Fax (802) 462-2663
firesafe@middlebury.net

FIREWISE (http://www.firewise.org)

Languages: English
Privacy Policy: No

Advertisements: No
Availability: Free
Direct Sales: No

Special Features: Information on wildland fires.

About: This Web site contains educational information for people who live or vacation in fire-prone areas of the United States. All information is supplied and approved by the National Wildfire Coordinating Group, a consortium of wildland fire agencies that includes the U.S. Department of Agriculture Forest Service, the Department of the Interior, the National Association of State Foresters, the U.S. Fire Administration, and the National Fire Protection Association.

Description: This is a very slick site that offers information, in many formats, about wildland fires. There are links to *Firewise* resources where visitors can learn what is new about the site, including information for the homeowner and the firefighter. Much of this information can also be applied to businesses. Next is the enhanced media where visitors can download images videos and screensavers. The forum allows visitors to chat, join a message board and view the message archives. There are downloads for self-running modules that do not require the Internet to run. *My Firewise* allows visitors to personalize their *Firewise* homepage. Other links include access to workshop series, *Firewise* communities in the United States, a catalog of publications, and *Firewise* for educators.

Contact:
Firewise
1 Batterymarch Park
Quincy, MA 02269
lcoyle@firewise.org

INTERNATIONAL FIRE INFORMATION NETWORK
(http://sres.anu.edu/au/associated/fire/index.html)

Languages: English
Privacy Policy: No
Advertisements: No
Availability: Free
Direct Sales: No

Special Features: International information sharing on fires.

About: *FireNet* is an online information service for any one interested in rural and landscape fires developed in 1993 by the Australian National University. The information covers all aspects of fire science and management, including fire behavior, fire weather, fire prevention, mitigation and suppression, plant and animal responses to fire, and all aspects of fire effects. This site should be of interest to professional rural and forest fire managers, educators and trainers, researchers, and students working in all aspects of fire, volunteer fire fighters and organizations, and all rural people concerned with rural and landscape fires.

Description: This is a site for communication, collaboration, education, and special services. A mailing list is provided for those interested in communicating with others about landscape fire hazards. There is also a registry of sites that focus on similar topics. Additionally, there are links to training resources, sites to download fire-specific software and emergency services and management.

U.S. FIRE ADMINISTRATION (USFA)
(http://www.usfa.fema.gov/index.shtm)

Languages: English, Spanish
Privacy Policy: Yes
Advertisements: No
Availability: Free
Direct Sales: No

Special Features: Fact sheets; information on grants; kids' page.

About: As an entity of the Department of Homeland Security and FEMA, the mission of the United States is to reduce life and economic loss due to fire and related emergencies through leadership, advocacy, coordination and support. Established in 1974 with the passing of P.L. 93–498, the U.S. Fire Administration and its National Fire Academy have helped reduce fire deaths by at least half through data collection, public education, research and training efforts, USFA has helped reduce fire deaths by at least half.

Description: Addressing portions of its site to separate audiences, the U.S. web site provides fire-related information for the fire service, the general public, the media. The "For the Public" pages contain the following: fire factsheets, a fire safety directory, kids' page, product recalls, campus fire safety, and a page specifying fire legislation regulating fire safety in hotels and motels. For the fire services, this site addresses such topics as: terrorism, hazardous materials, incident management, disaster planning, prevention, training, and wildfire.

Contact:
U.S. Fire Administration
16825 South Seton Ave.
Emmitsburg, MD 21727
(301) 447-1000
Fax (301) 447-1052

SOUTHERN REGION HEADQUARTERS
(http://www.srh.noaa.gov/default.html)

Languages: English
Privacy Policy: Yes
Advertisements: No
Availability: Free
Direct Sales: No

Special Features: Provides local information for the enite United States, links to local radar loops.

About: Southern Region Headquarters, a part of the National Weather Service (NWS), encompasses one-quarter of the land of the contiguous United States, yet, this area has one-third of all the rainfall in the United States; half of the nation's severe thunderstorm, flash flood, and tornado events; and the greatest number of tropical storm landfalls. This sector of the NWS focuses on weather events that occur in the Southern Region.

Description: While the Southern Region Headquarters was formed to investigate weather events that occur in the Southermost United States, it provides national information via clickable maps and a search by zip code. Of particular interest on this site is its Flood Safety page where information can be found on the types of flooding, the impact of flooding on automobiles, and what should be done before, during and after a flood.

Content: Flood Safety. http://www.srh.noaa.gov/lmrfc/education /safety .shtml. Find information on the types of flooding, the impact of flooding on automobiles, and what should be done before, during and after a flood.

Contact:
Links to local and regional offices found at http://www.stormready .noaa.gov/contact.htm.

ENVIRONMENTAL PROTECTION AGENCY (EPA)
(http://www.epa.gov)

Languages: English, Spanish
Privacy Policy: Yes
Advertisements: No
Availability: Free
Direct Sales: No

Special Features: Educational materials; databases and software; EPA Hotline.

About: The primary charge is to develop and enforce legislation that protects the environment.

Description: Included in this site is helpful information regarding dealing with emergencies that involve chemicals or other toxic substances. The EPA site provides databases that allow the user to obtain important information for local risk assessments.

Content: Small Business Ombudsman. http://www.epa.gov/sbo/. The Small Business Ombudsman serves as an effective conduit for small businesses to access EPA and facilitates communications between the small business community and the EPA.

Chemical Emergency Preparedness and Prevention. http://yosemite .epa.gov/oswer/ceppoweb.nsf/content/index.html. This site provides tools and resources for dealing with chemical emergencies including databases, publications, and links to laws and regualtions.

Hotlines. http://www.epa.gov/epahome/hotline.htm. The EPA has provided this list of hotlines to report chemical emergencies or receive help in such an event.

Contact:
Environmental Protection Agency
Ariel Rios Building
1200 Pennsylvania Avenue NW
Mail Code 3213A
Washington, DC 20460
(202) 260-2090

GEOLOGIC HAZARDS: LANDSLIDES
(http://landslides.usgs.gov)

> *Languages: English, Spanish (selected publications only)*
>
> *Privacy Policy: Yes*
>
> *Advertisements: No*
>
> *Availability: Free*
>
> *Direct Sales: No*

Special Features: This is a great site when seeking information on landslides. The information center has a number of landslide images and links to the tangential threats of avlanches, floods, and volcanoes.

About: U.S. Geological Survey scientists have worked to reduce long-term losses and casualties from landslide hazards through better understanding of the causes and mechanisms of ground failure both nationally and worldwide.

Description: This site links to the National Landslide Information Center, a bibliographic database, publications, landslide events, and a loss reduction module. The National Landslide Information Center provides an overview of this phenomena and resources for the classroom. Also provided by this portion of the site are images, publications, and state and local information on landslides. The searchable bibliographic database is continuously updated to provide reference information on the general topic of landslides.

Contact:
U.S. Geological Survey
12201 Sunrise Valley Drive, M.S. 908
Reston, VA 20192
(800) 654-4966

RADIATION EMERGENCY ASSISTANCE CENTER/TRAINING SITE (REAC/TS) (http://www.orau.gov/reacts/manage.htm)

Languages: English
Privacy Policy: No
Advertisements: No
Availability: Free
Direct Sales: Yes

Special Features: Radiation Accident Registry System, education in handling radiation accidents.

About: Since its formation in 1976, the REAC/TS has provided support to the U.S. Department of Energy, the World Health Organization and the International Atomic Energy Agency in the medical management of radiation accidents. A 24–hour emergency response program at the Oak Ridge Institute for Science and Education, REAC/TS trains, consults, or assists in the response to all types of radiation accidents or incidents. The Center's specially trained team of physicians, nurses, health physicists, radiobiologists, and emergency coordinators is prepared around-the-clock to provide assistance on either the local, national, or international level.

Description: Contained in this site are basics about radiation including how to detect a hazard of this nature. Important information is also included about managing radiation emergencies. This site addresses medical emergencies arising from radiation hazard including pre-hospital response and hospital and medical guidelines for managing this type of emergency.

Content: Radiation Accident Registry System. http://www.orau .gov/reacts/registry.htm. The Radiation Accident Registry System consists of five components: the U.S. Radiation Accident Registry; the U.S. Department of Energy Equal To or Greater Than 5 Rem Study Registry; the Diethylenetriaminepentaacetic Acid (DTPA) User Registry; the Prussian Blue Registry and Foreign Accident Registry. Data from the registry system is used to determine the efficacy of treatment protocols, to monitor trends in morbidity and mortality, and as a database for follow-up of accident survivors.

Contact:
Oak Ridge Institute for Science and Education
REAC/TS
P.O. Box 117, MS 39
Oak Ridge, TN 37831-0117
(865) 576-3131
Fax (865) 576-9522

CENTRAL INTELLIGENCE AGENCY (CIA)
(http://www.cia.gov)

Languages: English
Privacy Policy: Yes
Advertisements: No
Availability: Free
Direct Sales: No

Special Features: *Chemical/Biological/Radiological Incident Handbook*, which provides a good overview of the varying aspects of bioterrorism.

About: The CIA was created in 1947 with the signing of the National Security Act by President Truman. The National Security Act charged the Director of Central Intelligence with coordinating the nation's intelligence activities and correlating, evaluating, and disseminating intelligence which affects national security.

Description: The CIA site is a good source for international information with such resources as the *World Factbook, The Factbook on Intelligence* and a directory of Chiefs of State around the world. This site also contains a comprehensive and informative resource called the *Chemical/Biological/Radiological Incident Handbook*.

Content: Chemical/Biological/Radiological Incident Handbook. http://www.cia.gov/cia/reports/cbr_handbook/cbrbook.htm. Topics include: differentiating between a chemical, biological, or radiological event; personal safety considerations; indicators of a chemical, biological, or radiological incident; and a glossary of terms.

Contact:
CIA
Office of Public Affairs
Washington, DC 20505
(703) 482-0623
Fax (703) 482-1739

OFFICE FOR DOMESTIC PREPAREDNESS
(http://www.ojp.usdoj/odp/)

Languages: English
Privacy Policy: No
Advertisements: No
Availability: Free
Direct Sales: No

Special Features: Training and technical assistance, equipment acquisition grants, state-based needs assessment.

About: The Office for Domestic Preparedness (formerly The Office for State & Local Domestic Preparedness) is the program office within the Department of Justice responsible for enhancing the capacity of state and local jurisdictions to respond to, and mitigate the consequences of, incidents of domestic terrorism.

Description: Of particular interest at the the Office for Domestic Preparedness Web site is its library which contains fact sheets on domestic terrorisim, a training video and information on obtaining grants. Toward the bottom of the "Library" page are links to two reference books: *Medical Management of Biological Casualties Handbook* and *Critical Incident Report*.

Contact:
U.S. Department of Justice
950 Pennsylvania Avenue NW
Washington, DC 20530-0001
(202) 353-1555
AskDOJ@usdoj.gov.

U.S. DEPARTMENT OF STATE OFFICE OF INTERNATIONAL INFORMATION PROGRAMS (IIP)
(http://usinfo.state.gov/homepage.htm)

Languages: Arabic, English, French, Japanese, Korean, Russian, Spanish
Privacy Policy: Yes
Advertisements: No
Availability: Free
Direct Sales: No

Special Features: Current information source for terrorist activities in the United States.

About: A division of the U.S. Department of State, the IIP is the principal international strategic communications service for the foreign affairs community. IIP designs, develops and implements a variety of information initiatives and strategic communications programs, including Internet and print publications, traveling and electronically transmitted speaker programs, and information resource services. These initiatives reach key international audiences, such as the media, government officials, opinion leaders, and the general public in more than 140 countries around the world.

Description: This site provides information on U.S. international policy as well as information services such as electronic journals, e-mail delivery, publications and more.

Content: Response to Terrorism. http://usinfo.state.gov/is/international_security/terrorism.html. This site provides news reports, commentary, official documents, in-depth subject treatments, and photo galleries.

Travel Warnings. http://travel.state.gov/travel_warnings.html. This page provides warnings based on all relevant information, to recommend that Americans avoid travel to a certain country. Countries where avoidance of travel is recommended will have Travel Warnings as well as Consular Information Sheets.

Contact:
Office of Press Relations
Room 2109
U.S. Department of State
Washington, DC 20520-6180
(202) 647-1512

THE TORNADO PROJECT ONLINE
(http://www.tornadoproject.com)

Languages: English
Privacy Policy: No
Advertisements: No
Availability: Free
Direct Sales: Yes

Special Features: Information on tornado safety, shelters, past tornadoes.

About: Since 1970, the Tornado Project has been locating, organizing and publishing information and more recently video on tornadoes. To date, the Tornado Project has collected information on over 60,000 tornadoes.

Description: The Tornado Project site contains information on tornado safety and storm shelters. This site explains, in lay persons' terms, some of the technical storm information that you may have wondered about.

Contact:
The Tornado Project
P.O. Box 302
St. Johnsbury, VT 05819
info@tornadoproject.com

WEST COAST & ALASKA TSUNAMI WARNING CENTER
(http://wcatwc.gov)

Special Features: E-mail updates and warnings, historic seismicity map, FAQs.

About: The U.S. West Coast/Alaska Tsunami Warning Center was established in Palmer, Alaska in 1967 as a direct result of the great Alaskan earthquake that occurred in Prince William Sound on March 27, 1964. In 1982, the Center's area of responsibility was enlarged to include the issuing of tsunami warnings to California, Oregon, Washington, and British Columbia, for potential tsunamigenic earthquakes occurring in their coastal areas. In 1996, the responsibility was again expanded to include all Pacific-wide tsunamigenic sources which could affect the California, Oregon, Washington, British Columbia, and Alaska coasts.

Description: The West Coast & Alaska Tsunami Warning Center offers publications and brochures for Tsunami and Tsunami-related phenomena.

Contact:
West Coast & Alaska Tsunami Warning Center
910 S. Felton St.
Palmer, AK 99645
(907) 745-4212
Fax (907) 745-6071
wcatwc@wcatwc.gov

CASCADES VOLCANO OBSERVATORY
(http://vulcan.wr.usgs.gov/home.html)

Languages: English
Privacy Policy: Yes
Advertisements: No
Availability: Free
Direct Sales: No

Special Features: Information about volcano hazards that is not necessarily specific to the Cascades area.

About: The U.S. Geological Survey Cascades Volcano Observatory researches volcanoes and related events such as landslides and debris flow. This agency also provides hazard assessments based on information gathered from past volcanic eruptions and issues warnings during a volcanic crisis.

Description: If information on volcanoes—where they are located, how they are manifested, the hazards they presents—is required, then the Cascades Volcano Observatory is a good place to start when preparing for a volcanic hazard. This site provides hazard assessments reports and maps as well as educational and outreach activities. Also included are the real-time monitoring of volcanoes, images, and links to other volcano hazards programs across the country.

Contact:
U.S. Geological Survey—
David A. Johnston Cascades Volcano Observatory
1300 SE Cardinal Court, Building 10, Suite 100
Vancouver, WA 98683
(360) 993-8900
Fax (360) 993-8980

U.S. GEOLOGICAL SURVEY VOLCANO HAZARDS PROGRAM (http://volcanoes.usgs.gov)

Languages: English

Privacy Policy: Yes

Advertisements: No

Availability: Free

Direct Sales: No

Special Features: Weekly report of world-wide volcanic activity, types and effects of volcanoes, emergency planning.

About: U.S. Geological Survey Volcano Hazards program is a part of U.S. Department of the Interior and the U.S. Geological Survey located in Menlo Park, CA.

Description: The U.S. Geological Survey Volcano Hazards program site links to the following Volcano Hazards programs in the United States: The Cascades, Yellowstone, Hawaii, and Long Valley. As a part of its information services, this site provides volcano monitoring, tips on Emergency planning, and an explanation of the warning scheme. Resources include: volcanic events reports, fact sheets, videos, volcano products, and a photo glossary of volcano terms.

HAZMAT SAFETY (http://hazmat.dot.gov)

Languages: English
Advertisements: No
Availability: Free
Direct Sales: No

Special Features: Homeland Security Advisory of the current threat level, HAZMAT enforcement, risk management, grants.

About: The Office of Hazardous Materials Safety, a part of the U.S. Department of Transportation's Research and Special Programs Administration, coordinates the national safety program for the transportation of hazardous materials.

Description: The HAZMAT safety site contains an *Emergency Response Guidebook* that can be viewed online or users can order the print version, a state and local education site, a risk management guide, and a link to The Hazardous Materials Emergency Preparedness (HMEP) grant program.

Content: Emergency Response Guidebook. http://hazmat.dot.gov/gydebook.htm. This site provides information for "First Responders" at hazmat disasters including how to quickly identify specific materials and how to protect oneself and others during an incident. This guide can be viewed online or purchased from the Government Printing Office.

Hazardous Materials Emergency Preparedness Grants. http://hazmat.dot.gov/hmep.htm. The HMEP grant provides financial and technical assistance as well as national direction and guidance to enhance State, Territorial, Tribal, and local hazardous materials emergency planning and training. This page contains information about how to apply.

Contact:
Office of Hazardous Materials Standards
U.S. Department of Transportation/RSPA (DHM-10)
400 7th Street SW
Washington, DC 20590-0001
(800) 467-4922; (202) 366-4488

HURRICANE HUNTERS (http://www.hurricanehunters.com)

Languages: English, Spanish
Privacy Policy: No
Advertisements: No
Availability: Free
Direct Sales: No

Special Features: Multimedia gallery of photos taken inside hurricanes, aircraft weather reports, "Ask a Hurricane Hunter."

About: The 53rd Weather Reconnaissance Squadron, known as the Hurricane Hunters of the Air Force Reserve, is the only Department of Defense organization still flying into tropical storms and hurricanes. They have been flying into hurricanes since 1944. Ten Lockheed-Martin WC–130 aircraft and crews are part of the 403rd Wing, based at Keesler Air Force Base in Biloxi, MS.

Description: This group hunts not only Hurricanes but winterstorms as well. Providing more than factsheets and helpful tips for surviving these types of sever weather, Hurricane Hunters has also developed a gallery of photos of these events. There are links to videos from this site as well as tips for interpreting warnings.

Contact:
Hurricane Hunters
403rd Wing
Keesler Airforce Base
Biloxi, MS
(228) 377-1110

CABLE NEWS NETWORK (CNN) WEATHER
(http://www.cnn.com/WEATHER/index.html)

Languages: Arabic, English, German, Italian, Japanese, Korean, Portuguese, Spanish

Privacy Policy: Yes

Advertisements: Yes

Availability: Free

Direct Sales: No

Special Features: E-mail alerts for severe weather; ability to personalize your weather information.

About: CNN is staffed 24 hours, 7 days a week by the dedicated staff in its world headquarters in Atlanta, Georgia, and in bureaus worldwide, CNN .com relies heavily on CNN's global team of almost 4,000 news professionals. As a counterpart to its televised news programs, CNN provides a Web site that is updated throughout the day.

Description: Features on this site include current weather in North America and links to current weather in major world cities. To get local weather simply type your zip code in the weather search feature or browse a list of locations. Weather maps are available for eight regions around the world. To receive alerts for severe storms submit your e-mail address in the "Storm Watch" section.

Contact:
CNN
One CNN Center
Atlanta, GA 30303
(404) 878-2276
Fax (404) 827-1995

EXTREME WEATHER SOURCE BOOK
(http://sciencepolicy.colorado.edu/sourcebook)

> *Languages: English*
>
> *Privacy Policy: No*
>
> *Advertisements: No*
>
> *Availability: Free*
>
> *Direct Sales: No*

Special Features: Statistical information such as cost and frequency of specific disasters including hurricanes, floods, tornadoes, and lightening.

About: *The Extreme Weather Sourcebook 2001 Edition* was created at the National Center for Atmospheric Research in the Environmental and Societal Impacts Group in partnership with the Atmospheric Policy Program of the American Meteorological Society.

Description: A good statistical resource for weather-related damage. Information is provided by weather type (hurricane, flood, tornado, lightening, and composites), then by state. An explanation of data and methodology is provided.

Content: Societal Aspects of Weather. http://sciencepolicy.colorado.edu/socasp/toc_img.html. This site provides links to information on general weather resources, floods, hurricanes, tornadoes, lightning, El Nino/La Nina, injury and damage statistics, emergency management, weather policy, and insurance.

NATIONAL OCEANIC AND ATMOSPHERIC ADMINISTRATION (NOAA) (http://www.noaa.gov)

> *Languages: English*
>
> *Privacy Policy: Yes*
>
> *Advertisements: No*
>
> *Availability: Free*
>
> *Direct Sales: No*

Special Features: Photo Library; real-time weather; satellite images; *NOAA Magazine.*

About: In a July 1970 statement to Congress, President Nixon proposed creating NOAA to serve a national need "for better protection of life and property from natural hazards . . . for a better understanding of the total environment . . . [and] for exploration and development leading to the intelligent use of our marine resources . . ." On October 3, NOAA was established under the Department of Commerce. Thirty years later, NOAA still provides timely and precise weather, water and climate forecasts, to monitoring the environment, to managing fisheries and building healthy coastlines, to making our nation more competitive through safe navigation and examining changes in the oceans.

Description: This site provides warnings for severe weather, sky and sea charts, current events in weather, weather reports, real-time satellite images, and much more.

Content: National Climactic Data Center. http://lwf.ncdc.noaa.gov/oa/ncdc.html. National Climactic Data Center is a statistical resource for weather data. Some information is available online free. Other resources are available for purchase.

National Severe Storms Laboratory. http://www.nssl.noaa.gov. A partner of the National Weather Service, the National Severe Storms Laboratory provides resources to track severe weather and supports the National Oceanic and Atmospheric Administration in its effort to provide accurate and timely weather reports.

The National Tsunami Hazard Mitigation Program. http://www.pmel.noaa.gov/tsunami-hazard/. The National Tsunami Hazard Mitigation Program was developed as a state and federal partnership to reduce the impact of tsunamis through the implementation of specific recommendations. This site provides real-time data from the Deep-Ocean Assessment and Reporting of Tsunamis (DART) database. This site also links to the U.S. Geological Survey Earthquake Hazards Program that provides maps and other earthquake related data.

National Weather Service. http://www.nws.noaa.gov. This site provides current warnings, forecasts and forecast models, and resources for weather safety. Information of the National Weather Service is compiled in a database to service the information needs of government agencies, private industry, and the general public.

Contact:
NOAA
14th Street & Constitution Avenue, NW
Washington, DC 20230
(202) 482-6090
Fax (202) 482-3154

THE WEATHER CHANNEL (http://www.weather.com)

Languages: English (United Kingdom and United States), French, German, Spanish
Privacy Policy: Yes
Advertisements: Yes
Availability: Free
Direct Sales: Yes

Special Features: Weather glossary and encyclopedia; "Weather Magnet" for current weather conditions, five day forecasts, severe weather alerts, and maps on your own Web site; travel information; local weather.

About: The Weather Channel began in 1982 as a television network that provided continuous weather information. Currently, it provides weather information for 77,000 locations worldwide with local and regional radars. The Weather Channel also provides information through its Weather Channel Radio Network and the Weather Channel Newspaper Service.

Description: This site provides international weather information including real-time weather, weather forecasts, satellite imagry, and educational materials.

Content: Local Forecasts (United States). http://www.weather.com/common/welcomepage/local.html?from=globalnav. This site allows the user to enter a zip code or an area of interest to get local weather information.

World-Wide Weather. http://www.weather.com/common/welcomepage/world.html?from=globalnav. This site allows the user to enter a city or select a link for a geographic area or country. Links include: Brazil, France, Germany, Latin America, and Great Britain.

Weather News. http://www.weather.com/newscenter/?from=globalnav. This site provides news about weather events.

Maps. http://www.weather.com/maps/garden.html?from=globalnav. This site provides various types of weather maps specific to activity and interests.

Weather Tools. http://www.weather.com/services/?from=globalnav. This site provides software that can be downloaded to make weather information more accessible from your desktop or Web site.

Contact:
Contact information is subject specific. Go to http://www.weather.com/interact/contactus/?from=footer to find the best link.

SUMMARY

There is an ever-expanding array of disaster-related information on the World Wide Web. Using the tools that have been discussed in Parts 1–3, any library manager should be able to construct and implement a disaster preparedness plan that fits his or her library.

Don't wait for disaster to strike.

Do your planning now.

IV   THE DISASTER RECOVERY QUICK GUIDES

GUIDE 1

AMIGOS LIBRARY SERVICES, INC., DISASTER PLAN TEMPLATE

This document is designed to assist libraries and archives in preparing for emergency situations which may threaten the safety of persons, collections, and facilities. Whether your institution has a minimal amount of time to devote to emergency planning or is undertaking a comprehensive planning project, this disaster plan can help you to gather vital information which will be invaluable in the event of an emergency. Use this document as it is, or use selected parts. It may be reproduced without permission, provided that the Amigos Preservation Service is credited.

DISASTER PLAN

Institution: _____

Date of current revision: _____

IN-HOUSE EMERGENCY TEAM

Name	*Office Phone*
Home Phone	*Cell Phone*

Administrator _____

Disaster Team

Leader _____

Building

Maintenance _____

Disaster Team:

1) _____

2) _____

3) _____

4) _____

Department Head:

_____

Department Head:

_____

Department Head:

_____

Department Head:

_____

Department Head:

_____

FACILITIES: LOCATIONS OF EMERGENCY SYSTEMS

Building: _____

*List locations and attach floor plan
(use letters to indicate locations on floor plan).*

A. Main Utilities

1. Main water shut-off valve: _____

2. Sprinkler shut-off valve: _____

3. Main electrical cut-off switch: _____

4. Main gas shut-off: _____

5. Heating/cooling system controls: _____

B. Fire Suppression Systems (by room or area)

1. Sprinklers: _____

2. Halon: _____

3. Other: _____

C. Water Detectors _____

D. Keys

Key boxes: _____

Individuals with master and/or special keys (attach list with names, titles, and keys in possession).

E. Fire Extinguishers (Label by number according to type.)

1. Type A—Wood, paper, combustibles

2. Type B—Gasoline, flammable liquid

3. Type C—Electrical

4. Type ABC—Combination

F. Fire Alarm Pull Boxes (Use floor plan.)

G. Smoke and Heat Detectors (Use floor plan.)

H. Radios

1. Transistor radios (for news): _____

2. Two-way radio (for communication): _____

I. First Aid Kits _____

J. Public Address System _____

K. Nearest Civil Defense Shelter _____

EMERGENCY SERVICES

<u>Company/Service and Name of Contact</u>	<u>Phone number</u>
Security	
Fire Dept.	
Police/Sheriff	
Ambulance	
Civil Defense	
Other	

Maintenance/Utilities:

Janitorial Service _____

Plumber _____

EMERGENCY SERVICES (continued)

Electrician _____

Locksmith _____

Carpenter _____

Gas Company _____

Electric Company _____

Water Utility _____

Recovery Assistance:

Preservation Resource _____ <u>Amigos Imaging and Preservation</u>
<u>Service   (800) 843-8482</u>

Preservation Resource _____

Conservators/Specialists:

Paper and Book _____

Photographs _____

Computer Records _____

Local Freezer (1): _____

Local Freezer (2): _____

Disaster Recovery Service: _____

    Account pre-established? _____   Account Number: _____

    Services available: __ Water   __ Freezer   __ Vacuum
                      Recovery   Freeze Dryer

                           __ Fire   __ Mold   __ Environment
                             Recovery   Fumigation   Control

Disaster Recovery Service: _____

    Account pre-established? _____   Account Number: _____

    Services available: __ Water   __ Freezer   __ Vacuum
                      Recovery   Freeze Dryer

                           __ Fire   __ Mold   __ Environment
                             Recovery   Fumigation   Control

Exterminator: _____

Other Services: _____

Insurance (Attach copy of insurance policy.)

Insurance Company: _____

Agent/Contact: _____

Policy Number: _____

Self-Insured? _____ If yes, list contact:

Other

Legal Advisor: _____

Architect: _____

_____

_____

COLLECTION SALVAGE SUPPLIES

On-Site Location or Off-Site Source   (Source's Phone number)

__ Freezer or wax paper _____

__ Gloves, rubber _____

__ Interfacing (Pellon) _____

__ Masks _____

__ Milk crates, plastic _____

__ Mylar polyester sheets _____

__ Newsprint, blank _____

__ Notepads & clipboards _____

__ Nylon monofilament (fishing) line _____

__ Paper towels (no dyes) _____

__ Sponges _____

__ Trash bags, plastic _____

EQUIPMENT & SUPPLIES

On-Site Location or Off-Site Source   (Source's Phone number)

__ Aprons, smocks _____

__ Book trucks, metal _____

__ Boots, rubber _____

__ Brooms _____

__ Buckets & trash cans, plastic _____

__ Camera (to document damage) _____

__ Dehumidifiers _____

__ Extension cords, grounded _____

__ Fans _____

__ Flashlights _____

__ Forklift _____

__ Generator, portable _____

__ Hard hats _____

__ Lighting, portable _____

__ Mops, pails _____

__ Pallets _____

__ Paper towels _____

__ Plastic sheeting, heavy _____
  (stored with scissors, tape)

__ Refrigerator trucks _____

__ Safety glasses _____

__ Sponges, industrial _____

__ Sponges, natural rubber _____

__ Sump pump, portable _____

__ Tables, portable _____

__ Trash bags, plastic _____

__ Vacuum, wet _____

__ Water hoses _____

__ Water-proof clothing _____

Other:

_____   _____

_____   _____

_____   _____

_____   _____

ATTACHMENTS

___ 1. List of **SALVAGE PRIORITIES** for each department, area and/or office.

___ 2. **EMERGENCY PROCEDURES** and **EVACUATION PLAN**.

___ 3. Copy of **INSURANCE POLICY**.

___ 4. Copy of **DISASTER RECOVERY VENDOR CONTRACT**.

___ 5. Other **EMERGENCY PLANNING and RECOVERY DOCU-MENTS:**

_____

_____

_____

LOCATIONS WHERE THIS PLAN IS ON FILE

In-House:

Off-Site:

AGENCIES AND CONSULTANTS

Aggreko
15600 J.F.K. Boulevard, Suite 200
Houston, TX 77032
(877) 603-6021 U.S. Toll Free; (281) 985-8200 (outside United States)
www.aggreko.com

A global company with offices worldwide, Aggreko provides rental power, temperature control, and compressed air systems. Aggreko's equipment is designed to function in all continents and all types of terrain. By careful design and use of the most suitable technology, they aim to minimize the environmental impact of that equipment. All Aggreko's equipment and solutions are designed to comply with applicable laws, regulations, and industry standards wherever operated it in the world.[1]

Services: Disaster recovery, environmental control, temperature and humidity control.

American Freeze-Dry, Inc.
411 White Horse Pike
Audubon, NJ 08106
(609) 546-0777
www.americanfreezedry.com

American Freeze-Dry was established in 1976 and since it's inception has processed many priceless works of literature, as well as valuable contemporary volumes, archival material, and other records. Their clients come from throughout the United States and Canada. Each task, in it's own way, has enabled American Freeze-Dry to learn and grow, resulting in an expertise which is unmatched. They have processed volumes dating to the 16th century, historical manuscripts, sunken ship logs and currency, and wooden and leather artifacts. They also process standard library material and business documents.

Services: Vacuum freeze-drying, cleaning of materials affected by smoke or mold.

---

[1] Company information taken directly from Web pages or communication with representatives.

American Institute for Conservation of Historic and Artistic Works
1717 K Street NW, Suite 200
Washington, DC 20006
(202) 452-9545

The American Institute for Conservation of Historic and Artistic Works (AIC) is the national membership organization of conservation professionals dedicated to preserving the art and historic artifacts of our cultural heritage for future generations. Providing a forum for the exchange of ideas on conservation, AIC advances the practice and promotes the importance of the preservation of cultural property by coordinating the exchange of knowledge, research, and publications. AIC's Code of Ethics and Guidelines for Practice defines appropriate conduct for the field.

Services: Disaster planning, education.

American Interfile & Library Services, Inc.
165 Price Parkway
Farmingdale, NY 11735
(800) 426-9901
www.americaninterfile.com

Serving the record management and library community, American Interfile & Library Services, Inc., provides assistance in collection cleaning, collection storage, collection mapping, shelving and furniture layout, collection shifting, and moving.

Services: Disaster planning and recovery, collection cleaning, library relocation.

Americold Logistics, Inc.
10 Glenlake Parkway South, Suite 800
Atlanta, GA 30328
(678) 441-1400
www.americold.net

In 1998, AmeriCold Logistics, LLC was formed through the merger of URS Logistics and Americold Corporation. Today, they have over 500 million cubic feet of refrigerated capacity and over 100 facilities across the United States. AmeriCold's extensive network of public distribution centers provide a wide variety of value-added services such as blast freezing, transloading and crossdocking, plant support, and import/export services.

Services: Disaster recovery, blast freeze-drying, refrigeration.

Amigos Library Services
14400 Midway Road
Dallas, TX 75244
(800) 843-8482
www.amigos.org

Amigos Library Services, Inc. is dedicated to serving libraries. Amigos began in 1974 in Dallas as AMIGOS Bibliographic Council, when twenty-two libraries united to bring OCLC access to the southwestern United States. A nonprofit organization, Amigos is today one of the nation's largest library resource-sharing networks and a leader in providing information technology to libraries. The Amigos membership consists of over 800 libraries and cultural institutions, located primarily in the southwestern United States, who utilize Amigos' comprehensive line of services, including cataloging, reference, resource sharing, preservation, digital imaging, consulting, and training.

Services: Disaster planning and recovery, preservation services, consultation, disaster plan template (http://www.amigos.org/preservation/disasterplan.pdf).

Ansul, Inc.

1 Stanton Street
Marinette, WI 54143
(800) 862-6785
www.ansul.com

The Ansul mission is to save lives, protect property, and preserve the environment. They do this by providing superior-quality fire protection solutions in partnership with distributors, end-users, and suppliers. They are a worldwide industry leader in the creative application of innovative technologies in fire protection.

Services: Disaster recovery, environmental control, fire suppression.

Atlas Cold Storage & Logistics

5255 Yonge Street, Suite 900
Toronto, ON M2N 5P8
(888) 642-3333
www.atlascold.com

Atlas Cold Storage & Logistics operates the second largest temperature-controlled distribution network in North America with 55 facilities and 276 million cubic feet of refrigerated space. Atlas uses state-of-the-art radio frequency systems connecting computer terminals to onboard material handling equipment for real-time management control that offers small to large volume assembly and preparation services 24 hours a day. Temperatures can be maintained from –20° Fahrenheit to +68° Fahrenheit.

Services: Disaster recovery, blast freeze-drying, refrigeration.

BELFOR USA

2425 Blue Smoke Court South
Fort Worth, TX 76105
(800) 856-3333
www.belforusa.com

BELFOR is the global leader in restoration and reconstruction services. Our expertise comes from more than 50 years of successfully completed projects in virtually every area of property repair. Our 53 full-service offices throughout North America are always ready—24/7—to provide comprehensive, rapid response to mitigate property damage and get operations back on track quickly.

Services: Disaster recovery, fire recovery, environmental control, dehumidification, magnetic media recovery, mold removal, vacuum freeze-drying.

Blackmon-Mooring Steamatic (BMS) Catastrophe, Inc.

303 Arthur Street
Fort Worth, TX 76107
(877) 730-1948
www.blackmonmooring.com

Originally started in 1948 as a furniture and dye shop, Blackmon-Mooring Steamatic has grown to include a host of services ranging from fire and water restoration to air duct and carpet cleaning to mold remediation. Blackmon-Mooring is now an international company with 280 franchises located around the world.

Services: Disaster recovery, vacuum freeze-drying, fire and water damage recovery fumigation, soot and smoke odor removal, computer and magnetic media salvage.

Canadian Association of Professional Conservators

C/O Canadian Museums Association
280 Metcalfe Street
Ottawa, Ontario, Canada K2P 1R7
(613) 567-0099
www.capc-acrp.ca/

The Canadian Association of Professional Conservators (CAPC) is a non-profit association dedicated to the accreditation of professional conservators and the maintenance of high standards in conservation of art and cultural property in Canada. Membership is open to conservators and conservation scientists through defined professional membership requirements.

Services: Disaster planning, education.

Canadian Conservation Institute

1030 Innes Road
Ottawa, Ontario K1A OM5, Canada
(613) 998-3721
www.cci-icc.gc.ca/html/

CCI was created in 1972 to promote the proper care and preservation of Canada's cultural heritage and to advance the practice, science, and technology of conservation. The Institute has worked closely with hundreds of museums, art galleries, academic institutions, and other heritage organizations to help them better preserve their collections. As a special operating agency of the Department of Canadian Heritage, CCI has widened its scope of activities and now markets its services and products around the world.

Services: Disaster preparedness, education.

Conservation Center for Art and Historic Artifacts

264 South 23rd Street
Philadelphia, PA 19103
(215) 545-0613
www.ccaha.org

The Conservation Center for Art and Historic Artifacts (CCAHA) has grown to be one of the largest regional conservation laboratories in the country. Its mission is to provide expertise and leadership in the preservation of the world's cultural heritage. CCAHA specializes in the treatment of works of art and artifacts on paper, such as drawings, prints, maps, posters, historic wallpaper, photographs, rare books, scrapbooks, and manuscripts, as well as related materials such as parchment and papyrus. CCAHA also offers on-site consultation services, educational programs and seminars, internships, and emergency conservation services.

Services: Treatment of art and historical artifacts, including drawings, prints, maps, posters, architectural drawings and musical scores, training in disaster planning and recovery.

Cutting Corporation

4940 Hampden Lane
Bethesda, MD 20814
(301) 654-2887
www.cuttingarchives.com

The Cutting Corporation is dedicated to making preservation transfers of audio recordings of historical significance in order to ensure the preservation of these materials for generations to come. Since 1979, they have preserved over 25,000 hours of audio recorded in wide variety of tape, disc, and belt formats. Their laboratories are capable of both preservation and restoration work and they are able to extract audio from any format of recorded media.

Services: Conservation and preservation of recorded sound collections.

Detex Corporation

302 Detex Drive
New Braunfels, TX 78130
(800) 729-3839
www.detex.com

Detex Corporation is a world-class manufacturer and distributor of products that protect people, secure property, and assure the life safety and security objectives of our customers. We will create the highest customer value in our worldwide markets while obtaining the highest possible return for our other stakeholders.

Services: Disaster recovery, environmental control, security.

Document Reprocessors, Inc.
5611 Water Street
Middlesex, NY 14507
(800) 437-9464
www.documentreprocessors.com
Document Reprocessors has been in the restoration business serving the library and institutional community since 1979. They use the latest in technology and methods in the restoration of books, documents, and magnetic and micrographic media.
Services: Disaster recovery, vacuum freeze-drying, salvage of computers, fumigation, smoke removal.

Dorlen Products
6615 West Layton Avenue
Milwaukee, WI 53220
(414) 282-4840
www.dorlenproducts.com
Dorlen Products Inc. has supplied companies with simple and reliable water leak detection equipment and systems since 1975.
Services: Disaster recovery, water alarms.

DuPont Corporate Information Center
Chestnut Run Plaza
Wilmington, DE 19880-0705
(800) 441-7515
www.dupont.com
DuPont Safety Resources offers services in workplace safety, contractor safety, ergonomics, operational excellence, and emergency. The Safety Training Observation Program™ (STOP) series teaches safety auditing skills for observing people while they work, reinforcing safe work practices, and correcting unsafe acts and conditions.
Services: Disaster recovery, hazardous material response, safety training.

Dust Free, Inc.
1112 Industrial
Royse City, TX 75189
(800) 441-1107
www.dustfree.com
Dust Free®, is a family owned and operated business headquartered in Royse City, Texas. Dust Free® was established in July of 1982 specializing in air filtration equipment designed to benefit allergy patients who needed a clean indoor environment. Today, Dust Free® manufactures a wide variety of air purification equipment for both residential and business locations.
Services: Disaster recovery, environmental control, air filters, mold test kits.

Eastman Kodak Quality Control Laboratory
1901 West 22nd Street
Oak Brook, IL 60652
(800) 352-8378
www.kodak.com

The Kodak Disaster Recovery Program rescues and restores damaged film by recreating damaged documents, overnight, if necessary. If disaster strikes, call any time night or day. When you call, the people at the lab will respond quickly to assess your situation and advise you on how to proceed. Personnel and equipment will be scheduled to deal with your microfilm when it arrives.

Services: Digital imaging, disaster recovery, reprocessing of Kodak film and microfilm.

Epic Response
103 Executive Drive
Woodstock, GA 30188
(877) 277-4647
www.epicresponse.com

Epic Response offers a turnkey approach to disaster response. Their goal is to minimize the negative impact of unexpected emergency situations on offices and buildings. By providing 24/7 rapid response, they reduce the likelihood of business interruption and accompanying negative effects on your employees and business operations.

Services: Disaster recovery, dehumidification, mold remediation.

Etherington Conservation Center
7609 Business Park Drive
Greensboro, NC 27409
(877) 391-1317
www.donetherington.com

The Etherington Conservation Center, Inc., is an internationally recognized conservation laboratory specializing in the preservation and conservation of books, documents, vellum and parchment objects, photographs, and works of art on paper. Their goal is to preserve our common cultural heritage. The Center's comprehensive services are available to individuals, libraries, museums, institutions, and collectors of all types.

Services: Preservation and conservation of books, documents, vellum and parchment objects, photographs, and works of art on paper.

FPC, Inc.
6677 Santa Monica Boulevard
Hollywood, CA 90038
(800) 814-1333
www.fpcfilm.com

Since the 1950s, the Film Salvage Company (FSC) has provided anti-piracy support to the motion picture film industry through the secured destruction and environmental disposal of used motion picture film. Approximately 20 million pounds of film are destroyed and recycled annually, and in March of 2000, the Academy of Motion Picture Arts and Sciences recognized FSC for its recycling program. FSC is a division of FPC, Inc., which happens to be a subsidiary of the Eastman Kodak Motion Picture Group. They are located in Hollywood, California; Mountain City, Tennessee; and Milan, Italy.

Services: Conservation and preservation, disaster recovery, film restoration.

Film Technology Company, Inc.
726 North Cole Avenue
Los Angeles, CA 90038
(323) 464-3456
www.filmtech.com

Film Technology Company, Inc., has restored thousands of motion pictures over its 30–year history. Film Technology has worked on projects photographed on 70mm, 35mm, 16mm, 9.5mm, and 8mm film. Vitaphone discs, optical and magnetic film tracks, wire recordings, and various magnetic audio tapes have all been handled by the company's staff. These wide and varied recordings of moving pictures and sound have been brought to Film Technology by major archives throughout the world. Motion picture studios, broadcast organizations, historical societies, and private individuals also use the services of Film Technology Company.

Services: Disaster recovery, motion picture film restoration.

Getty Conservation Institute
1200 Getty Center Drive, Suite 700
Los Angeles, CA 90049-1684
(310) 440-7702
www.getty.edu/conservation/

The Getty Conservation Institute works internationally to advance the field of conservation through scientific research, field projects, education and training, and the dissemination of information in various media. The mission of the Institute is to enhance and encourage the preservation and understanding of the visual arts in all of their dimensions—objects, collections, architecture, and sites—by addressing unanswered questions, demonstrating best conservation practice, and contributing to the development of sustainable conservation solutions.

Services: Conservation and preservation, disaster recovery, consultation services.

Halotron, Inc.
3770 Howard Hughes Parkway, Suite 300
Las Vegas, NV 89109
(702) 735-2200
www.halotron-inc.com

The Halotron Division of American Pacific Corporation is the manufacturer of environmentally acceptable clean fire extinguishing agents that are replacements for halons. The American Pacific Corporation is a specialty chemical company.

Services: Disaster recovery, environmental control, fire extinguishers, fire suppression.

Heritage Preservation
1730 K Street, NW, Suite 5666
Washington, DC 20006
(202) 634-0031

Heritage Preservation provides a forum for discussion, understanding, and awareness of national conservation and preservation needs. Their programs and publications provide advice and guidance on the proper care and maintenance of historic documents, books and archives, works of art, photographs, architecture, monuments, anthropological artifacts, historic objects, and family heirlooms.

Services: Disaster preparedness, education.

International Institute for Conservation of Historic and Artistic Works
6 Buckingham Street London, England WC2N 6BA
01-1441-839-5975

For more than 50 years The International Institute for Conservation (IIC) of Historic and Artistic Works has promoted the knowledge, methods, and working standards needed to protect and preserve historic and artistic works throughout the world. IIC members belong to an international community of professionals who aim to provide the highest possible level of care for the world's cultural heritage.

Services: Disaster preparedness, education.

Industrial Cold Storage
2625 West Fifth Street
Jacksonville, FL 32203
(904) 786-8038
www.icslogistics.com

The Industrial Cold Storage mission is to provide world class expertise and services for the global supply chain through timely, accurate, and professional performance. Services include blast freezing and cold storage to −20° Fahrenheit.

Services: Disaster recovery, blast freeze-drying, refrigeration.

Insects Limited, Inc.
16950 Westfield Park Road
P.O. Box 40641
Westfield, IN 46074
(800) 992-1991
www.insectslimited.com
Insects Limited was established in 1982 with the motto "The future of pest control is without the use of toxic chemicals." Today, the company researches, tests, develops, manufactures, and distributes pheromones, a unique niche of pest control for protecting stored food, grain, tobacco, timber, museums, and fiber worldwide.
Services: Disaster recovery, environmental control, pest control.

Kidde-Fenwal, Inc.
400 Main Street
Ashland, MA 01721
(508) 881-2000
www.fenwalcontrols.com
Founded in 1938, Fenwal has led the way in designing and manufacturing high quality temperature controls for 65 years. Today, they offer engineers solutions to diverse temperature control, gas ignition, and heat detection challenges.
Services: Disaster recovery, environmental control, fire suppression.

Library of Congress
Preservation Directorate
Washington, DC 20540
(202) 207-5213
www.loc.gov/preserv
The mission of the Preservation Directorate at the Library of Congress is to assure long-term, uninterrupted access to the intellectual content of the library's collections, either in original or reformatted form. The Preservation Directorate has a strong outreach program and provides information about preservation to the Congress, government agencies, other libraries (both national and international), and to the general public. It also provides programs for library staff and patrons that raise preservation awareness and increase the level of knowledge about the library's preservation policies and practices.
Services: Resource center for conservation and restoration.

MBK Consulting
60 North Harding Road
Columbus, OH 43209-1534
(614) 239-8977
www.mbkcons.com
MBK Consulting was founded by Miriam Kahn, MLS in 1991. The

company specializes in providing consulting and educational services to libraries, archives, historical societies, museums, and other cultural institutions. Workshop topics include disaster preparedness and preservation.

Services: Disaster and conservation planning, consulting, workshops.

Midwest Freeze-Dry, Ltd.
7326 North Central Park
Skokie, IL 60076
(847) 679-4756
www.midwestfreezedryltd.com

Midwest Freeze-Dry, Ltd. is industry leader utilizing non-chemical methods of vacuum freeze-drying and a proprietary plasma technology for drying wet materials, mold remediation, pest infestations, and odor removal. Their 20 years of experience have enabled them to develop advanced concepts which can be applied to the conservation and restoration of water, fire, mold, or smoke damaged vellum books, textiles, wooden objects, vellum documents, paper documents, artwork, memorabilia, and photographs.

Services: Conservation and preservation, disaster recovery, deacification, fumigation, vacuum freeze-drying.

Munters Moisture Control Services
341 Dartmouth Avenue
Swarthmore, PA 19081
(800) 422-6379
www.munters.com

Munters is a world leader in humidity control with products and services for water and fire damage restoration, dehumidification, humidification, and air cooling. Customers are found in a wide range of segments, the most important being insurance, utilities, food, pharma, and electronics industries.

Services: Disaster recovery, dehumidification, freeze- and air-drying books and manuscripts, mold remediation, and magnetic media recovery.

National Fire Protection Association
1 Batterymarch Park
Quincy, MA 02169-7471
(800) 344-3555
www.nfpa.org/home/index.asp

The mission of the international nonprofit National Fire Protection Association (NFPA) is to reduce the worldwide burden of fire and other hazards on the quality of life by providing and advocating scientifically-based consensus codes and standards, research, training, and education. NFPA membership totals more than 75,000 individuals from around the world and more than 80 national trade and professional organizations. Established in 1896, NFPA serves as the world's leading advocate of fire prevention and is an authoritative source on public safety.

Services: Disaster recovery, fire safety.

New Pig
One Pork Avenue
Tipton, PA 16684-0304
(800) 468-4647
www.newpig.com

In 1985 New Pig invented the world's first contained absorbent—the PIG® Absorbent Sock—to help clean up oil spills and leaks around machinery, and revolutionized industrial cleanup forever. Today they have grown into a multi-channel, multi-brand supplier of products designed specifically for spill containment, industrial safety, and plant maintenance to industrial, institutional, and governmental facilities. New Pig is committed to keeping workplaces clean and safe worldwide, and now serves more than 170,000 customers in over 40 countries.

Services: Disaster recovery, leak and spill problems.

Northeast Document Conservation Center
100 Brickstone Square
Andover, MA 01810-1425
(978) 475-8140
www.nedcc.org

The Northeast Document Conservation Center (NEDCC) is the largest nonprofit, regional conservation center in the United States. Its mission is to improve the preservation programs of libraries, archives, museums, and other historical and cultural organizations; to provide the highest quality services to institutions that cannot afford in-house conservation facilities or that require specialized expertise; and to provide leadership to the preservation field.

Services: Disaster recovery, environmental control, conservation and preservation, consulting, microfilming, preservation field services.

OCLC
6565 Frantz Road
Dublin, OH 43017
(800) 848-5878
www.oclc.org

The OCLC Preservation Service Centers are staffed by experienced technicians and consultants who work closely with you to identify your needs and provide custom microfilming, scanning, and digital services so you can provide broad access to your collections while preserving them for generations to come. (See also: Amigos & Solinet.)

Services: Digitization services, microfilm production and preservation project planning.

Pest Control Services, Inc.
14 East Stratford Avenue
Lansdown, PA 19050
(610) 284-6249
www.termitesonly.com

Pest Control Services, Inc., is an entomological consulting practice in the structural pest control industry. It is devoted to providing technical advice and training in a variety of entomological disciplines. A major area of expertise is the inspection and analysis of actual and potential pest problems for museums, historic properties, libraries, archives, and their collections. This work culminates in the development of tailored, integrated pest management programs for the protection of these valuable structures and the collections housed within.

Services: Disaster recovery, environmental control, consulting, pest control.

ProText, Inc.

P.O. Box 30423
Bethesda, MD 20824
(301) 320-7231
www.protext.net/

The mission of ProText, Inc., is to minimize the damage caused by natural or manmade disasters by helping the caretakers of collections to be prepared with effective products and information. Their years of experience in the field and collaboration with other preservation specialists led them to create REACT-PAK™ a disaster preparedness kit, and RESCUBE® a disaster recovery book container.

Services: Disaster recovery, emergency response kits.

Reliable Automatic Sprinkler Company, Inc.

525 North MacQuesten Parkway
Mount Vernon, NY 10552
(800) 431-1588
www.reliablesprinkler.com

In the past 80 years The Reliable Automatic Sprinkler Company, Inc., has grown from a small company founded by a mechanical contractor, to the internationally respected leader in fire sprinkler manufacturing it is today. Three goals are at the heart of the corporate mission: to be the leading worldwide manufacturer of innovative, quality-oriented fire sprinklers and system devices; to be a leading supplier of fire sprinkler system components; and to be the leader in providing the highest level of operational excellence in customer service, exceeding all customer expectations.

Services: Disaster recovery, environmental control, fire suppression, water mist.

ServiceMaster Company

3250 Lacey Road, Suite 600
Downers Grove, IL 60515
(888) 937-3783
corporate.servicemaster.com/

The ServiceMaster Company provides service to residential and commercial customers in the United States where they serve 10.5 million homes and businesses each year. Their core service capabilities include termite and pest control, plumbing, heating and air conditioning maintenance, and repair and cleaning and furniture maintenance.

Services: Disaster recovery, cleaning, fire and water damage recovery, pest control.

Solinet
1438 West Peachtree Street, Suite 200
Atlanta, GA 30309
(404) 892-0943
www.solinet.net

The mission of the preservation services program of Solinet is to improve institutions' abilities to maintain long-term, cost-effective access to information resources in both traditional and networked collections. The field services program has been providing education, training, information, and consulting to cultural institutions since 1984. The microfilm service, established in 1990, enables libraries to preserve the intellectual content of endangered and brittle volumes.

Services: Disaster planning, emergency disaster assistance, consulting.

SPECS Brothers
P.O. Box 5
Ridgefield Park, NJ 07660
(800) 852-7732
www.specsbros.com

A video and audio restoration since 1983, SPECS Brothers offers services in disaster planning and recovery of damaged audiovisual materials.

Services: Disaster recovery, reformatting services, magnetic media restoration and reformatting.

SunGard Recovery Services, Inc.
1285 Drummers Lane
Wayne, PA 19087
(800) 247-7832
www.recovery.sungard.com

The mission of SunGard Availability Services is keeping people and information connected. With a full continuum of services, from assessing availability requirements or delivering recovery solutions, to providing managed IT solutions or professional services, SunGard helps you maximize and safeguard your IT investments.

Services: Computer data recovery.

Unsmoke Systems
1135 Braddock Avenue
Braddock, PA 15104-1706
(800) 332-6037
www.unsmoke.com

Founded in 1972, Unsmoke Systems offers services in odor control and mold remediation excellence. Unsmoke began as a service firm performing the removal and neutralizing of odor problems resulting from fire-related smoke, water damage, death and decomposition, and animal urine. In 1987 Unsmoke opened the industry's first hands-on training program/ facility.

Services: Conservation and preservation, disaster recovery, fire and water damage recovery, smoke removal, mold remediation, education.

VidiPax

450 West 31st Street, 4th Floor
New York, NY 10001
(800) 653-8434
www.vidipax.com

Pioneering the magnetic media restoration process in the early 1990s, VidiPax™ successfully identified the disintegration of video and audiotape and invented a remedial process. This process involves temporarily or permanently restoring the tape to playable condition. Through a proprietary cleaning process, VidiPax™ technology provides restoration of the tape in a noninvasive manner. The technique preserves the integrity of the original tape signal without using chemicals in the process. Transfers can be produced from the restored masters in modern video or audio formats.

Services: Disaster recovery, reformatting services, consulting, and magnetic media restoration.

GUIDE 3

AGENCY AND CONSULTANT GRID

	Disaster Planning	Disaster Recovery	Environment Control	Fire Damage	Haz-Mat	Temp & Humidity Control	Vacuum Freeze Drying	Blast Freeze Drying	Refrigeration	Consultation/Training	Images/Film	Reformatting	Water Damage	Conservation/Preservation	Fire Suppression	Smoke Damage	Mold Damage	Computer Salvage	Collection Cleaning	Pest Control	Security	Library Relocation
Aggreko, Inc.			•			•																
American Freeze-Dry							•									•	•					
American Interfile & Library Services																			•			•
Americold Logistics, Inc.		•						•	•													
Amigos Library Services									•				•									
Ansul, Inc.	•	•													•							
Atlas Cold Storage		•						•	•													
Belfor USA	•	•				•	•									•	•	•				
Blackmon-Mooring Steamatic Catastrophe		•					•						•			•						

219

	Disaster Planning	Disaster Recovery	Environment Control	Fire Damage	Haz-Mat	Temp & Humidity Control	Vacuum Freeze Drying	Blast Freeze Drying	Refrigeration	Consultation/Training	Images/Film	Reformatting	Water Damage	Conservation/Preservation	Fire Suppression	Smoke Damage	Mold Damage	Computer Salvage	Collection Cleaning	Pest Control	Security	Library Relocation
Canadian Association of Professional Conservators	•									•												
Canadian Conservation Institute	•									•												
Conservation Center for Art and Historic Artifacts										•				•								
Cutting Corporation														•								
Detex Corporation		•	•																		•	
Document Reprocessors		•					•											•	•			
Dorlen Products		•																				
Dupont Corporate Information Center		•			•					•												
Dust Free, Inc.		•	•														•					
Eastman Kodak Quality Control Laboratory		•									•											
Epic Response		•					•										•					
Etherington Conservation Center		•									•			•								

	Disaster Planning	Disaster Recovery	Environment Control	Fire Damage	Haz-Mat	Temp & Humidity Control	Vacuum Freeze Drying	Blast Freeze Drying	Refrigeration	Consultation/Training	Images/Film	Reformatting	Water Damage	Conservation/Preservation	Fire Suppression	Smoke Damage	Mold Damage	Computer Salvage	Collection Cleaning	Pest Control	Security	Library Relocation
FPC, Inc.		•									•			•								
Film Technology Company, Inc.		•									•											
Getty Conservation Institute		•								•				•								
Halotron, Inc.		•	•												•							
Heritage Preservation	•	•								•												
Industrial Cold Storage		•						•	•													
Insects Limited		•	•																	•		
International Institute for Conservation of Historic and Artistic Works	•	•								•												
Kidde-Fenwal		•	•												•							
Library of Congress										•												
MBK Consulting										•												
Midwest Freeze-Dry		•					•									•		•				
Munters Moisture Control Services		•				•		•									•	•				

	Disaster Planning	Disaster Recovery	Environment Control	Fire Damage	Haz-Mat	Temp & Humidity Control	Vacuum Freeze Drying	Blast Freeze Drying	Refrigeration	Consultation/Training	Images/Film	Reformatting	Water Damage	Conservation/Preservation	Fire Suppression	Smoke Damage	Mold Damage	Computer Salvage	Collection Cleaning	Pest Control	Security	Library Relocation
National Fire Protection Association		•													•							
New Pig		•			•																	
Northeast Document Conservation Center			•							•	•			•								
OCLC										•				•								
Pest Control Services, Inc.		•	•							•										•		
ProText, Inc.	•	•								•												
Reliable Automatic Sprinkler Company		•	•												•							
ServiceMaster Company		•											•							•		
Solinet	•									•												
SPECS Brothers		•																•				
SunGard Recovery Services, Inc.																		•				
Unsmoke Systems		•								•			•	•		•	•					
VidiPax		•								•							•					

SOLINET DISASTER PREVENTION AND PROTECTION CHECKLIST

The inspection checklist provided on the following seven pages is designed to be used as part of an institutional disaster preparedness program. Through the periodic inspections and information-gathering activities outlined here, staff can reduce an institution's vulnerability to disaster. Some of this information may be gathered in regular tours of the building, while other elements can be ascertained in conversations with others in the organization.

The information gathered is of use in two primary ways. First, some conditions will require repair, replacement, or other maintenance activity. For example, if drains are not flowing freely from the roof, a simple cleaning will remedy that condition. Or if fire extinguishers are missing from a critical area, they may be purchased and installed. Second, staff will identify some conditions that are not easily remediable. The existence of such conditions will alert the institution to vulnerabilities that must be considered in the institution's disaster plan. For example, if there is no automatic fire suppression capability, it may not be immediately installed. But this vulnerability should signal the disaster preparedness team to plan carefully for other strategies that will reduce the risk of fire.

In actual use, an institution may create its own checklists based on the frequency with which each item needs to be checked. Some will need attention only once or every few years (e.g., identifying the type of roof on the structure). Others will require annual or semi-annual inspections, as is the case with furnace and boiler inspections. Still others will merit monthly or quarterly attention, such as fire extinguisher inspections and examination of the plumbing.

Many of the inspections outlined here are likely to be the duty of personnel responsible for facilities maintenance. In those cases, the repository staff need only develop mechanisms for learning of remedial actions that are needed and verify that the inspections are done as scheduled. Those areas not included in inspections by facilities staff should be assigned to staff in the library or archives. One individual should keep copies of the completed checklists and track progress in completing repairs and other actions noted on the forms—this may be done by the administrator responsible for the building or by the chair of the disaster preparedness committee.

Most librarians and archivists require some education in order to carry out a disaster preparedness program. A bibliography of readings (available from SOLINET Preservation Services) will provide a good starting point.

Training programs on disaster preparedness are offered by SOLINET and other organizations throughout the country. Contact the Preservation staff at the above address for further information.

Area/Item to be Inspected	Condition OK?	Action Required (Describe in detail)	Action Complete (date and initial)
1. Outdoor hazards:			
* Railings, benches, planters, light/flag poles well anchored?	yes / no	_____	_____
* Overhanging trees/branches trimmed?	yes / no	_____	_____
2. Building:			
* No sign of cracks/seepage visible in exterior or interior walls?	yes / no	_____	_____
* Compliance with seismic, fire, electrical, and other codes?	yes / no	_____	_____
3. Roof:			
* "Sloped" or "pitched" (i.e., not flat)?	yes / no	_____	_____
* Roof covering sound? No buckling/bubbles, leaks, cracks, standing water?	yes / no	_____	_____
* Flashing/caulking intact?	yes / no	_____	_____
* Equipment on roof prohibited? or (if present) properly anchored?	yes / no	_____	_____
4. Drainage: (eaves, gutters, downspouts, scuppers, drains, interior columns)			
* Connected into sewer system? Water directed away from building footings?	yes / no	_____	_____

Area/Item to be Inspected	Condition OK?	Action Required (Describe in detail)	Action Complete (date and initial)
* Draining freely?	yes	_____	_____
	no	_____	_____
* Good drainage around doors?	yes	_____	_____
	no	_____	_____
5. Windows and skylights:			
* Caulking/sealants sound?	yes	_____	_____
	no	_____	_____
* Trees/limbs trimmed away?	yes	_____	_____
	no	_____	_____
6. Fire safety:			
* Fire-resistant structure?	yes	_____	_____
	no	_____	_____
* Concrete flooring, with no air passages between floors?	yes	_____	_____
	no	_____	_____
* Concealed spaces (e.g., false ceilings) identified?	yes	_____	_____
	no	_____	_____
* Fire detection in all concealed spaces?	yes	_____	_____
	no	_____	_____
* Stairways and pipe shafts enclosed?	yes	_____	_____
	no	_____	_____
* Electrical wiring in good condition?	yes	_____	_____
	no	_____	_____
* Appliance cords in good condition?	yes	_____	_____
	no	_____	_____
* Appliances unplugged nightly?	yes	_____	_____
	no	_____	_____

Area/Item to be Inspected	Condition OK?	Action Required (Describe in detail)	Action Complete (date and initial)
* Do staff have keys to mechanical rooms and janitorial closets?	yes no	———————— ————————	———————— ————————
* Regular Fire Marshall visits?	yes no	———————— ————————	———————— ————————
* Fire Marshall visits used productively? (e.g., floor plans given to Fire Department; high priority collection areas noted; appropriate follow-up on observed Code violations)	yes no	———————— ————————	———————— ————————
* Detection systems:			
- appropriate type(s) present?	yes no	———————— ————————	———————— ————————
- wired to 24-hour monitoring station?	yes no	———————— ————————	———————— ————————
- tested regularly?	yes no	———————— ————————	———————— ————————
* Appropriate extinguishers present? Inspected appropriately and on schedule?	yes no	———————— ————————	———————— ————————
* Automatic suppression system (i.e., sprinklers, Halon) present and operating?	yes no	———————— ————————	———————— ————————
* Staff trained in:			
- sounding alarms?	yes no	———————— ————————	———————— ————————
- interpreting annunciator panels (if present)?	yes no	———————— ————————	———————— ————————

Area/Item to be Inspected	Condition OK?	Action Required (Describe in detail)	Action Complete (date and initial)
- notifying Fire Dept. and others as called for?	yes	_____	_____
	no	_____	_____
- using extinguishers?	yes	_____	_____
	no	_____	_____
- turning off power, HVAC, sprinklers, gas main?	yes	_____	_____
	no	_____	_____
- closing fire doors?	yes	_____	_____
	no	_____	_____
- overseeing evacuation?	yes	_____	_____
	no	_____	_____

7. Heating, ventilation, and
air-conditioning (HVAC) system:

* Automatic shut-off capacity in event of fire?	yes	_____	_____
	no	_____	_____
* Furnace/boiler inspected each fall?	yes	_____	_____
	no	_____	_____
* Air conditioning:			
- no leaks?	yes	_____	_____
	no	_____	_____
- no mold present?	yes	_____	_____
	no	_____	_____
- effective drainage from condensation-collecting pans?	yes	_____	_____
	no	_____	_____
- dehumidification capacity?	yes	_____	_____
	no	_____	_____

Area/Item to be Inspected	Condition OK?	Action Required (Describe in detail)	Action Complete (date and initial)
- capable of operating on exhaust to reduce smoke?	yes no	_____ _____	_____ _____
8. Stack areas:			
* Shelves well braced?	yes no	_____ _____	_____ _____
* No water sources located above collections?	yes no	_____ _____	_____ _____
* Books shelved snugly?	yes no	_____ _____	_____ _____
* Shelving 4–6" off floor?	yes no	_____ _____	_____ _____
* "Canopies" atop shelving units?	yes no	_____ _____	_____ _____
* No valuable materials in basement?	yes no	_____ _____	_____ _____
* Exits unobstructed?	yes no	_____ _____	_____ _____
* Important collections away from windows?	yes no	_____ _____	_____ _____
9. Protection from water damage:			
* Pipes and plumbing well supported?	yes no	_____ _____	_____ _____
* No pipe/plumbing leaks?	yes no	_____ _____	_____ _____
* Water detectors present?	yes no	_____ _____	_____ _____

Area/Item to be Inspected	Condition OK?	Action Required (Describe in detail)	Action Complete (date and initial)
* Sump pumps and back-ups present?	yes	_____	_____
	no	_____	_____
* Appropriate dehumidifiers available?	yes	_____	_____
	no	_____	_____
* No leakage/seepage through walls?	yes	_____	_____
	no	_____	_____
* Valuable materials stored above ground level?	yes	_____	_____
	no	_____	_____
* Valuable and fragile media stored in protective enclosures?	yes	_____	_____
	no	_____	_____
* Do staff have keys to mechanical rooms and janitorial closets?	yes	_____	_____
	no	_____	_____
* Do staff know location of water main and have appropriate tools (if needed) for shut-off?	yes	_____	_____
	no	_____	_____

10. Security:

Area/Item to be Inspected	Condition OK?	Action Required	Action Complete
* Book drops (if any) located away from building or in fire resistant enclosure?	yes	_____	_____
	no	_____	_____
* Building exterior well lighted?	yes	_____	_____
	no	_____	_____
* Locks/alarms on all windows and doors?	yes	_____	_____
	no	_____	_____
* Intrusion detectors/alarms present and monitored 24 hours?	yes	_____	_____
	no	_____	_____
* Effective closing procedures to ensure building is vacant?	yes	_____	_____
	no	_____	_____

Area/Item to be Inspected	Condition OK?	Action Required (Describe in detail)	Action Complete (date and initial)
11. Housekeeping:			
* Cleaning supplies and other flammables stored safely?	yes / no	_____ / _____	_____ / _____
* Trash removed nightly?	yes / no	_____ / _____	_____ / _____
* Staff room cleaned daily and well?	yes / no	_____ / _____	_____ / _____
* Smoking prohibited?	yes / no	_____ / _____	_____ / _____
* Food and drink prohibited? And prohibition enforced?	yes / no	_____ / _____	_____ / _____
* Pest management strategies in place and effective?	yes / no	_____ / _____	_____ / _____
12. Insurance:			
* Policy up to date?	yes / no	_____ / _____	_____ / _____
* "Acts of God" covered?	yes / no	_____ / _____	_____ / _____
* Replacement costs specified as needed?	yes / no	_____ / _____	_____ / _____
* Staff aware of records required for claim, and those records maintained safely?	yes / no	_____ / _____	_____ / _____
* Duplicate shelflist, catalog, inventory, and/or back-up computer tapes for entire collection?	yes / no	_____ / _____	_____ / _____

Area/Item to be Inspected	Condition OK?	Action Required (Describe in detail)	Action Complete (date and initial)

13. Construction projects:

* Responsibility for fire safety precautions clearly specified in contract?

    yes   _____   _____

    no   _____   _____

* Fire guards used in all cutting/welding operations?

    yes   _____   _____

    no   _____   _____

* Debris removed nightly?

    yes   _____   _____

    no   _____   _____

* Fire-resistant partitions used?

    yes   _____   _____

    no   _____   _____

* Extra fire extinguishers on hand?

    yes   _____   _____

    no   _____   _____

Julie Arnott
Manager, Preservation Services
SOLINET, Inc.
Atlanta, GA

HOW TO USE THE CD-ROM

PURPOSE

The CD-ROM portion of this book contains:

- A template for a disaster plan draft that lays out the rudimentary elements of a strategic response to emergency events presenting potential threats to a particular facility.
- A directory of consultants that aid in recovery operations.
- A Web site kit containing files, images, and links that provide guidance in developing a disaster mitigation Web site.

These items serve as tools for the development of a cohesive plan to aid in the mitigation of a disaster event. Users should feel free to take as much or as little from the CD-ROM as is needed to put together an informative and functional disaster plan.

HOW TO ACCESS THE CD-ROM

*These instructions describe how to access the contents of the CD-ROM for Windows Operating Systems.

Insert the CD-ROM in the computer's disc drive. Click on the **Start** (Figure 1) button, then the **Run** (Figure 2) command. Type "d:/" at the prompt. This will bring up the file contents of the CD-ROM.

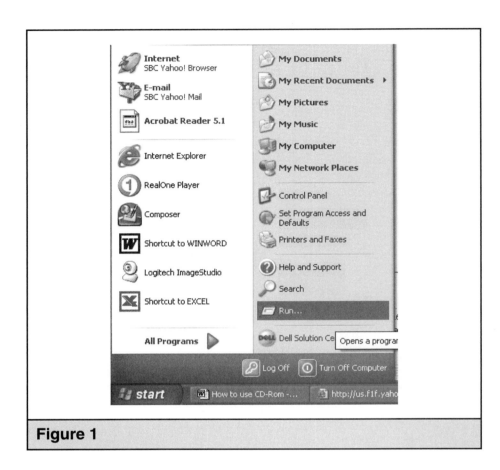

Figure 1

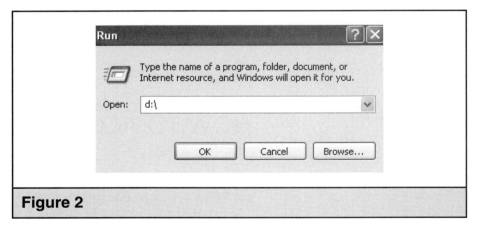

Figure 2

HOW TO USE CD-ROM CONTENTS

This CD-ROM contains 2 documents: the disaster plan template and a folder containing the Web site kit. The disaster plan template lays out the rudimentary elements of a strategic response to emergency events that present a potential threat to a particular facility. The disaster Web site kit uses the document created for the template to build a more sophisticated site with links to the Internet.

DISASTER PLAN TEMPLATE

The Disaster Plan Template is a Word document that provides the layout of a comprehensive approach to responding to emergency events. The template asks the plan's developer to enter information. Simply, place the cursor wherever you need to fill in the exact information and enter the required information. The remainder of this section will look at the different components of the plan and how they should be completed.

The **Introduction** should include the scope and purpose of the plan as well as the following key elements:

- Disaster definitions
- How often the plan will be updated
- Identification of the main author
- The location of the print and electronic copy of the disaster plan

Members of the **Disaster Team** should be listed by position along with their corresponding duties. The matrix found in this section allows for the insertion of contact information and provides suggested duties for each member of the disaster team. Key members of the team include the director or deputy director, collections manager, accountant, security officer, human resource representative, systems head, public relations representative, and facilities manager.

Emergency Contacts portion of the plan contains a directory of local, state, and national agencies. Simply click on the "click here to type" prompt and enter the phone number of the agency.

The next section of the disaster plan template addresses **Library Closure Procedures**. Click on the prompt in order to insert information about the closing authority, media notification and evacuation procedures.

The template has a checklist of **Communications Equipment** and **Disaster Supplies for Immediate Response**. Click in the box next to the items that are available at your facility.

The **Emergency Systems** section of the plan provides ideas about the sort of mechanisms in a facility that mitigates disaster events. List those systems that are available in your institution.

The section **Emergency Plan for Specific Emergencies** provides cues for developing a strategy for reacting to disasters specific to a particular geographic area. Complete this section with regard to disaster events that could threaten your facility using the **Preparing By Knowing Your Disaster** chapter.

The final portion of the template asks for information about your disaster recovery consultants. Information should include the Company name, address, phone number and, if available, the Web address.

DISASTER WEB SITE KIT

The **Disaster Mitigation Web** provides a framework on which to build an online version of the disaster plan. Its purpose is to keep employees informed whether they are at their desktops or at remote locations. The site, if updated regularly, can:

- Propagate details of and changes to the plan quickly.
- Connect employees with information about conditions that can affect a facility locally.
- Grant easy access to downloadable print copies of the plan.
- Serve as an effective communication tool during a disaster.

NOTE: You may need to obtain assistance from your technology department if you are not familiar with developing and/or posting Web sites.

In the event of a computer network attack or catastrophic damage to your facility, it would be reasonable to have a backup of site kept both on and off site for ready retrieval. If your Web site is in any degree dynamic, it makes sense to schedule regular backups. Backups are simple and can be done within a short period of time as opposed to the time it would take to rebuild your site from scratch.

Blackouts pose a different sort of problem that can be overcome by installing a backup power supply before the blackout occurs. Your site will remain available to employees who are offsite and hopefully in areas not affected by the blackout. Backup power supply units actually run on battery power—not generators—and can cost as little as $70 or run into the tens of thousands of dollars. They can be purchased at most computer and electronic stores.

Another helpful precaution in the event of a blackout (to be used in conjunction with the backup power supply) is to have key portions of the site accessible by a *Personal Digital Assistant* (PDA). PDAs use wireless technology and they are battery-operated. What is more, many of today's cell phones have some of the same capabilities as PDAs. Should you have to rely on information from your Web site for communications, having principal elements of the site PDA compatible would provide a useful fall-back. The Disaster Mitigation Web has not been designed to be PDA accessible, however your site can be customized using HTML and XML.

THE DISASTER WEB KIT INDEX

In the Disaster Web Kit Site, you will find an index to a number of templates for pages in your Web site. You are able to edit these pages so that they reflect the issues facing your institution.

EDITING PAGES IN THE WEB SITE

To edit the pages on the Disaster Web you should first create a Disaster Web Kit folder on you computer's hard drive, then copy the files on the CD-ROM to it. Using your Web editor go to File > Open. Browse to files that are found in the folder that you have created for your Disaster Web. Open the file that you would like to edit. At this point, you may add or modify the content to the center column.

Note:
If your knowledge of HTML is limited, you may want to use a WYSIWYG (pronounced *WIS-ee-wig*) or What You See Is What You Get. In this type of application, as a page is created or edited, the page displays as it would in a browser. This use of this type of editor makes it easy to cut and paste information your web pages. Examples of WYSIWYGs include: Dreamweaver, Microsoft Frontpage, and Netscape Composer.

These pages can also be created using Notepad. However, you must know how to use HTML.

CREATING NEW PAGES

The **Disaster Mitigation Web** site is designed to be expandable. For this reason, templates (Figure 4) are provided so that new pages can be created while maintaining the look and feel of the site. To see the **Page Template** (page_template.html), open the **template** folder (**DisasterWebKit\ template**). The template contains links to other files in your site in the **Left Menu**. The center column is left blank for the main text of your page. The **Right Menu** contains helpful tools to keep your site dynamic and your visitors abreast of current conditions.

To use the template, add your content to the center column. Then go to **File>Save As . . .** and name your new file. Be sure to save it in the correct directory. *Do not* save your file in the template directory.

VIEWING THE WEB FILES ON THE INTERNET

When viewing the site on the CD-ROM, the **Index** page should be loaded first. It is the starting point in any directory when the site is loaded onto a Web server. To get to the *index.html* in the main directory of the Disaster Web Kit follow these steps:

1. Open your Internet browser
2. Go to **File > Open . . . (Ctrl + O)**
3. Browse to the **d:** drive and click on the **Disaster-WebKit** folder
4. Select **index**
5. Click on the **Open** button

HOME PAGE

index.html

The **Index** page—also called the Home page—serves as the jumping off point for the site (Figure 4). An area has been provided for announcements such as drills, training, and changes to the site. This is also a good place to alert site visitors to potential hazardous events as the season or situation presents itself (i.e., hurricane season, winter/summer storms). In the introduction, discuss the purpose and scope of your disaster plan just as it is discussed in the print version of the plan that was drawn up using the **Disaster Template**.

At the bottom of the page are links to pages that provide instructions for specific hazards that could threaten a particular facility. You will need to create these pages, and then link to them from the Home page. We will look at this more closely when we address the **Hazards** directory.

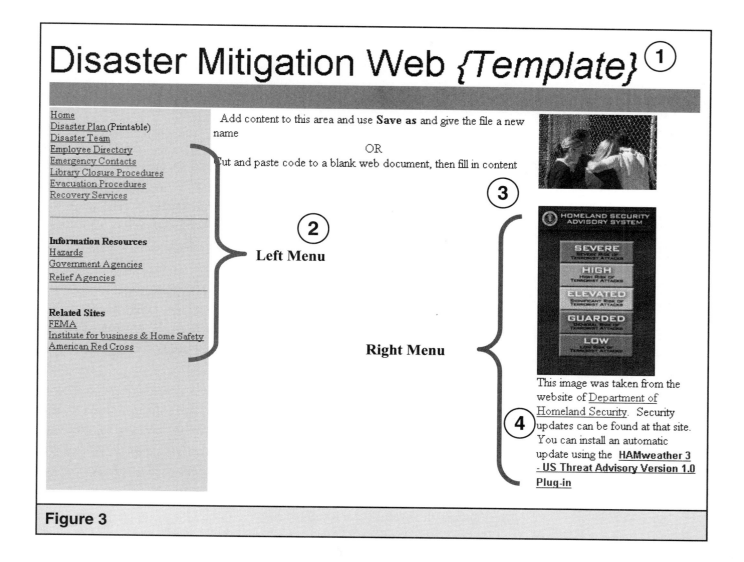

Figure 3

FIGURE 3

Elements of a page

The **Disaster Mitigation Web** follows a basic template (Figure3). The look and feel of the site is controlled by a Cascading Style Sheet (CSS) found in the template.css file.It defines the positioning and the style of the web pages.

To access the CSS file: right-click on the Start button, select Explore, and browse the DisasterWebKit folder for the **template.css** file.

The elements of the Disaster Web template are as follows:

1. Site Title: Replace the generic title with the name of your library and/or add your library's logo. Change the

position and style of this using the element h1.pagetitle in the **template.css** file.

2. Left Menu: The Left Menu is comprised primarily of links to internal pages that are the basic components of a disaster web site. This menu can be modified to include as many or as few of the links that may be necessary for the implementation of your web site. Use the element **p.lmenu** in **template.css** file to change the look of this section.

3. Main: This is the focal point of each page in your site. It contains the page title and all of the information that you will be presenting. You can write the content for the page in WORD, then cut and paste the content to the **Main** section of the page. Modifications to the style can be made using the element **div.main** in the **template.css** file.

4. Right Menu: The Right Menu contains alerts and services that you may want to provide to your users. These are applications that must be downloaded. If you would like to include any of the services referenced in this menu, links to the site where the services can be downloaded are provided. The style elements are **div.rmenu** and **p.features.**

To use the template, add your content to the center column or the Main section. Then go to File>Save or, if you are creating a new page, go to File>Save As... and name your new file.

Viewing the Web Files on the Internet

When viewing the site on the CD-ROM, the Index page should be loaded first. Follow these steps in order to get to the index.html in the folder that you have created for the Disaster Web Kit:

1. Open your Internet browser.
2. Go to **File>Open**... (Ctrl + O)
3. Browse to the **DisasterWebKit** folder
4. Select **index**
5. Click on the **Open** button

Migrating Your Site to the Server

Once you have made all of the modifications required to get your Disaster website going, your site is ready to be published. You will need access to a web server and a means of uploading your files. Your web server may contain an existing web site or you will have a site dedicated to your Disaster site, simply upload the entire **DisasterWebKit** directory to your server. Otherwise upload the contents of the main directory of the DisasterWebKit to the root directory of your newly created website.

Files are uploaded using a File Transfer Protocol (FTP) application such as WS_ftp, or Secure Shell (SSH). Some web editors such as Frontpage or Dreamweaver have their own file transfer mechanism. Once you have established assess to your server, file transfers are as simply as a click of a button. For more information on file transfers, consult with your Information Technology staff. Also, PageResource.com (http://www.page resource.com/putweb/ftpmain.htm) has a good tutorial regarding this process.

Disaster Web Index
index.html

The **Disaster Web Index** main section contains an area where you can post announcements such as drills, training, and/or changes to the site. This is also a good place to alert site visitors to potential hazardous events as the season and/or situation presents itself (i.e. hurricane season, winter/ summer storms).

Disaster Plan (Printable)
disastertemplate.doc

A link to the print version of the disaster plan can be found in the left menu. This enables visitors to download their own copy of the disaster plan. You should not make accessible any of the attachments (i.e. insurance documents) that are sensitive in nature.

The template is in Word Document format primarily so that it can be completed before it is loaded on the web. Once the disaster plan has been completed, convert the file to a Portable Document Format (.PDF). This requires the full version of Adobe Acrobat.

Disaster Team
Disaster_Team.html

This page lists the members of the disaster team, their position and contact information, and their responsibilities during a disaster. This page lists the suggested duties for each member. Please modify to suit your organization's need.

Employee Directory
Employee_Directory.html

An empty template is found on this page. It is up to the individual organization as to what format the Employee Directory should take. The following are possible format:

- An alphabetical listing of employees and their contact information.
- A phone tree that indicates the order in which employees should be notified. According to this model each employee is required to call the next person on the list.

Emergency Contacts
Emergency_Contacts.html

The Emergency Contacts page contains a directory for essential emergency agencies at the local, state, and national level. Enter the appropriate phone numbers the agency that should be associated with your organization.

Closure Procedures
Closure_Procedures.html

The Closure Procedures page contains cues for entering your organization's procedures for closing operations in the event of an emergency. Information about the closing authority and media notification should be provided here.

Evacuation Procedures
Evacuation_Procedures.html

This page provides procedures that can be made specific to every section of the library. List the staff from each department that is responsible for evacuation of that department as well as the public areas near the department. Provide information about the location of emergency exits and gathering place. Link to floor plans if available.

Government Agencies
Government_Agencies.html

This page contains links to government agencies that can provide assistance before, during or after a disaster.

Relief Agencies
Relief_Agencies.html

The Relief Agencies page provides links to organizations that can assist in recovery efforts.

Images Directory

All of the images on the site are located in the **images** folder.

Web Development Resources

> Writing HTML
> http://www.mcli.dist.maricopa.edu/tut/lessons.html
> W3Schools HTML Tutorial
> http://www.w3schools.com/html/default.asp
> Useit.com: Jakob Nielson's Website
> http://www.useit.com/
> HTML Goodies: HTML Primer
> http://www.htmlgoodies.com/primers/html/
> W3Schools CSS Tutorial
> http://www.w3schools.com/css/default.asp
> EchoEcho.com CSS Tutorial
> http://www.echoecho.com/css.htm
> CSS Tutorials
> http://www.htmlcenter.com/tutorials/index.cfm/css/

BIBLIOGRAPHY

BOOKS

Alire, Camila. *Library Disaster Planning and Recovery Handbook.* New York: Neal-Schuman, 2000.

Buck, George. *Preparing for Terrorism: An Emergency Services Guide.* Albany, NY: Delmar/Thomson Learning, 2002.

Genovese, Robert, Taylor, Trish, and White, Edward. *Disaster Preparedness Manual.* Buffalo, NY: W.S. Hein, 2003.

George, Susan C. *Emergency Planning and Management in College Libraries.* Chicago: Association of College and Research Libraries, 1994.

Kahn, Miriam B. *Disaster Response and Planning for Libraries.* 2nd ed. Chicago: American Library Association, 2003.

Kunreuther, Howard and Rose, Adam Zachary. *The Economics of Natural Hazards.* Cheltenham, England: Edward Elgar Publishers, 2004.

Matthews, Graham and Feather, John. *Disaster Management for Libraries and Archives.* Aldershot, England: Ashgate Publishers, 2003.

McCracken, Peter H. *The Crucial Inadequacy: Disaster Planning in Libraries and Museums.* Chapel Hill: University of North Carolina Masters Thesis, 1995.

Merrrill, Andrea T. *The Strategic Stewardship of Cultural Resources: To Preserve and Protect.* New York: Haworth Information Press, 2003.

Ogden, Sherelyn. *Preservation of Library & Archival Materials: A Manual.* Andover, MA: Northeast Document Conservation Center, 1999.

Ruzicka, Glen. *Disaster Recovery: Salvaging Books.* Philadelphia: Conseration Center for Art and Historic Artifacts, 2002.

Shuman, Bruce A. *Library Security and Safety Handbook: Prevention, Policies, and Procedures.* Chicago: American Library Association, 1999.

Spignesi, Stephen J. *The 100 Greatest Disasters of All Time.* New York: Citadel Press, 2002.

Sturges, Paul and Rosenberg, Diana. *Disaster and After: The Practicalities of Information Service in Times of War and other Catastrophes: Proceedings of an International Conference Sponsored by IGLA (The International Group of the Library Association), 4–6 September 1998, University of Bristol*. London: Taylor Graham, 1999.

Switzer, Teri R. *Safe at Work?: Library Security and Safety Issues*. Lanham, MD: Scarecrow Press, 1999.

Wellheiser, Johanna G. and Scott, Jude. *An Ounce of Prevention: Integrated Disaster Planning for Archives, Libraries, and Record Centres*. Lanham, MD: Scarecrow Press, 2002.

VIDEOS

Business Continuation and Disaster Recovery. Washington, D.C.: Federal Library and Information Center Committee, Library of Congress, 2002.

Disaster Recovery: The Pentagon Library Experience. Federal Library and Information Center Committee, Library of Congress, 2002.

McColgin, Michael and Slusar, Linda. *Disaster Planning: Soaring to Excellence Videos*. Chicago: American Library Association, 2000.

ARTICLES

"ALA Responds to Terrorist Attacks." *American Libraries* 32, no. 10 (November 2001): 8.

"Amigos IPS Helps Houston Members Recover from Tropical Storm Flooding." *Que Pasa* 22, no. 3 (Fall 2001): 1.

Amirkhani, Gholamreza. "Visitors Find War-Weary Kabul Librarians Struggling to Rebuild." *American Libraries* 33, no. 11 (December 2002): 30.

Baker, Aidan. "Disaster and After." *Library Management* 20, no. 1 (1999): 54–55.

Baker, Whitney. "Preservation Perspectives: Preparing for the Imminent: Protecting Your Collections From a Disaster." *Kentucky Libraries* 66, no. 2 (Spring 2002): 18–19.

Balas, Janet. "Useful Resources for Writing Library Policies." *Computers in Libraries* 22, no. 6 (June 2002): 30–33.

Balik, Vojtech and Polisensky, Jiri. "The National Library of the Czech Republik and the Floods of 2002." *Alexandria* 16, no. 1 (2004): 17–24.

Beinhoff, Lisa A. "Library Earthquake Preparedness Planning: How to Make Sure That Your Library is Ready for the Big One." *Journal of Library Administration* 31, no. 1 (2000): 67–83.

Benefiel, Candace R. and Mosley, Pixey Anne. "Coping with the Unexpected: A Rapid Response Group in an Academic Library." *Technical Services Quarterly* 77, no. 2 (1999): 25–35.

Boccaccio, Mary. "Flood of the Century." *North Carolina Libraries* 58, no. 3 (Fall 2000): 73.

Bodin, Greg. "Malicious Code: Viruses, Worms and Trojan Horses." *Network News* 58 (January 2002).

Bradley, Lynne E. "New Developments Since September 11." *College & Research Libraries News* 62, no. 10 (November 2001): 1012.

Breeding, Marshall. "Defending Your Library Network." *Information Today* 18, no. 8 (September 2001): 46–47.

Butler, Rebecca P. "Software Piracy: Don't Let It Byte You!" *Knowledge Quest* 31, no. 2 (November/December 2002): 41–42.

Chadwell, Faye A. "Planning for the Worst: When Disaster Strikes." *OLA Quarterly* 6, no. 3 (Fall 2000): 16–17.

Childress, Schelley H. "Planning for the Worst: Disaster Planning in the Library." *Southeastern Librarian* 44 (Summer 1994): 51–56.

Clay, Edwin S. "Attack of the Virus: A Library Survival Guide." *Virginia Libraries* 48, no. 4 (October/November/December 2002): 5–7.

Collins, Janet. "One Approach to Earthquake Preparedness." *Information Bulletin (Western Association of Map Libraries)* 27 (July 1996): 128–29.

"Complying With New Enhanced 9–1–1 Requirements: What You Need to Know." *Illinois Library Association Reporter* 19, no. 5 (October 2001): 18–19.

Courtois, Martin P. and Rubin, Claire B. "Crisis, Disaster and Emergency Management." *College & Research Libraries News* 63, no. 10 (November 2002): 723–26.

Crispen, Patrick. "The Weekly Fab Five: Things You Should do Every Week to Keep Your Computer Running in Tip-Top Shape." *Book Report* 20, no. 1 (May/June 2001): 36.

Davis, Mary and Kyger, Ellen. "Flood Destroys North Dakota State University's Main Library." *College & Research Libraries News* 61, no. 8 (September 2000): 661.

DeCandido, GraceAnne Andreassi. "Digital Disaster Planning: When Bad Things Happen to Good Systems." *Public Libraries* 39, no. 5 (September/October 2000): 258–59.

DeLong, Linwood R. "Collections Development and the Red River Flood of 1997: A Case Study in Collecting Information on a Natural Disaster." *Feliciter* 43, no. 10 (October 1997): 18–21.

DiMattia, Susan Smith. "Planning for Continuity: Disaster Plans." *Library Journal* 126, no. 19 (November 15, 2001): 32–34.

Doran, Amanda-Jane. "U.K. Feels the Impact of Terrorist Strikes." *Publishers Weekly* 248, no. 39 (September 24, 2001): 10.

Dropkin, Murray. "Continuing Series on Disaster Planning: Fundraising in the Aftermath." *Nonprofit Report* 11, no. 8 (February 2002): 1–3.

Dropkin, Murray. "Crisis Intervention for Nonprofits: Responding to the Events of September 11, 2001 and Updating Your Organization's Disaster Plan." *Nonprofit Report* 11, no. 5 (November 2001): 1–4.

Eberhart, George M. "The Flood of '97 Wreaks Havoc on Ohio River Valley Libraries." *American Libraries* 28, no. 4 (April 1997): 15–16.

Eberhart, George M. "Floods Devastate Prague's Libraries." *American Libraries* 33, no. 10 (October 2002): 30.

Eberhart, George M. "Floods from Floyd Swamp Eastern Libraries." *American Libraries* 30, no. 11 (November 1999): 13–14.

Eberhart, George M. "German Library Fire Destroys Thousands of Rare Books." *American Libraries* 35, no. 9 (October 2004): 12.

Eberhart, George M. "Libraries Forego Funds to Aid Flood-Ravaged Pendleton County." *American Libraries* 28, no. 10 (October 1997): 14.

Eberhart, George M. "South Dakota Tornado Demolishes Library." *American Libraries* 29, no. 8 (August 1998): 15–16.

Eberhart, George M. "Washington Earthquake Topples Books, Skews Shelving." *American Libraries* 32, no. 4 (April 2001): 22–23.

Eberhart, George M. "West Virginia Libraries Hit Hard by Floods." *American Libraries* 32, no. 8 (August 2001): 15.

Eden, Paul and Matthews, Graham. "Disaster Management in Libraries." *Library Management* 17, no. 3 (1996): 5–12.

Egerton, Angela, Kendall, Ellen and Resnik, Rhea. "From the Bottom Up: School Library Media Centers and the Flood of 1999." *North Carolina Libraries* 58, no. 3 (Fall 2000): 64–66.

Ekhaml, Leticia T. "Protecting Yourself from Internet Risks, Threats and Crime." *Journal of Educational Media & Library Sciences* 39, no. 1 (September 2001).

Eng, Sidney. "How Technology and Planning Saved My Library at Ground Zero." *Computers in Libraries* 22, no. 4 (April 2002): 28–35.

Estabrook, Leigh S. "Coping, View 2: Response Disappointing." *American Libraries* 33, no. 8 (September 2002): 37–38.

Ezennia, Steve E. "Flood, Earthquake, Libraries and Library Materials." *Library & Archival Security* 13, no. 1 (1995): 21–27.

Fineberg, Gail. "Surviving the War: Library Sends a Team to Aid Iraqi Librarians." *Library of Congress Information Bulletin* 62, no. 12 (December 2003): 298–301, 305.

Fisher, Steven P. and Fry, Thomas K. "Security and Emergency Preparedness in a University Library: Planning Works." *Colorado Libraries* 23 (Spring 1997): 9–11.

Flagg, Gordon. "Flooding Closes Library at University of Maryland." *American Libraries* 31, no. 10 (October 2000): 15.

Flagg, Gordon. "Most Libraries Spared in Oregon Floods." *American Libraries* 27, no. 3 (March 1996): 11.

Flagg, Gordon. "Nimda Worm Hits Library Computers." *American Libraries* 32, no. 10 (November 2001): 21–22.

Flagg, Gordon. "North Dakota State University Fights to Salvage Flooded Materials." *American Libraries* 31, no. 8 (August 2000): 16.

Flagg, Gordon. "Oklahoma City Bomb Explosion Closes Downtown Library." *American Libraries* 26, no. 6 (June 1995): 490–91.

Flagg, Gordon. "Rainstorm Floods Stanford University's Main Library." *American Libraries* 29, no. 3 (March 1998): 14.

Flagg, Gordon. "Red River Flood Takes Toll on North Dakota, Minnesota Libraries." *American Libraries* 28, no. 6/7 (June/July 1997): 16–17.

Flagg, Gordon. "Torrential Rains Flood Libraries in Illinois, Pennsylvania." *American Libraries* 27, no. 9 (September 1996): 12.

"Flood Recovery Health Concerns." *The Unabashed Librarian* 104 (1997): 17–18.

"Flooded Library Has New Home, Far From River's Reach." *School Library Journal* 42, no. 8 (August 1996): 14.

"The Floods: Huge Losses at Lewes." *Library Association Record* 102, no. 12 (December 2000): 663.

Friedman, Ann M. "Libraries in Times of Emergency—Lessons Learned." *Virginia Libraries* 48, no. 1 (January/February/March 2002).

George, Susan C. "Library Disasters: Are You Prepared?" *College & Research Libraries News* 2 (February 1995): 80.

Gillespie, Karen. "Elements in Developing a Library Emergency Plan." *Kentucky Libraries* 58 (Summer 1994): 10–11.

Giovannini, M. Andrea. "Pour un Plan de Prevention et D'Intervention en Cas de Catastrophe." *Arbido* 17, no. 1 (January 2002): 5–12.

Goldberg, Beverly. "Flood Rings in Soggy Year at Olympic College Library." *American Libraries* 28, no. 2 (February 1997): 21.

Goldsborough, Reid. "Keeping Hackers Away with Personal Firewalls." *Teacher Librarian* 29, no. 2 (December 2001): 40.

Goodes, Pamela A. "California Libraries Offer Fire-Recovery Assistance." *American Libraries* 34, no. 11 (December 2003): 16–17.

Grant, Alison M. "Benighted! How the University Library Survived the Auckland Power Crisis." *Australian Academic & Research Libraries* 31, no. 2 (June 2000): 61–68.

Greene, Harlan. "Build It and They Will Come: Libraries and Disaster Preparedness." *North Carolina Libraries* 52 (Spring 1994): 6–7.

Haislip, Ron. "Knee Deep in North Carolina: A Disaster Planning Manual." *North Carolina Libraries* 58, no. 3 (Fall 2000): 54–56.

Halsted, Deborah. "HAM-TMC Library Recovery Efforts." *Texas Medical Center News* 23, no. 14 (August 1, 2001): 10, 25.

Halsted, Deborah and Keeney, Mike. "Libraries in Crisis: Accounts of the Houston Floods: Damage from Tropical Storm Allison at the Houston Academy of Medicine and the Aldine Independent School District." *Texas Library Journal* 77, no. 3 (Fall 2001): 112–14.

Hane, Paula. "Information Professionals Respond Following Terrorist Attacks." *Information Today* 18, no. 9 (October 2001): 3.

Hane, Paula J. "Update: More Disaster Recovery Resources." *Information Today* 18, no. 10 (November 2001): 14–15.

Harger, Elaine. "Reflections on a Firebombing." *School Libraries in Canada (Online)* 23, no. 4 (2004): 1.

Hayes, Laura. "Coping, View 1: Programs Laudable." *American Libraries* 33, no. 8 (September 2002).

Higginbotham, Barbra Buckner. "Before Disaster Strikes; Be Prepared." *Technicalities* 15 (July 1995): 4–5.

Higginbotham, Barbra Buckner. "It Ain't Over 'Til It's Over: The Process of Disaster Recovery." *Technicalities* 16 (May 1996): 12–13.

Higginbotham, Barbra Buckner. "Managing Emergencies: Small Construction Projects: Concrete Dust at Brooklyn College Library." *Technicalities* 16 (October 1996): 1.

Hinegardner, Patricia Gail and Mayo, Alexa A. "Selected Bioterrorism Web Sites for the Health Care Community and Consumer." *Internet Reference Services Quarterly* 6, no. 3/4 (2002): 1–15.

Hobbs, Lenora. "Chaos Limitation: Emergency Response Plans." *Public Libraries* 38, no. 5 (September/October 1999): 277.

Holt, Eric A. "Making Your Network Secure." *Louisiana Libraries* 64, no. 1 (Summer 2001): 28–30.

Intner, Sheila S. "After September 11th." *Technicalities* 21, no. 6 (November/December 2001).

Johnson, Doug. "The Hoax on You." *Book Report* 21, no. 1 (May/June 2002).

Jordan, Amy. "Water-Damaged Texas Library Condemned, Closed." *American Libraries* 33, no. 5 (May 2002).

Junion-Metz, Gail. "In Tragedy's Wake." *School Library Journal* 47, no. 11 (November 2001): 31.

Kahn, Miriam. "Fires, Earthquakes and Floods: How to Prepare Your Library and Staff." *Online (Weston, Conn.)* 18 (May 1994): 18.

Kalyan, Sulekha, Bao, Xue-Ming and Deyrup, Marta M. "Academic Libraries' Emergency Plans for Inclement Weather." *Library Administration & Management* 15, no. 4 (Fall 2001): 223–29.

Kane, Kim. "You Too Can Do a Disaster Plan." *Library Mosaics* 12, no. 2 (March/April 2001): 12–13.

Keiser, Barbie E. "Safety First: Part Two." *Searcher* 12, no. 6 (June 2004): 21–25.

Keiser, Barbie E. "Safety First: Where? When? Why Me?" *Searcher* 12, no. 5 (May 2004): 16–23.

Keiser, Barbie E. "The Web as Safety Net: Weather-Related Catastrophes and Other Natural Disasters." *Searcher* 10, no. 1 (January 2002).

Kemp, Barbara E. "Tropical Storm Allison." *College & Research Library News* 62, no. 9 (October 2001): 899.

Kenney, Brian. "Central Libraries in Uncertain Times." *Library Journal* 126, no. 19 (November 15, 2001): 36–37.

Kim, Taeock and Goodwater, Leanna. "Submerged: How a California Library was Invaded by Rising Groundwater—and Survived." *American Libraries* 34, no. 10 (December 2003): 50–52.

Kniffel, Leonard. "Flood Toll at Colorado State Could Reach $100 Million." *American Libraries* 28, no. 9 (September 1997): 16.

Kniffel, Leonard. "Floods Devastate Libraries in Southwestern Poland." *American Libraries* 28, no. 9 (September 1997): 28.

Kniffel, Leonard. "A Moving Target in the War on Terrorism." *American Libraries* 33, no. 11 (December 2002): 18–19.

Kniffel, Leonard. "Nation on Alert." *American Libraries* 32, no. 12 (December 2001): 14–17.

Kniffel, Leonard. "Remembering September 11." *American Libraries* 33, no. 8 (September 2002): 30–34.

Kniffel, Leonard. "Terrorist Attacks Shatter American Sense of Security." *American Libraries* 32, no. 9 (October 2001): 20–21.

Kniffel, Leonard. "Traumatized by Terrorism." *American Libraries* 32, no. 10 (November 2001).

Kresh, Diane Nester. "Courting Disaster: Building a Collection to Chronicle 9/11 and its Aftermath." *Library of Congress Information Bulletin* 61, no. 9 (September 2002): 151–55.

Kristl, Carol. "Fort Worth Public Library Tornado Damages Top $1.2 Million." *American Libraries* 31, no. 5 (May 2000): 20.

Lau, Debra, Jones, Trev, and Minkel, Walter. "Librarians Cope with Post-9/11 World." *School Library Journal* 48, no. 8 (August 2002): 14–15.

Lederer, Naomi and Ernest, Douglas J. "Managing the Media During a Library Crisis." *American Libraries* 33, no. 11 (December 2002): 32–33.

Levack, Kinley. "Digital Darwinism: Piracy Pushes Progress." *Econtent* 25, no. 9 (September 2002): 6, 8–9.

Loving, Matthew. "The War on Terror: Darkest Days." *American Libraries* 33, no. 5 (May 2002): 68–72.

Mahony, Alan P. "Federal Office Bombing Closes Downtown Oklahoma City Library." *Wilson Library Bulletin* 69 (June 1995): 14.

Manley, Will. "Freedom or Security?" *American Libraries* 32, no. 11 (December 2001): 112.

Matthews, Graham and Eden, Paul. "Disaster Management Training in Libraries." *Library Review (Glasgow, Scotland)* 45, no. 1 (1996): 30–38.

Matthews, Graham and Eden, Paul. "Heading Off Disaster." *Library Association Record* 97, no. 5 (May 1995): 271.

McCormick, Edith. "Tornadoes Sock Libraries in Southern Minnesota." *American Libraries* 29, no. 5 (May 1998): 18–19.

McDermott, Irene E. "Danger, Will Robinson!: Emergency Alerts, Warnings and Advisories on the Web." *Searcher* 9, no. 9 (October 2001): 58–62.

McPherson, Keith. "Emergencies and School Libraries: Making Safety a Priority." *School Libraries in Canada (Online)* 23, no. 4 (2004): 1.

Melville, Keith. "Coming to Terms with Terrorism." *Kettering Review* 20, no. 1 (Winter 2002): 23–50.

Meraz, Gloria. "Libraries After 9/11." *Texas Library Journal* 77, no. 4 (Winter 2001): 128–29.

Milliot, Jim, Zeitchik, Steven M., and Baker, John F. "After the Attack, Industry Moves Forward." *Publishers Weekly* 248, no. 39 (September 24, 2001): 9–10.

Miltner, Terrence C. "Libraries Damaged in Maryland Tornado." *American Libraries* 32, no. 10 (November 2001): 21.

Minkel, Walter. "Is Your Server Safe?" *School Library Journal* 47, no. 11 (November 2001): 25, 27.

Morgan, G. Gillian and Smith, J. Gretchen. "Disaster Management in Libraries: The Role of a Disaster Plan." *South African Journal of Library and Information Science* 65 (March 1997): 62–71.

Muir, Adrienne and Shenton, Sarah. "If the Worst Happens: The Use and Effectiveness of Disaster Plans in Libraries and Archives." *Library Management* 23, no. 3 (2002): 115–23.

Mullin, Christopher G. "Planning for Disaster: Some Ideas About Where to Begin." *PNLA Quarterly* 60 (Spring 1996): 11–12.

Mutter, John, Howell, Kevin and Nawotka, Edward. "Bookstores Regroup as Customers Seek Answers." *Publishers Weekly* 248, no. 39 (September 24, 2001): 16–17.

Myles, Barbara. "The Impact of a Library Flood on Computer Operations." *Computers in Libraries* 20, no. 1 (January 2000): 44–46.

Novacek, Julie. "Coping in New York." *American Libraries* 32, no. 10 (November 2001): 18–19.

Oder, Norman and Kenney, Brian J. "Attack on NYC, DC Victimizes, Strains Libraries, Librarians." *Library Journal* 126, no. 16 (October 1, 2001): 16–17.

Ogden, Sherelyn. "Security From Loss: Water and Fire Damage, Biological Agents, Theft, and Vandalism." *Rare Books & Manuscripts Librarianship* 11, no. 1 (1996): 43–47.

Ojala, Marydee. "Net Crisis." *Online (Weston, Conn.)* 25, no. 6 (November/December 2001): 7.

"Oklahoma City Library Children's Staff Responds to Crisis." *School Library Journal* 41, no. 6 (June 1995): 17.

"Oklahoma City Library Reopens." *American Libraries* 26, no. 7 (July/August 1995): 632.

"Oklahoma City Library Reopens Following Terrorist Bomb Attack." *Library Journal* 120, no. 12 (July 1995): 16.

"Oklahoma City PL Recovers in Wake of Horrific Bombing." *Library Journal* 120, no. 9 (May 15 1995): 12–13.

Owens, Brian M. and Brown-Syed, Christopher. "Not in Our Stars: the University of Windsor Archives and Library Disaster Plan." *Library & Archival Security* 14, no. 2 (1998): 61–66.

Pack, Thomas. "Virus Protection." *Link-Up* 19, no. 1 (January/February 2002): 25.

Page, Julie A. "Exercising Your Disaster Plans." *PNLA Quarterly* 66, no. 1 (Fall 2001): 18.

Page, Julie A. "When Disaster Strikes: First Steps in Disaster Preparedness." *Serials Librarian* 36, no. 3–4 (1999): 347–61.

Pelser, Janeen C. and Culpepper, Penny. "What If—." *Florida Media Quarterly* 27, no. 2 (Winter 2002): 33–35.

Pierce, Jennifer Burek. "Recovery in Washington." *American Libraries* 32, no. 10 (November 2001): 16–18.

Rasmus, Francesca Lane. "Earthquake Rocks Pacific Northwest Libraries." *College & Research Libraries News* 62, no. 4 (April 2001): 382.

Ratledge, David D. "Solutions for Library Public PC Security." *Tennessee Librarian* 52, no. 3 (Summer 2001): 5–15.

Reid, Calvin, Zeitchik, Steven M., and Milliot, Jim. "Publishing in the Wake of the WTC Attack." *Publishers Weekly* 248, no. 38 (September 17, 2001): 9–12.

Reinertson-Sand, Mary. "What I Learned From the Flood of 1997; or, Why Archival Class is Essential." *American Libraries* 30, no. 3 (March 1999): 40–45.

Rightmyer, Sandra P. "Disaster Planning; Or, The 'What Next' Attitude." *New Jersey Libraries* 28 (Summer 1995): 3–18.

Riley, Cheryl A. "In an Emergency: Salvaging Library Collections: Report of a Program at the 2000 NASIG Conference." *The Serials Librarian* 40, no. 1/2 (2001): 19–30.

Riley, Julie and Meadows, A. J. "The Role of Information in Disaster Planning: A Case Study Approach." *Library Management* 16, no. 4 (1995): 18–24.

Robertson, Guy. "Hoping for the Best, Preparing for the Worst: A Disaster Planner's Experience." *Feliciter* 41 (1995): 20–25.

Robertson, Guy. "Investigating Risk: Assessing and Analyzing Trouble Before it Strikes." *Feliciter* 48, no. 1 (2002): 30–32.

Robertson, Guy. "Lights Out! Dealing with Power Outages in Your Library." *Feliciter* 50 (2004): 156–58.

Rogers, Michael. "Colorado State University Library Closed by Flooding." *Library Journal* 122, no. 14 (September 1, 1997): 104.

Rogers, Michael. "Nimda Virus Slams Fairfax County, Virginia." *Library Journal* 126, no. 17 (October 15, 2001): 16.

Rogers, Michael. "Tornado Destroys Minnesota Libraries." *Library Journal* 123, no. 8 (May 1, 1998): 14.

Rogers, Michael and DiMattia, Susan Smith. "Heavy Floods Devastate Western/Midwestern Libraries." *Library Journal* 122 (June 1, 1997): 12–13.

Ruyle, Carol J. and Schobernd, Elizabeth M. "Disaster Recovery Without the Disaster." *Technical Services Quarterly* 14, no. 4 (1997): 13–26.

Safran, Franciska and Vaughan, Barbara. "The Charting of the Western New York Disaster Preparedness Network." *Conservation Administration News* 61 (April 1995): 10–13.

Samek, Toni. "Destruction of United Talmud Torah Grade School Library." *School Libraries in Canada (Online)* 23, no. 4 (2004): 1.

Schink, Michael Lee. "Selecting Disaster Recovery Software." *Colorado Libraries* 25, no. 1 (Spring 1999): 38–39.

Schneider, Karen G. "With all Our Heart." *American Libraries* 32, no. 10 (November 2001): 68.

Schuyler, Michael. "A Serious Look at Systems Security." *Computers in Libraries* 22, no. 1 (January 2002).

"A Silver Lining for Two Flood-Soaked Oregon Libraries." *School Library Journal* 42, no. 4 (April 1996): 12.

Smith, Sherrie Kline. "Earthquake Strikes El Salvador Libraries." *American Libraries* 32, no. 3 (March 2001): 24.

Spiegel, Pamala. "Arson Damages Minnesota High School Library." *American Libraries* 33, no. 4 (April 2002): 22.

Stevens, Terri J. "Surviving Terrorism and Other Disasters." *Link-Up* 19, no. 1 (January/February 2002).

Stoneham, Laurie. "Immeasurable Losses: Baylor and UT-Houston Lose more than Animals and Equipment." *Texas Medicine* 97, no. 9 (September 2001): 58–62.

Strickland, Lee S. "Information and the War Against Terrorism." *Bulletin of the American Society for Information Science and Technology* 28, no. 2 (December/January 2002).

Swartz, Betty Jean. "Nuclear Terrorism: A Selection of Internet Resources." *Internet Reference Services Quarterly* 6, no. 3/4 (2002): 87–98.

Taylor, Dee Dee. "Hurricane Survival Tactics: A Public Library Offers Emergency Service of EPIC Proportions." *American Libraries* 35, no. 10 (November 2004): 42–43.

Tennant, Roy. "Digital Libraries: Coping with Disasters." *Library Journal* 126, no. 19 (November 15, 2001): 26–28.

Todaro, Julie Beth. "Managing Through Tragedy." *Library Administration & Management* 16, no. 1 (Winter 2002): 40–43.

"Traumatized by Terrorism." *American Libraries* 32, no. 10 (November 2001): 12–15; 40, no. 1/2 (2001): 19–30.

Verba, Sidney. "Thoughts About the Library, Librarians, and Our Hopes and Fears." *College & Research Libraries News* 62, no. 10 (November 2001): 978.

Volesko, Michele Mary. "It Wasn't Raining When Noah Built the Ark: Disaster Preparedness for Hospitals and Medical Librarians Post September 11." *Internet Reference Services Quarterly* 6, no. 3/4 (2002): 99–131.

Watkins, Christine. "Chapter Report: Disaster Planning Makes (Dollars and) Sense." *American Libraries* 27, no. 9 (September 1996): 9.

Watkins, Christine. "Chapter Report: A Flood of Books for a Damaged Library." *American Libraries* 29, no. 1 (January 1998): 13.

Watt, Marcia A. "2200 Gallons of Water." *Southeastern Librarian* 44 (Summer 1994): 67–68.

Welch, John T. "The Fire Next Time: Disaster Planning & Recovery." *North Carolina Libraries* 58, no. 3 (Fall 2000): 48–73.

Wessling, Julie E. and Delaney, Thomas. "After the Flood, Colorado State Reaps a Harvest of Invention." *American Libraries* 31, no. 10 (November 2000): 36–37.

Wettlaufer, Brian. "Preparing a Library Disaster Plan." *Library Mosaics* 6 (November/December 1995): 8–10.

Whelan, Debra Lau. "California Fires Shut Libraries." *School Library Journal* 49, no. 12 (December 2003): 22.

Whelan, Debra Lau. "Vandals Firebomb Jewish School Library." *School Library Journal* 50, no. 5 (May 2004): 19.

Will, Barbara H. "The Public Library as Community Crisis Center." *Library Journal* 126, no. 20 (December 2001): 75–77.

Wood, Larry. "1000 Easy Steps Toward Developing a Disaster Recovery Plan; or, The Boss Must Like Me Because He Gave Me the Job of Writing the Disaster Plan." *Conservation Administration News* 58–59 (July/October 1994): 16–20.

Zeitchik, Steven M. "Book Industry Adapts to Anthrax Scares." *Publishers Weekly* 248, no. 45 (November 5, 2001): 10.

INDEX

ABOUT
THE AUTHORS

Deborah D. Halsted is Associate Director, Public Services & Operations, Houston Academy of Medicine-Texas Medical Center Library. At the time of the June 2001 flood, she was in charge of the recovery and reconstruction efforts.

Richard P. Jasper is a Special Projects Librarian in Monograph Acquisitions at the University of Michigan Library in Ann Arbor. In June 2001 he was Assistant Director for Collections at the HAM-TMC Library.

Felicia M. Little is a librarian at the Michael E. DeBakey Veteran Affairs Hospital in Houston, TX. In June 2001 she was the Web librarian for the HAM-TMC Library.